CONSTRUCTING THE CANON OF
CHILDREN'S LITERATURE

Children's Literature and Culture

Jack Zipes, Series Editor

CONSTRUCTING THE CANON OF

CHILDREN'S LITERATURE

BEYOND LIBRARY WALLS AND IVORY TOWERS

ANNE LUNDIN

ROUTLEDGE
NEW YORK AND LONDON

Published in 2004 by
Routledge
270 Madison Avenue
New York, NY 10016
www.routledge-ny.com

Published in Great Britain by
Routledge
2 Park Square
Milton Park, Abingdon
Oxon OX14 4RN
www.routledge.co.uk

Routledge is an imprint of the Taylor & Francis Group.

Printed in the United States of America on acid-free paper.
Typesetting: BookType

Lundin, Anne H., 1944–
    Constructing the canon of children's literature : beyond library walls and ivory towers / by Anne Lundin.
        p.   cm. — (Children's literature and culture ; 31)
    Includes bibliographical references and index.
    ISBN 0-815-33841-4 (alk. paper)
    1. Children's literature, American —History and criticism—Theory, etc. 2. Children's literature, English—History and criticism—Theory, etc. 3. Children—Books and reading. 4. Canon (Literature) I. Title. II. Series.
    PS490 .L86   2004
    810.9'9282—dc22
                                                        2004001366

To Emily, Karl, and Tom—
The Sweetness of Life

Contents

Series Editor's Foreword

Dedicated to furthering original research in children's literature and culture, the Children's Literature and Culture series includes monographs on individual authors and illustrators, historical examinations of different periods, literary analyses of genres, and comparative studies on literature and the mass media. The series is international in scope and is intended to encourage innovative research in children's literature with a focus on interdisciplinary methodology.

Children's literature and culture are understood in the broadest sense of the term *children* to encompass the period of childhood up through adolescence. Because the notion of childhood has changed so much since the origination of children's literature, this Routledge series is particularly concerned with transformations in children's culture and how they have affected the representation and socialization of children. Although the emphasis of the series is on children's literature, all types of studies that deal with children's radio, film, television, and art are included in an endeavor to grasp the aesthetics and values of children's culture. Not only have there been momentous changes in children's culture in the last fifty years, but there also have been radical shifts in the scholarship that deals with these changes. In this regard, the goal of the Children's Literature and Culture series is to enhance research in this field and, at the same time, point to new directions that bring together the best scholarly work throughout the world.

—Jack Zipes

Acknowledgments

My life's work, that's what I've called this book, as it weaves together so many threads. My family and my department are loving people behind me.

I am grateful to the University of Wisconsin, School of Library and Information Studies, for summer research grants and a semester sabbatical. My department, led by Louise Robbins, is very supportive. Colleagues Christine Pawley and Wayne Wiegand inspired me to explore children's library history and print culture history. Jack Zipes encouraged this research out of his own interest to know more, and Beverly Lyon Clark and I share conjoined interests. My relationship with the Children's Literature Association has been vital to my sense of community in the field.

Intertextually, this book draws together material from earlier publications on Victorian picture books and women's library history. I am grateful to the editors of *The Lion and the Unicorn* for permission to reprint "Everygirl's Good Deeds: The Heroics of Nancy Drew" from the January 2003 issue.

Prologue

Reading has always been used as a way to divide a country and a culture into the literati and everyone else, the intellectually worthy and the hoi polloi. But in the fifteenth century Gutenberg invented the printing press, and so began the process of turning the book from a work of art for the few into a source of information for the many. But it was not impossible, and it continued to be done by critics and scholars.

—Anna Quindlen, *How Reading Changed My Life*

The printing press promised the democratization of a print culture. Elizabeth Eisenstein's landmark study, *The Printing Press as an Agent of Change*, illuminates the far-reaching, revolutionary implications of the printing inventions of the fifteenth century. Some of these phenomenal effects were the widening of scholarship, a collaborative approach to the collection of data, an ability to improve and correct texts once published, and an interchange between disciplines. She suggests that these cultural transformations are an ongoing process, effecting a museum without walls. Movable type meant the possibilities of a peaceable kingdom of scholarship, where the arts and sciences could unite in a shared discourse in print. While the causes of the modern fall of Babel are complex indeed, we have opportunities anew if we sense our rich shared culture. Professions seem particularly isolated from each other even in our interdisciplinary web of ideas. Only connect the prose and the poetry, the profession and the practice, the child and the book.

I wish to offer a kind of map where professionals engaged in the study and services of children's literature would build a community of scholars, practitioners, hosts of readers, a cloud of witness. We have two stories on parallel lines. Once upon a time that was and never was, a brave woman or two or three stepped into a new world: a professional life apart from family, perhaps far from family, an adventurous, risky endeavor, a living out of dreams, an experience with bringing books and children together. At first, they had to fight to let the children in. No dogs or children allowed. But they persisted even in the limited, gendered world of middle-brow culture and bureaucracy. They found a space for some books and then a larger shelf and a room even, as inviting as a living room, a sense of place where children and books mattered. They fought for space and then for collections and then for child-centered causes. They lived in settlement houses, traveled rough-and-tumble routes to bring books to city neighborhoods and small lanes. These were educated, cultured, bright, creative women who fortunately through their efforts entered one of the only professions open to them. We will be grateful for a long while that these extraordinary women were both missionaries and managers of a new narrative. This story would be the gift they could give.

These revolutionary changes were somewhat like the invention of the printing press because the public could access books, readers could seek information for their lives, and be transported through stories to far-flung places. The fledgling women librarians who began this movement were indeed brave souls. They took the standards they had known in a cultured home, in their own education, and sought to bring these advantages to the less fortunate. They were a high-minded lot, full of ideals, ready to cross boundaries, to make a difference in the lives of children.

They certainly experienced the slings and arrows of outrageous patriarchal ideologies well in place that discouraged such women from working, especially in the grimy city streets, filled with immigrants, strange languages, and a fair amount of risk to their sheltered upbringing to be ladies. They were feminists by all means, whether they fought for voting rights or fought for books for children. They chose this campaign to be where they brought their strengths, their vision. Not only would these new children's rooms have materials to use, but books to discover through the guidance of a librarian who saw herself as a teacher, a cultural guide, and a critic. Unlike other librarians with more custodial, care-taking jobs, they would actually read the books and write about them and know good from bad. And they would go where the children were on whatever means: traveling librarians with their books at hand. The story of children's librarians at the turn of the century and many decades into the twentieth century is remarkable, an extraordinarily successful venture into literacy and literature for children and youth. Library ladies they were indeed, and books—good books—were their business. You would have a hard time finding a more creative group of women taking the world in their arms, filled with books.

I tell this rather triumphant story because their ventures into a culture resisting their mission and missing their potential is somewhat like another story: the academics treading lightly to establish a footing in a culture unreceptive to children and their literature. The struggles of academics to be taken seriously in their research, study, and teaching of children's literature is somewhat parallel to the path taken by librarians. Both gathered their resources, organized, and set high goals. While the librarians wanted to tackle their mission with the zeal of a social worker or a politician or an artist, the academic scholars wanted to use their scribal and pedagogical tools—and their political savvy to stake a claim for the study of children's books and the cause of children's reading in this culture. Not too dissimilar, although they went their own ways, fought their own battles, and built their empires of books, readers, teaching, and writing, both groups organized—both knew to do that—and both sensed what would work in their setting. They had a common goal to promote children's books as literature, and they fixed on classics, old and new, as a way to make a name, to set a place at the table.

Curiously, they never met, or hardly ever. The children's librarians prevailed for almost a half-century of growth and change. They witnessed the awakening of publishers to fine books for children; they even had a voice in what was published. When children's libraries were an entity needing development—books on the shelf for a wide variety of interests—the publishers saw the potential of a new market. Most of the publishers were in the eastern United States, and most of the librarians were too. They had a lot in common, and together they promoted their wares and their mission. Librarians not only knew their books, but also wrote about them to a broad public. Women of Letters in a grand tradition of American Victorian literati shared that faith in the power of literature to shape lives, especially of the young and innocent.

The academics came into their own rather speedily. In just three decades they made their subject be felt within the academy. They wrote and wrote: scholarly articles, journals, whole books on the subject. They met colleagues in related fields and shared their knowledge. They taught vigorously, especially the classics that were so associated with their own childhood reading and with the Great Books. Together, alone, the librarians and the scholars set their sights on the Best, and the story that follows tells how and what they chose and the difference it makes.

I am intrigued with this blind partnership that exists in two collegial fields, which could easily collaborate. Those librarians were quite enterprising and knew how to spread the word in the media and to write their own sacred texts. The academics knew a lot about literature, and together they set out to demonstrate that acumen to the waiting world. Here is their story.

This book has been long in the making for me, as it weaves together so much of my background as a teacher and librarian—and a scholar and a writer. I started my career way back when, as an English teacher attracted to the classics, I taught *Alice in Wonderland* to seventh graders (imagine!) and coordinated a whole school curriculum around the finest of literature that would prepare these children for higher culture and higher education. On a summer leave to England, I experienced children's literature in its full regalia, its rich resonance, its ivy walls and flower boxes—so many gardens, which evoked for me my own affinity for enclosed, verdant places, for a sense of place I associated with books and landscapes I had known. I branched out in my literary life by becoming a librarian, who happened into a lovely position at a special collection of children's literature, where I could not only help eager scholars who came my way, but also help my own intellectual hunger for old books, manuscripts, art work, and all the ephemera of a special library with very generous collecting goals.

In the course of my work as a curator, I became aware of how much the other books on the shelf were important to the scholar interested in the one book.

I found great reward in bringing a wide context of materials to visiting scholars, all the while broadening my own horizons and longing for a life surrounded by books and readers wanting more. I merged my interests in teaching, curating, collecting, and researching the culture of books, the culture of children. Working on assessing a collection of original materials—a rare collection of Kate Greenaway items—I became intrigued with the thought: What did the Victorians think of her? She was phenomenally popular, and I sensed that they read her with different eyes. I started the search for the critical and commercial reception of Greenaway's first book, *Under the Window,* and then was hooked on Victorian periodicals and the thrill of turning the dry, foxed paper and meeting history all about. Working on my doctorate, I became interested in the field of cultural studies, drawing on postmodern studies that made me see the world differently, to see literature in terms of anthropology as well as aesthetics. Through cultural approaches, I could see that rich world of text and context at play and those tissues that tether literature and librarianship, so interwoven. I began plotting this book as a way to take these threads and weave a crazy quilt of the roles and contributions of both in defining a high standard—an adult standard—for the cultural valorization of the book in their midst. I saw the construction of a canon—a selective tradition—to be the way to begin to see these institutional cultures and their effects as a field, as a child-centered, literature-centered enterprise.

I became even more fascinated with power relations and cultural authority as I sat on various award committees: the Newbery, the Caldecott, the Hans Christian Andersen, and the Phoenix. My work in both organizations—the American Library Association and the Children's Literature Association—gave me more insight and skepticism about the whole process of valuing, whether it be in a ceremony with a sticker on every book and that book enshrined for a lifetime, or whether it was all the fuss on the best of this, the best of that. I bring some of that questioning spirit into this book, although my main focus is on relating the two professions in terms of institutional history and canonical resolve. This work is part of a larger discourse that critiques the canon as an ideological construct in its curriculum, its field of power, its choices to represent or not certain groups, certain ideas, which in a democratic society need the definition of print and the expression of story, poetry, art.

I am so convinced that values—those universals I was so sure about—are contingent and certainly not fixed. No list or award or selection or library collection or scholarship can change that shifting sense of truth. Classics are indeed political. The dynamic of a shared culture through literature is the Victorian idyll we wish to recover, and how to do that involves power relations and identity politics.

As I interchangeably use the words "canon" and "classic," I offer some definition in a highly ambiguous cultural context. The idea of a literary canon is a fairly recent phenomenon, although its roots are in scriptural texts of law and religion. The word "canon" means "of the first class, of acknowledged excellence," and derives from the ancient Greek word "reed," used in classical times as measuring rods, a shift in usage whereby the object of measurement becomes the object measured. In the fourth century, the canon signified the books of the Bible and writings of early theologians that were selected for their orthodoxy as genuine and inspired. In the world of musical traditions, a repertory of commonly performed pieces is considered a canon. In literature, the word "canon" was used primarily to discuss a body of works by one author. The word increasingly means "Literature," with a capital L. and a certain resonance of tone. While considered to be timeless and universal, the canon is quite unstable, with works moving in and out of repute according to the taste and theory of the time. If a work fails to sustain critical and pedagogical fealty, it slips from the canon, largely a search engine of time and taste.

The canon's main function is to position texts in relation to one another—and to exclude more than include. As a classificatory construct, the canon is a collection, much like a library collection. Despite its investment in perpetuity, a classic depends on changing standards of perceived needs for educating the next generation. The canon is a political proving ground where its uses shift according to the rhetorical and reading audience. Our sense of what is "literature" is a product of ideological struggles for a selective tradition at work. Just have a look around.

While canon wars have waged in the humanities, the family tree of children's classics has remained relatively unshaken amid the storms about. Perhaps that stasis says something about our isolation from the discourse that engages the larger literary culture. I appreciate Beverly Lyon Clark's work because she explores professions as intricately involved in literature for children. Jack Zipes also questions the nature of a classic, and questioned it at least three decades ago in a cultural critique of *Heidi*. In *Sticks and Stones,* Zipes asks questions about value and the institutions that assume such cultural authority, even mentioning the need for a social history of the female librarians of the early twentieth century. That was all the charge I needed, although I have been working on this project seemingly for a lifetime. I find his thinking and writing to be such a clarion call, as are the voices of Beverly Clark, Peter Hunt, Alison Lurie, Uli Knoepflmacher (my first teacher), and the late, dearly missed Mitzi Myers. In the library field, Wayne Wiegand, Christine Jenkins, Christine Pawley, Besty Hearne, Virginia Walter, Kay Vandergrift are just a few of the best and brightest I know in these parts.

The book is divided into three categories of meaning-makers in children's books: the librarian, the scholar, and the reader. My interest is to connect the fields in theory and practice, centering on their role and contribution as critics in the field. I wish to use that ubiquitous term "field" in new ways, following the wisdom of Pierre Bourdieu with his layers of social interaction, of systematic rules and relationships, of cultural production in a commercial culture. Individuals in this field aspire to position themselves by their literary taste and hierarchical standards of what literature is and does. I trace the origins of the canonical movement in librarianship, which was appropriated in the same, shared breath. I look at the matriarchs who made much of quality and relate where they found their stimulation as self-appointed cultural authorities. I look for the ideas that moved them, a kind of intellectual history, a women's history. I spend a fair amount of time presenting the logic of literary criticism, in particular the scaffolding of a canon. I let the critics speak, which they do so eloquently. My hope is that these two critics, so sensitive to children and to literature as empowering, might see some traces where they meet and greet in the saving grace of a favorite book. I have at least introduced you. Now hand each other on.

Chapter One

Best Books: The Librarian

"Only the rarest kind of best of anything can be good enough for a child."

—Walter de la Mare, *Bells and Grass*

What story to tell of Anne Carroll Moore, the great star in the sky over the landscapes of children's libraries? Legends abound of her power over the national publishing scene, her children's literature empire on 42nd Street, and her eccentricities and alter egos. I will tell one anecdote that illustrates the imagistic talents of Anne Carroll Moore. When New York Public librarian Anne Carroll Moore was offered the rare opportunity to write her own children's book page in 1924 in the *New York Herald Tribune*, the first full-page spread on children's books in the American press, she chose the title, "The Three Owls," inspired by a library weathervane and symbolizing the equal powers of *author, artist,* and *critic* in the making of children's books. The author is easy to figure; the artist is the illustrator, but who exactly is the critic in the early 1920s? Who but the children's librarian in her prime, hooting in the dark?

When Moore later wrote a column for the *Horn Book* and compiled her writings into book form, she again chose that predatory night bird as her emblem. Not only did she regard owls as the most picturesque and human of all birds, according to her biographer Frances Clarke Sayers, but she also raised to an apogee of art the criticism of books for children.[1] Books were written, illustrated, and then appraised by none other than the children's librarian as artist in her own right. Here was a dynamic profile of the librarian: not the mere custodian of books looking elsewhere for expertise, not the timid, bespeckled spinster dusting books on the shelf, but instead a figure of great prowess, of swooping cultural authority, equal to creators of art. Hardly a meek image, the owl is a sign of wisdom, and this third owl was indeed wise in the ways of the world.

This is the larger story I wish to tell: how children's librarians took over the children's book world in the first half of the twentieth century and made their mark on the literature, especially on a high standard for children's books, one

1

equal or superior to general literature—high standards that only a classic, old or new, could meet. I survey the history of this specialty in American librarianship, focusing on the matriarchal Caroline Hewins and Anne Carroll Moore. Children's librarianship was imbued with tenets of Romanticism and emerged in the art revivals of the late nineteenth century, when the child became the apotheosis of art and literature. And where else did librarians receive their inspiration beyond the Romantic poets? I recount the contextual influences of five formative figures in shaping the aesthetics that bound children's librarians to humanism. A mingling of social reform, a romantic spirit, a humanistic ideology, and a growing professionalism of women conflated in the high ideals of children's librarianship. Women sought a field that could be their own where they would recreate an ideal domesticated space, a utopia of literature and the arts, a peaceable kingdom.

The children's librarian was the odd-woman-out in the fledgling field of librarianship, which had its official beginnings in 1876, with the institution of the American Library Association (ALA) and Melvil Dewey (1851–1931) as auteur. Public libraries were not initially conceived to be a family institution, but as adult education with multiple purpose, multiple motivation: "The People's University." Children inched in through the door until they were at last granted physical space, collections to fill that space, and specialized library staff responsible for their appropriate rearing into literature. These three features of space, collections, and staff were critical in validating this fledgling field. While heightened cultural interest in the child advanced the cause, the agency of pioneer women librarians was instrumental in establishing a field of children's literature *within* a field of children's librarianship (the merger matters), with a series of sites, a public sphere. The gradual awareness of need coincided with the growing professionalism of women, who turned to new career possibilities in fields associated with female nurture: teaching, nursing, social work, and librarianship. That some powerfully motivated women took interest in bringing books and children together makes a story, a narrative sufficiently profound and far reaching as intellectual history, as women's history on the making of children's culture in the twentieth century.

Children's librarianship was a stepchild of the library movement, the Cinderella who through magic and derring-do regains her true identity and position in the world. While trained in "the Library Spirit" of Melvil Dewey to be apostles of reading for the social good, they were unique in autonomy and authority, startlingly so. In reformist spirit, they aimed to acculturate the immigrants streaming into the cities, to uphold the highest standards of literature, and to reach new groups needing service. Dewey gave the children's realm a freedom to develop in a gendered direction that would be natural to women who understood children. While librarians in general have been regarded as neutral, passive gatekeepers or custodians of culture, the children's librarian was fairly autonomous in her own domain granted by default. The children's room—a significant symbol and sign system within the library setting—exuded a spirited sense of ritual and rhyme from on high: the children's librarian as a self-determined cultural authority within the garden walls of children's literature.

Children's librarians created a dominant ideology that privileged certain texts within a romanticized construction of the literature of childhood. The idea of Nature, a romanticized nature, offered an acceptable critique of industrialized society and search for utopia, a familiar and popular literary passion of this late-century period. Celebration of nature's beauty took on patriotic significance in association with leaders like Jefferson, who described nature as a monument to American identity, and writers as quintessentially American as Emerson and Thoreau. Popular Romanticism in the late nineteenth and early twentieth centuries sent families "back to nature" in the suburbs, national parks, in scouting, and in consumption of innumerable literary evocations of Arcadia. So close to Nature, children must grow like a garden, and their books a child's garden of fanciful fiction and verse. Library service to children implied knowing the literature (which presumably only women might know) and recommending the best (again, who else?). They chose as their jurisdiction knowledge and experience with *literature* rather than knowledge and experience with *education*: the best of books rather than the best of reading, literature over literacy—the Book as conveyer of meaning more than the Child as maker of meaning with particular wants and needs. This choice to be more one way rather than the other inexorably shaped the direction librarians took for the next century.

The secret garden of their labors shaped not only *how* but *what* literature emerged for children in the early decades of the twentieth century, its greenest growing season. I focus on a period of roughly fifty years: starting with Caroline Hewins's labors in the 1880s through Anne Carroll Moore's prime in the 1930s, with some references to the network of women who followed in their selective tradition. These were the years when children's librarianship established its jurisdiction over criticism of literature. The reputation of children's librarians as movers and shakers in literary and commercial culture is a longer story than I can tell, but I believe it is connected to their own cultural authority in perpetuating a selective tradition. Their metaphor was one of growth with all the redolence of a garden.

Frances Jenkins Olcott (1872–1963), a matriarch of the children's library movement and librarian of Carnegie Library of Pittsburgh, shaped the garden into a grand vision of landscape:

> The guiding of children's reading is of great importance because it is fundamental. It strikes at the roots of many weedy growths that weaken and hamper the healthy development of character. For even as when desiring a beautiful garden we prepare the selected seeds, and pluck out the weeds, so should we carefully prepare the children's minds, root out the tares, and fill their imaginations with the noble thoughts and ideals of these great books which will help the developing men or women to resist ignoble and corroding influences.[2]

How did this fierce determination to implant and improve construct a hierarchical value structure based on selections they made and promoted through a variety of venues? How did children's librarians become the professionals charged with canon-making in their cultivation of the garden of children's literature in the years between the 1880s and the 1930s? How did librarianship affect literature? To ask these questions is to offer a dynamic approach to library/literary history: not as static entities but as agents of growth and change, of challenge and response, what we call *culture*.

As metaphors shape perceptions, I trace the verdant years of early children's librarianship, a half-century from the formative 1880s through the first three decades of growth, as the garden grew. This story constructs a new profession with its identity rooted in a policy and practice of selection and selectiveness: the markings of a canon. Librarians selected the standard of evaluation that examined a child's book in the same way as an adult book; their canon was geared toward "best books" from an adult perspective, and with a female slant at that. The ideology that inspired such institutional growth was Romanticism, a pervasive belief in "the child within" as the locus of adult power and childhood as the apotheosis of wonderment in nature. Children's librarianship tells a story that constructs ideals, prescribes rules, specifies sources of authority, and offers a sense of purpose and continuity. Romanticism fit these parameters as a cultural language that shaped the child's garden of books as subject and object. The cultural context of children's librarianship within this child myth is a critical part of the story that offers explanations of the growth and future of books and children in this country. The child as exemplum, as redeemer of a fallen world, is a seductive yet weighty image. In Anne Scott MacLeod's view, romanticized children persisted generationally, appearing "like emissaries from a better world to improve the lives of joyless adults."[3]

ROMANTICISM

The garden trope evokes the fertile Romanticism of late-nineteenth-century America, an ideology deriving from literary influences, social change, and institutional construct. Philologically derived from *romaunt* ("romance," "roman," i.e., novel), Romanticism has deep associations with the imaginative, fantastic, revolutionary, utopian—the sense of the good life. The mythic "Age of Romanticism" was an expression of an age of revolutions, a dynamic period of aesthetic, political, economic, social, and philosophical movements that together transformed the Western world. Romanticism privileges the creative function of the Imagination, seeing Art as an intuitive form of higher truth and Nature as the revelation of divine nature and the subject of the most primitive and pure arts. Romanticism is perceived as an exercise in the freedom to explore, to move beyond the community, to encounter Nature in her rough-and-ready form, to commune with this Nature for personal revelation. This literary landscape is grounded on a particular freedom and autonomy to move, to venture—what Judith Plotz calls "supra-social independence."[4] The emphasis is on the search for the Absolute, the Ideal, the transcendence of the actual.

Traditionally, Romanticism's literary roots are the six male British poets of the period of 1780 to the 1830s: Wordsworth, Coleridge, Blake, Byron, Shelley, and Keats, as a group associated with a philosophical stance on creativity, perception, and cognition and with popular tropes of pastoral bliss and childhood reverie. The title "Age of Romanticism" is strictly considered to be the four decades after 1790, a time when writers spoke of "the spirit of the age," aware of the charged atmosphere of innovation and new birth; in actuality the movement lasted long in the nineteenth and twentieth century. With the Romantics' "discovery" of the child, we are confronted with something new: the phenomenon of major literary figures expressing their most profound thoughts through the image of the child, a veritable Golden Age when "the majors wrote for minors." Within a few decades, the child emerged from cultural diminution to become the cultural icon of imaginative literature and philosophical speculation.

Romanticism persisted as myth, particularly in the identification of children and Nature. The idea of Nature, a Romanticized nature, offered an acceptable critique of industrialized society and search for utopia, a familiar and popular literary passion of this late century. Children's librarianship was organized within the parent organization (ALA) the very year that Baum's *Wizard of Oz* burst on the scene. This was an era of expansive possibilities for America as a better place, a utopian vision of the Child and Nature. Celebration of nature's beauty took on patriotic significance in association with leaders like Jefferson, who described nature as a monument to American identity, and writers as quintessentially American as Emerson and Thoreau. Popular Romanticism in the late nineteenth and early twentieth centuries sent families "back to nature" in the suburbs, national parks, in scouting, and in consumption of innumerable literary evocations of Arcadia. Burgeoning interest in the acculturation of children using a metaphor of growth, a favorite trope of John Dewey's educational reforms, fit with this new designed space for children, so close to Nature itself. The child in the book, the child in Nature, and the child in the library conflated into a profession in charge of a body of literature.

Notions of Romanticism colored the very fabric of children's literary culture in the nineteenth and twentieth centuries. James Holt McGavran stresses the influence of the Romantic concept of childhood in its content, psychological power, and narrative structure.[5] Revisionist critics speak of "the Romantic ideology" that has shaped much of the historiography of children's literature into a conflicting paradigm of instruction versus amusement, with imaginative writings privileged over more educational works. F. J. Harvey Darton, who shaped the way we view children's book history, defined children's books as "printed works produced ostensibly to give children spontaneous pleasure," with a subsequent devaluation of works deemed less than pleasurable, such as the genre of books known in the history as "The Moral Tale," many of which were written by women reformers of the late eighteenth century.[6] These stories were considered too prosaic and didactic in character to be considered pleasing. This bias toward one form of writing—adventurous and fantastic fiction and verse—precluded a serious consideration of other genres and other readers' pleasures. Children's librarians appropriated Romanticism in their privileging of a certain imaginative paradigm for a profession and a literature of childhood that translated "the child in nature" to "the child in the library," and so the garden grew.

The two writers most associated with the revolutionary vision of romanticized childhood are William Blake (1757–1827) and William Wordsworth (1770–1850), whose writings were appropriated to the image of children's literature and librarianship in the United States at the turn of the century. The Romantic ideology suited the reformist impulse, the nature reverie, and the Anglophilia that characterized turn-of-the-century American literary culture. The Romantics' utopian image resonated with librarians' aspirations for cultural ascendance, a good green space of their own. The children's librarians appropriated the rhetoric, but in their practice revealed a more feminist model, a perspective that emphasized the values of domesticated nature and community, of shared rather than solitary experiences. Women lacked the leisure, the freedom, to wander from home, to adventure into the depths of Nature for a sense of mystical communion or adversarial conflict. Women tended to stay close to home, to build gardens, to create communities, to espouse harmony, values associated with feminist Romanticism. Anne Mellor characterizes this approach as privileging nature not as "a source of divine creative power as much as a female friend or sister with needs and capacities," a more quotidian celebration of common life.[7] To scholar Mitzi Myers, the Romantic paradigm is "our foundational fiction, our ordinary myth ... the 'always already' saidness of the Romantic literary discourse on childhood."[8] While male tropes of wilderness have been valorized as Romanticism in its finest spirit, women's developmental stories and envisioned communities have been relegated to nonliterary status, as educational treatises, pictures of everyday life, simple nursery fare, and, significantly, as children's collections and library services.

More than the other Romantic poets, Wordsworth and Blake became the mentors and muses became to the early children's librarians who saw in their library work a visionary Golden Age. The language of children's librarians resembles a Romantic text, full of childhood reverie, paeans to the power of imagination, commitment to a revolutionary cause, and a legitimization of a canon and character to literary selection and guidance. Anne Carroll Moore's prolific reviews and essays on children's literature were punctuated with references to Wordsworth and Blake, with an occasional reference to Maria Edgeworth, associated with feminist Romanticism. To Moore, Wordsworth's poetry marked the discovery of childhood, when "poetry and childhood emerged at the same time to claim their naturalization papers."[9] She eulogized Wordsworth and Blake for their witness to visionary childhood. To Moore, Blake was "the first great explorer of childhood."[10] Wordsworth's celebration of a folkloric childhood in *The Prelude* privileged fairy tales and imaginative literature, a curriculum not lost on children's librarians who championed a comparable literature for children of modern America: a canon composed of books of romanticized America, of books that privileged the child in Nature, of books that stood timeless as the fabled and storied lore of classics and traditional tales. Romanticism persisted in other cultural movements of the day that influenced the ascendancy of childhood and its literature. As an ideology, Romanticism blossomed into the domesticated spaces where children read, following Matthew Arnold's cultural prescription for "sweetness and light": beauty in all its forms as truth.[11]

Throughout the nineteenth century, the child/father figure "trailing clouds of glory" summoned impulses toward reform and nostalgia for the child extolled by Wordsworth as prophet and priest. The child retained an earlier divinity, while the aura surrounding childhood faded into the common light of adulthood. As Jackson Lears writes in his social history of the Gilded Age, Wordsworth's ideas became widely popularized in America, with the "Ode" a formative text for cultural attitudes toward children.[12] Tracing its appearance in sermons and speeches, Barbara Garlitz compares its impact on the Victorian culture to that of Darwin's *Origin of Species* or of Freud's work on the modern temper. As the catalyst of child focus in the nineteenth century, the "Ode" attains the status of fact:

> The ideas in the "Ode" that the child is fresh from God and still remembers his heavenly home, that the aura which surrounds childhood fades into the common light of adulthood, that the child has a wisdom which the man loses—these ideas became the most common ideas about childhood in the nineteenth century.[13]

William Blake shared Wordsworth's passion for the child as symbol of innocence and naturalness. Considered the first poet of genius to write for children, Blake in his companion works, *Songs of Innocence* (1789) and *Songs of Experience* (1794), illustrates in word and image the child as a bright angelic spirit, a contradiction to the repressive forces of urbanization, mechanization, and Puritanism, which repressed nurture and growth for the child and the adult. Blake was appreciated by this cadre of librarians as a unique creative genius who spoke from the child's voice and vision, setting down what a child thought as representing human nature—as "innocent experience recorded, not as an offering to innocence," as Harvey Darton states.[14] Straddling these contraries, the dialectic between innocence and experience, child and adult, Blake depicts the life journey to be one of restoring innocence, which could be called the ideal of the children's librarianship. Darton's monumental history, *Children's Books in England* (1932), elevated Blake to a transcendent status as the "living spark in poetry meant for children."[15] Other historians have concurred, such as Mary Thwaite in *From Primer to Pleasure in Reading* (1963), which grouped him with the Romantics as instrumental in changing the conception of the nature and needs of children and thus the books written for them.[16]

Although children's librarians would appropriate masculine, high Romantic ideology in their canonical vision of library collections, they would demonstrate a more feminine Romanticism in their community of practice. Children's librarians privileged Wordsworth and Blake for their vision of lost childhood within the more feminized Romanticism of the domesticated domain of a children's room and shared collections. Within their romantic rhetoric, children's librarians composed what Mildred Batchelder called a "Leadership Network," mobilized through their attitude toward children and their access to libraries, the early availability of specialized training, and their professional organization in 1900 of the ALA Section for Library Work with Children.[17] These pioneering librarians, whom Betsy Hearne and Christine Jenkins name as "Foremothers," were united in their understanding of the book and the child as mutually constructed. They expressed their convictions in a canon of professional writings called "sacred texts: psalms, proverbs, precepts, and practices."[18] The librarians in this classification have a name (foremothers), a concept (the child and the book), and a canon of literary works: eleven influential books representative of their writings.[19]

The librarians selected by Hearne and Jenkins for their influential intertextual writings are Annis Duff, Margaret A. Edwards, Paul Hazard (the one male), Bertha E. Mahony and Elinor Whitney, Anne Carroll Moore, Amelia Munson, Frances Clarke Sayers, Ruth Sawyer, Marie L. Shedlock, Lillian Smith, and Ruth Hill Viguers. I would add Alice M. Jordan to their list, for her scholarly study *From Rollo to Tom Sawyer*, her list of classics, and her close relationship to Bertha Mahony and the *Horn Book*. For the purposes of my study of canonical influence over the years, from the 1880s to 1930s, I am focusing on the formative voices of Caroline Hewins and Anne Carroll Moore, whom I name as "matriarchs" for their legacy in the ideological world of children's literature, librarianship, and publishing, including professional journalism, criticism, readers advisory services, bookselling, and editing. Their influence was synergistic, stretching into adjacent fields beyond library walls to reveal the agency of children's library work in the world. As heirs to Romantic conceptions of nature, art, imagination, and the child, Hewins and Moore passed on a tradition of homage to an invented past, a utopian place where books and children could unite for the good. The construction of a book community by these matriarchs and foremothers—a veritable clan—created a "literary spirit" as well as a "library spirit" that shift the focus from the *self* to the *self-in-relation*. Their ideology includes the essence of traditional and feminist Romanticism: a utopian vision of an idealized childhood in a community of readers. Romanticism was their secular faith, and classics the scriptures. The fact that we still a century later retain a romanticized appreciation of children's literature shows the persistence of their cultural imprinting.

When children's libraries emerged as a phenomenon at the turn of the century, the array of books for children was slim pickings. Publishers overlooked children's books as a serious market and rarely showed books in shops except for the Christmas holiday season. The preponderance of books was British, reflecting a dependent cultural relationship to the mother country and the American marketplace that privileged foreign authors over home-grown. Classics for children stood out amid a morass of popular pulp fiction, and librarians were intent on distinguishing their selections from the general fare. That the matriarchs came largely from cultural, upper-class backgrounds privileged their own childhood reading, which consisted of classical works of myth and folklore, English classics by the grand masters, and a sprinkling of picture books considered to be artistic. When Caroline Hewins composed her groundbreaking 1882 publication, *Books for the Young, A Guide for Parents and Children*—the first of its kind—there were few possibilities other than classics of the period and a few current items. Notice the title: the audience was parents and children, not librarians, who had yet to be invented.

The matriarchs of children's librarianship were born into a Victorian culture and class that perceived childhood as a secular paradise, a walled world separate from, even opposed to, the world of adults, or, in Humphrey Carpenter's terms, a "secret garden" of refuge and restoration.[20] Children's librarianship was one construction of a cultural preoccupation with the child, which contributed to literary as well as extra-literary formations. Children's literature was the product of their domesticated spaces, whereby they appropriated Romantic ideology into their own conception of the right books for children. These domesticated spaces and institutional constructs in the form of collections and control of literature were shaped by the origins and ends of Romanticism, a metaphysical departure from the concept of human nature as fallen. Their sensibilities and rhetoric reveal an acquaintance with Romantic poets within a context sentimentalizing child-hood. The Victorians defined childhood as a separate stage of life and the child a locus of literary and philosophical speculation—as well as commercial exploita-tion. Peter Coveney, one of the first modern scholars to study the child in literature, expressed childhood for the Victorians as a symbol of mediation in a period of spiritual crisis.

> The child could serve as a symbol of the artist's dissatisfaction with the society that was in the process of such harsh development about him. In a world given increasingly to utilitarian values and the Machine, the child could become the symbol of Imagination and Sensibility, a symbol of Nature set against the forces abroad in society actively de-naturing humanity. Through the child could be expressed the artist's awareness of human Innocence against the cumulative pressures of social Experience.[21]

And, increasingly, that artist's vision converged on the child, and soon that artist would be the self-anointed children's librarian. Any profession claiming expertise over this highly charged landscape was treading lightly. The child meant so much more, as art and commerce took note.

AESTHETICISM

The zeitgeist of the age was a spirit of Romanticism in art, literature, and commerce with the child as synecdoche, a small significant part representing the whole. Contextually, the late nineteenth century mixed the elements of Roman-ticism into artistic movements that influenced the ideology and cultural production of books for children. As children became associated with art, blending image into object, the notion of children's books as rarefied material culture emerged as desiderata. The artistic, architectural, and commercial movement of aestheticism served as a decorative cultural pedestal with sensational designs. The idea of book as art shaped Anne Carroll Moore's conception of the ideal and inspired her passion for image as well as text.

The aestheticism of the last third of the nineteenth century was a movement of heightened emphasis on art principles, represented in the architecture of the "Queen Anne style" and in domestic manufacturing, including furniture, ceramics, textiles, wallpapers, and books. The aesthetes had a spacious, encompassing vision: the structures we build, the spaces we inhabit, the designs we incorporate, the books we read—all are art objects that influence our lives. aestheticism in America grew out of a similar reform movement that began in the mid-century in England. Its translation to American soil was enhanced by America's new urbanized and industrialized society. The shifts from urban to rural, from local to national, from peace to Civil War intensified questions of authority, gender, and opportunity, which glorified earlier rural America as a simpler, innocent world. Women as consumers and creators became an issue as women assumed more control over their own lives with increasing demands for opportunity; design reform became synchronous with gender reform, at least in terms of art education. The vast natural landscapes were being threatened and transformed. The centennial of America's republic renewed a sense of America's childhood. One journalist remarked in the *Dial* (1899) on the contemporary trend of historical fiction—tales of colonial times—to romantic yearnings for a nation's childhood at a time of enormous growth into maturity. Leaving behind simpler times, the country looked back to its origins, "when the nation was still in swaddling clothes."[22] The 1876 Philadelphia Centennial Exposition inspired nostalgia for a colonial revival: to reinstate the craftsmanship as well as the character of a bygone era.

As a critique and expression of contemporary American culture, aestheticism functioned as a way to reinstate natural forms into new purposes: leaf-like contours recall a Nature—and Culture—transformed. Indeed, small decorative children depicted in nature, indoors and out, could work wonders. The aestheticism movement sought to balance "art" with materialism, with aesthetics as material culture consonant with a Romantic subtext. The marketing and consumption of objects as ideology brought the book as symbolic object to the fore. The Arts and Crafts movement pursued the book arts at a time when libraries were extolling collections and building a literary culture. Authors and artists participated more fully in the design of works as a unified art; illustrations as art and commerce flourished. In late Victorian America, aesthetics mattered in all aspects of life and for all ages.

Children's books too were transformed from utilitarian fare to objects of art. Children's books were held high as exemplars of the credo of Beauty in the making. Mark Girouard, architectural historian, finds picture books done in aesthetic touches to be "secret persuaders" that "scattered sweetness and light beyond the nursery into every corner of the house."[23] The *Dial* (1881) admired the beautiful volumes designed for children, resplendent in gilt covers and exquisite illustrations, heaped on the booksellers' shelves and recalled, in contrast, the books of his own childhood, "plain and clumsy to ugliness in their exterior."[24] The *Art Journal* (1881) noted, too, the startling change between the toy-books of twenty years earlier and those of the present. Earlier books were "clumsy" and "primitive" in conception and craftsmanship, devoid of beauty; "Art for the nursery has become Art indeed."[25] Attention to aesthetics for children was heralded by books nominally written for children, particularly the work of Walter Crane, Randolph Caldecott, and Kate Greenaway. R. Gordon Kelly, who has written widely on this period in American literature, notes that this new conception of literature illustrated—the picture book—was instrumental in refining the quality of books for children. As Kelly says: "Art promised a kind of secular salvation through works of imaginative genius."[26] With a backward glance, the Aesthetes of the Queen Anne movement popularized a literature of childhood as a contrast to the excesses of modern technology, its commercial vulgarity and industrial blight. Country life, peopled by children and rustics, was preferable. The old-fashioned became fashionable. The adjectives "delicate," "quaint," and "old-fashioned" became high praise, epitomizing a nostalgic romanticism of the past. Writers, artists, and librarians indulged themselves in an imaginary return to the simplicity and enchantment of childhood. The historian Holbrook Jackson, in his history of the 1890s, found it quite natural that a period so intent on discovering—or rediscovering—romance would glorify childhood.[27]

CULT OF THE CHILD

The popular press articulated this passion as epochal in word and image. The *National Review* (1891) repeated the description of the period as "the Age of Children."[28] *Good Words* (1904) described the nineteenth century as "the Children's Century," noting the enhanced value placed on the child, as the subject of reform movements as well as scholarly studies and fictional narratives.[29] *Scribner's* (1898) explored the literary preoccupation with the child as "a second childhood in literature," in which writers looked back to a "golden age" for solace in uncertain times.[30] *Scribner's* (1896) also noted the outpouring of child literature, which seemed to be more about the child than for the child, more an expression of a state of mind than a dramatic literature. Adults seemed to be receiving "unalloyed enjoyment" from this new literature, which was enjoying "a kind of Elizabethan age."[31] The *Atlantic Monthly* (1894) observed the trend as well, noting in a review of Frances Hodgson Burnett's *The One I Knew Best of All* the prevalent fashion of interpreting the life of the imaginative child not as "juvenile literature" but as "books for the big about the little."[32] The *Critic* (1901) expounded on the "Literary Cult of the Child" as a discovery of childhood's "dramatic" and "picturesque" possibilities, with the effect of the child-cult as not moral but artistic.[33] Horace Scudder's *Childhood in Literature and Art* (1894) extolled certain children's books "as literature in which conceptions of childhood are embodied, and as literature that feeds and stimulates the imagination of children," what we might take today as the dual audience or cross-writing.[34] And, as the century turned, Ellen Key in 1909 entitled her book, *The Century of the Child*, a language of latent possibilities.[35]

Authors secularized the faith in the child as exemplum in a variety of popular and elite literary texts. British critic Humphrey Carpenter explores the intertexuality of the pastoral garden of childhood for a whole framework of authors making up "the Golden Age" of children's literature: Charles Kingsley, Lewis Carroll, George MacDonald, Louisa Alcott, Richard Jeffries, Kenneth Grahame, E. Nesbit, Beatrix Potter, J. M. Barrie, and A. A. Milne. Carpenter argues that children were celebrated for their clear, even heightened vision of the world and that by the end of the century, children and childhood became critical, conflicting elements in the literary imagination.[36] The critical is easily demonstrated, but the conflictual is more elusive and underlies cultural movements of the time. James Holt McGavran's two collections of essays on Romanticism in children's literature in the nineteenth and twentieth centuries reveal persistent continuations and postmodern contestations.[37] That texts can be simultaneously subversive and conservative as instruments of social change suggest subtle connections between Romanticism and postmodernism.

Romanticism is the undercurrent of new ideas in education that shaped the progressive education movement in the United States in a parallel, although divided, development with children's librarianship. John Dewey appropriated certain views of the child that were gaining force in the late nineteenth century into his pragmatic philosophy and school reforms. Believing that education could redeem the larger society, he positioned the child, as critical to that remaking, at the very center of the school. Defining education essentially as growth, Dewey believed that the realization of the individual child would foster the fulfillment of democratic society. The matriarchs of children's librarianship turned elsewhere for their inspiration, to belles-lettres instead of child development, to become authorities in literature rather than literacy. Both approaches developed through Romanticism and the utopian conviction that the child could grow through education toward civic good. To Dewey, education is the experience of the individual child in the world in an endless cycle of growth and development. To the pioneer children's librarians of the period, education is the experience of the child within the book and the child with the book in forming certain kinds of subjectivities, which privileged the imagination. Dewey's philosophy was experiential and manifest in movements like the Bank School College of Education, whose "here and now" books became anathema to the fantasy and folk ideal of the librarian's choice. Curiously, the children's librarians resisted Dewey, a choice with impact on their paradigmatic expertise in literature rather than child development.

Librarians chose books with their own inscribed Romanticism in a utopian drama of cultural transformation—the world made right by a child in the children's room, "the nursery of citizenship."[38] This messianic role of book and reader motivated the pioneer librarians who crusaded for the place for children and their literature: a mutuality of domestic and literary arts. In their study of the writings of these mavericks, Betsy Hearne and Christine Jenkins reveal the richness of this ideology in the spirituality of their prose, the sense of mission that imbued their good works with good words, a high-minded idealization of "child" and "literature."[39] Drawing on the feminist writings of literary historian Mitzi Myers, who views children's literature as "a narrative space encoding a wish for remothering," I would argue that the institutional history of children's libraries reveals a similar incarnation: the re-creation of children's literature in a space encoding a similar desire.[40] Structurally and symbiotically, the children's library was the library's child in Nature. The matriarchs labored long and hard for that space.

Children's librarianship grew up in the prime of Romanticism and the stirrings of reform. As children's book historian Anne Scott MacLeod notes, turn-of-the-century America was a high point in the Romanticism of childhood, with the popular culture sentimentalizing children's beauty and innocence, and aesthetes embracing childhood in nature with a mythic aura.[41] Children's librarians shaped Romantic strands into their conception of the ideal book and the ideal reader. Inaugurative children's librarians like Anne Carroll Moore embraced Romanticism with rhetorical fervor in privileging the creative imagination in children's literature as exemplum. The Romantic myth of childhood as transhistorical innocence, uncorrupted by the adult world persisted in the children's library. Their institutionalization of Romanticism at the turn of the century produced a body of literature that performed cultural work, in Jane Tompkins's words, which expressed a radical discourse of power in its "attempt to redefine the social order."[42] Children's literature in twentieth century America was the product of library labors, specifically female children's librarians, who, unique to the larger, more bureaucratic parent profession, not only selected and accessed literature but became its cultural authority. Canon walls fortified the child's garden of books.

A CONTEXT FOR CLASSICS

Books for children have traditionally been associated with classics. Indeed, the first fiction or fantasy children read were books written for adults: *Robinson Crusoe*, *Pilgrim's Progress*, *Gulliver's Travels*, among others. When there were no books written specifically for a child's pleasure, children found delight by appropriating an adult book and reading the text as their own story. These books that children adopted became designated as classics, with the allure of young and old. A canon in books for children can be traced to the 1880s. American periodicals document interest in the late nineteenth century in the historiography of children's literature and in educational reforms, which became linked to the regulation of reading. In

1881, Horace E. Scudder, then editor of *The Atlantic Monthly*, published a compilation called *The Children's Book*, an anthology of "the classics of juvenile literature." In the same year was also published *Shakespeare for the Young Folk*, by Robert Haymond. So many reprint editions of classics were appearing that Edward Hale, in the *Critic* of 1884 wrote: "Every large jobbing house in the book trade, I am told, has its own plates of *Robinson Crusoe*, and even the librarians have long since ceased the effort to catalog the various editions." He added that he doubted the popularity of the book with "people we call literary people," but instead with "the rank and file."[43] The first textbook anthology of "Classics for Children" appeared in 1885 by the firm of Ginn, Heath & Company, to rave reviews by the *Dial.*

These publications represent an attempt to divert young readers from sensational fiction by the introduction of traditional literature adapted for children. "Purity in print" was clearly the elusive ideal, as revealed in Paul Boyer's study of censorship by that title.[44] By the end of the nineteenth century, a canon is being formed of books children should read as well as their own selected favorites. Such figuring was fraught with anxiety, as educators and critics debated the deluge of popular serials, sensational fiction, and a less hegemonic literature for youth. Horace Scudder wrote an impassioned article, "American Classics in School" in an *Atlantic Monthly* of 1887, in which he described the reforms by which classics were being incorporated into the classroom. To Scudder, students were benefiting from a fuller exposure to American authors rather than the previous practice of graded reading, in which the "individuality of literature was subordinated" to "occasional specimens, but all the while keeping them from the real thing."[45] That few students found "the real thing" in schools is suggested in a remark in an 1883 *Critic*, in which a children's author, Eliot McCormick, surveyed the reading of youths in the New York City public schools with those in the Polytechnic Institute of Brooklyn and concluded that "a lower class of literature is read by the pupils of the public school than by those of the Institute" because they live in homes where "the standard authors and the standard magazines" are read by family members and so "there is no occasion for the children to supply their own needs in the matter of fictitious literature."[46] A columnist in the 1898 *Critic* remarked on receiving the latest Harper & Bros. catalog devoted entirely to books for the young and recalled the classics of his youth: *Pilgrim's Progress, Arabian Nights, Gulliver,* and *Robinson Crusoe* formed the bulk of most youths' libraries, with a sprinkling of *Rollo* books and *Franconia* stories.[47] Anna Hamel Wiekel, writing in the journal *Education* in 1900, cited the books necessary to introduce in kindergarten: *Mother Goose,* myths, Hans Christian Andersen, Grimm Brothers, *Aesop's Fables, Arabian Nights, Alice in Wonderland,* and *Pilgrim's Progress.* She quickly added *The Brownies,* Oliver Herford's *Child Primer,* Peter Newell's *Rhymes and Pictures,* Mrs. Ewing's books, which when Homer, Dante, and Shakespeare were added later, "verily they will not find the foundation unworthy or unstable."[48]

A stable and worthy foundation was there for a new profession to build an empire.

EARLY LIBRARY HISTORY

This most feminized field of children's librarianship emerged in the 1890s as a stepchild of the fledgling field of librarianship that commenced officially with the creation of the ALA in 1876 in Philadelphia in that memorable centennial year. Libraries existed for thousands of years for the purpose of acquiring and preserving objects of cultural authority. The Sumerians five thousand years ago created writing and established libraries to preserve the rituals and records needed for progress in religion and commerce. Libraries in their conserving or disseminating knowledge continued as cultural reflection and construction. Librarianship is a modern field that arose out of educational reforms after the French Revolution and the professionalization of the late nineteenth century. That librarianship took shape as a field was the result of a complex of circumstance and multiple motivations. An expanding country of aggressive industrialization demanded a labor force and a knowledge industry for acculturation. The rise of industry, urbanization, and immigration heightened concern for education, health care, and family values. The influx of immigrants from alien cultures aroused concern for their assimilation into the political and educational life of an industrializing and urbanizing country. Chaos was looming, and new structures for social progress and social control were needed. These perceived needs conjoined with the greater availability of print to bring books to remote areas and larger cities needing enrichment. The public library emerged as a charitable institution embraced by New England's business leaders who saw the potential for keeping working people safe from taverns and training them in new skills as a good investment. Books were the panacea for "the People's University," as well as the "American Dream." And what possibilities! Books could be provided on agriculture, technology, geography, and commerce, and literature of quality to raise tastes and to cultivate middlebrow culture in the pursuit of civic good. The choice of books depended on the use of authoritative—and conventional—intellectual and cultural canons to sort wheat from chaff, to spread the broadest diffusion of knowledge for all the people.

As a part of American intellectual history, the growth of librarianship as a profession conjoined with growth in intellectual institutions. To collect a body of materials, we must first need them and then create them. America was being transformed by the growth of literacy, the free public school movement, and changes in higher education. Universities had retained the old curriculum of liberal arts and religion inherited from the colonial era where textbook recitation was the principal mode of instruction. Interest in the natural sciences brought a spirit of inquiry with special schools arising as historical societies with collecting zeal. The Morrill Land Grant Act of 1862 promised federal funds for higher education in science, technology, and agriculture. Modern languages were appearing in the curriculum. The influence of German universities with their use of lecture and seminar attracted interest. The idea that the pursuit of truth and the extension of knowledge through research fostered a demand for specialization and structure. Johns Hopkins University was established in 1876 with a graduate school and research at the center. The assimilation process led to a broadening of curriculum to include science, technology, and professional education. Universities replaced classical liberal arts with new sciences of humankind: history, political economy, sociology. Applied knowledge led to the creation in the 1880s of specialized institutions such as the Smithsonian, the Department of Agriculture, the Bureau of Mines, the National Institutes of Health. Scholarship became institutionalized. Scholars no longer worked independently, relying on their own resources, but with the university as a focal point. A by-product of specialization was a change in publishing with greater number of monographs and journals. By accepting research as one of its basic functions, the university enabled the emergence of a new class: the professional scholar with cultural authority to establish a body of literature and a canon of writers to be included. Not until a new spirit changed the character of American higher education could the library be transformed into an instrument of use in its custodianship of cultural capital. And not until commerce and industry were in full force could there be surplus enough for new public institutions.[49] Toward the end of the nineteenth century, these same economic forces conflicted with labor and political unrest. "Bread and roses," the women textile workers cried. Democracy itself was perceived to be at risk, and the library a steadying social force, a life raft in stormy seas. Upholding tradition defined the library's mission, with consequent emphasis in building collections.

The philosophy of American libraries emerged from beliefs in nationalism, philanthropy, economic growth, and the ideology of infinite progress, the American Dream. Historian Sidney Ditzion chronicles a wide range of forces converging in the creation of the library movement. The subsequent range of theories runs from the metaphysical to the pragmatic:

> They run from a postulation of an unexplained, spiritually determined renaissance to an analysis based purely on the socialistic trend which resulted in bath houses, public school buildings, and adequate health inspection, along with public libraries. More generally the free library is associated with the development of a national culture and with the expansive mood of the country. These ideas are connected variously with cultural currents of the time.[50]

These currents include structures like Horace Mann's educational movement, lyceums, the Chautauqua Institution, settlement houses, as well as the cultural authority of writers as diverse as Emerson, Mark Twain, Bret Harte. The authors stimulated reading just as a booming economy enabled the mass production and distribution of books. But what books and who to decide, were problematic questions indeed.

The field of librarianship grew on this unstable landscape of the late nineteenth century, the time we witness, in Lawrence Levine's words, "the emergence of cultural hierarchy in America."[51] In his book *Highbrow/Lowbrow*, Levine shows how reverence for a safer past and the wish for a more secure future (socially and financially) led to a sacralization of high culture in new institutions arbitrating taste and tradition. The debate over the nature of libraries moved beyond the matter of accessibility to encompass the matter of quality of books made available. The initial impulse to promote libraries as social and philanthropic agencies serving the working classes was converted into an increasing emphasis on the educational value of public libraries as a respectable refuge. As a stimulus to political progress and economic boon, the library became a house of culture with the librarian as tradition bearer. Edward Shils speaks of "substantive traditionality"— the appreciation of the past and the desirability of using models from the past as guides—as "one of the major patterns of human thought"[52] Librarians inherited a tradition of literature based on general beliefs acquired from tradition: that literature determined character and civic good, that the stock of current knowledge essentialized the wisdom of the past, not the immediate past, but a remote, imagined past memorialized in books and pictures. Literature as a written tradition entailed a long sifting process and a large social organization for managing what to be added, what to be denied. And the gatekeeper would be culturally positioned to transmit normative tradition through selective endogenous change.

Who to be the prime mover but a man reared in the academy's inherited tradition, the "irrepressible reformer" Melvil Dewey (1851–1931)?[53] While he was not the lone voice in promoting librarianship and library education, his ethical ideas and technological innovations shaped the traditions of the field, including the public's perception of received knowledge. While working as a young librarian at Amherst College, Dewey deduced a contextual structure where materials and disciplines could be organized through his Dewey classification systems. He was also instrumental in articulating a professional identity. While others had introduced the concept, the time was ripe when in 1876 Dewey helped assemble a national meeting of librarians in Pennsylvania. From that emerged the ALA, characterized as "a kind of men's club aimed at educating the masses."[54] Sociologists have noted that the creation of a national professional association is a landmark that shapes identity, raises important issues, and sets standards of service and conduct. The creation of ALA also elevated the stature of the field in relation to other professions, also taking shape at this time. The American Medical Association was established in 1883, the American Historical Association in the following year. The professions were staking out their territory.

Professional organizations grew from original jurisdictions into a system. Sociologist of professions Andrew Abbott, in a case study of three professions, chooses librarianship to illustrate his theoretical model on the creation of jurisdiction and the changes brought by external and internal forces. He cites public and academic libraries as particularly important in relationship to the profession. As custodians of cultural capital, librarians historically had three basic approaches to their use: access, education, and entertainment. In access, the library is geared to retrieve user-requested information; in education and entertainment, the librarian chooses for patrons which information they should retrieve. In the educational outreach, the librarian, the criterion is improvement; in the entertainment realm, the focus is on user pleasure. Abbott contends that mid-nineteenth century librarians stressed the educational role, organizing collections for retrieval and defining what should be retrieved. Claiming control of acquisitions and collections, the librarian disdained "sensational fiction" for the "great books." Inevitably, the public will prevailed, and librarians retreated to the function of access, of a more technical librarianship. The possibility of bibliothecal art conflated to clerical craft, with subsequent change in cultural image.

To Abbott, librarians, like other professionals, have a core of power and a vague periphery. Academic libraries and special librarians are central by their association with prestigious universities, their interrelationship that necessitates standardization in format, and their elite clientele that insists on access only. The periphery of small public and school libraries is more local in mission and maintains educational outreach, which the core libraries abandoned. While all librarians contend with clients, those users who populate the core are also professionals (even more elite), which causes an interpersonal competition that "shaped both the substance and the organizational structure of the overall profession."[55]

Historian and biographer of Dewey, Wayne Wiegand argues that the question of cultural authority affected the stature of librarians (then and now). Librarians sought to create a niche apart from other professional jurisdictions and framed the profession around requisites of character, experience, and institution—not of knowledge, not of determining value, which was relinquished to others. These authorities were the scientists, intellectuals, culture critics, canonical authors, and scholarly elite, who constructed a publication system designed to classify into hierarchies and identify the "best." Librarians were expected to read the reviews in the periodical and scholarly publications to rely on their judgment; librarians were not expected to be themselves the determinants of value. While their own library press crafted volumes listing sources gathered from reviews and recommendations to reinforce the notion of the librarians' knowledge of best reading, these books failed to impress the cultural elites, who clung to their expertise and jurisdiction as the locus of power. The one exception was children's librarians, who with their gendered sensibilities would instinctively know the best books for children.[56] The claiming of this locus of power by children's librarians, in distinction to the more technical and passive role of other specialties, shaped their destiny in a different direction, which we will see.

While Dewey focused on classifying rather than claiming knowledge, he was driven by a passionate commitment to what he perceived as "the Library Spirit," "the Library Faith" apotheosized in the humanitarian and educational ideals of this new professional. Librarians' expertise could improve society by providing the best of literature in the diffusion of knowledge. In an 1876 article in *Library Journal* entitled "The Profession," Dewey argued for cultural influence through proper print. As moral crusader and social engineer, he projects the power of books. Speaking of the librarian, he writes:

He must see that his library contains, as far as possible, the best books on the best subjects, regarding carefully the wants of his special community. Then, having the best books, he must create among his people, his pupils, a desire to read those books. He must put every facility in the way of readers, so that they shall be led from good to better.... Such a librarian will find enough who are ready to put themselves under his influence and direction, and, if competent and enthusiastic, he may soon largely shape the reading, and through it the thought, of the whole community.[57]

This ambitious mission to shape a community's thinking implied the power of books for good or ill and the necessity for guidance to provide the "best books on the best subjects." Librarians' role functioned within their particular moral and pedagogical ideology: honoring the dictates of outside expertise, mastering their own unique professional expertise of delivering services, and accepting the validity of the institution itself.[58] Dewey counted on the middle-class backgrounds of his students to serve and support the reading canons of a middle- and upper-class audience and to educate the masses. Upholding the established order was unquestioned in the library's educational and social mission; only traditional texts were represented, and even newspapers were suspected of possible political agitation. Large reading rooms were built to attract and accommodate workers with little heat or light at home; the library beckoned as a domesticated place, an improving place, and one designed for adults after their public school education. Libraries could be offering wholesome and profitable books to the vocational-technical needs of industry and commerce while raising reading level and reading tastes, essential to the humanitarian ideals in a progressive era and gilded age. The library's highest goal was to conform to its interpretation of democratic ideals, to be, in the title of Sidney Ditzion's history, "Arsenals of a Democratic Culture." The primacy of select reading in the overall civic good of the nation encouraged the privileging and promoting of the best books, the classics. As a preserver of democracy, these very classics represented so much more than time-honored books; the classics were tradition itself, a single version of cultural value and truth. While adult librarians looked upward and outward for sure knowledge and solid footing, another specialist emerged to stake the claim for high ground.

CHILDREN'S LIBRARIANSHIP

Libraries for children evolved from the reform movements for kindergartens, social settlements, child welfare, and female professionalism associated with such causes. Children were an afterthought to these social architects who envisioned only youth of working age using library services like circulation and reference. Libraries were slow to encompass children as audience. The first public libraries saw their mission to further the independent learning of high school graduates. The warning that "children and dogs not admitted" tagged some library doors. Librarians did not originally envision their collections for home use but rather as a reference and reading room for adults. The major public libraries began to inch-open their doors to children, although few offered direct services of any kind. Many powerful library leaders felt that their mission could be best served by building collections in classroom libraries and providing reference service to teachers. One of the first women to challenge this policy was Minerva Sanders (1837–1912) of Pawtucket, Rhode Island, who in 1877 provided seating for children in her reading room, began lending books, created reading lists of children's books, and became a vocal presence at the ALA conferences. Caroline Hewins (1846–1926) of Hartford, Connecticut, raised the consciousness of the library field to the necessity of paying attention to children's reading needs; she addressed the august ALA, the first woman to do so, and challenged members with a survey to report on their activities to foster reading in youth. Lutie Stearns (1866–1943) of Milwaukee, Wisconsin, aroused concern with her "Report on Reading for the Young," which addressed the need for special children's rooms, without age limits, attended by a trained assistant. These years between 1876 and the turn of the century demonstrate a growing campaign to institutionalize library services to children, a brave new world. These three stand out for their early advocacy of books for children in libraries and in a new profession needing direction and cause. Their successes reveal the agency of female librarians in making book history, women's history, too long overlooked by diminished status associated with work with children.

The origins of children's librarianship coincided with a changing social posture toward women and their roles along with a new emphasis on the condition of children, particularly in urban settings. Women were more welcomed in fields related to children. The prevalence of women on the staff of public libraries encouraged the growth of children's services. Professional women tended to diversify into specialties other than those already subsumed by men, such as schools, settlement houses, hospitals, and library service. Sheila Rothman's *Women's Proper Place* shows the connection between changing ideas of women's proper roles and changing principles of American social policy toward women.[59] Barbara Brand's research on female-intensive professions notes the connections between children's services and kindergarten work—both areas considered to be in the female domain.[60] The autonomy granted to women in the child-care field enabled them to develop their own philosophy of service and heightened library roles. As Dee Garrison writes, "Here, as in no other area, library women were free to express, unchallenged, their self-image."[61] Women's perceived affinity for children permitted the profession to grow when women were granted little mobility in the job world. Women were entrusted with educating children and caring for the poor, more and more of whom flocked to public libraries for literacy, social programs, and access to books. At the same time, children's rooms were being recognized as a necessary accompaniment to regular adult services, even if just to lessen the chaos of children underfoot. As Sara Fenwick points out, the origins of children's services within a library setting was shaped by the changing status of children in the family and in community relationships that emphasized education.[62] The nineteenth century witnessed an ever-expanding awareness of childhood as a separate state, one that warranted special treatment: the provision of the best books as well as institutions to house and maintain those collections. Children's librarianship became woven into the progressive reform movement, part of a political context that Suzanne Hildebrand explores in her feminist writings. As she succinctly states, "Women library leaders and women library leaders generally have received unsatisfactory treatment in library history."[63]

The task of critique involves the radical examination of a tradition that is premised on the exclusion of its history, especially the history of women in librarianship. Children's literature, as well as the whole field of children's services, has been limited by its gendered specialization, which, in addition to its subject matter and audience, has diminished its status. As Elizabeth Minnich writes in *Transforming Knowledge*, the existence of curricular particularity—the prefixing of studies such as "Children's Literature" or "Women's History," instead of "Literature" or "History"—has distanced these fields from what is perceived as essential and ideal. As Minnich says, "The more prefixes, the further from the real, the significant, the best."[64] So, at best, children's literature and services suffer from a perceived sense of irrelevance, which further isolates the history of the significant women pioneers in the field.

In addition, the preoccupation of the profession with current technology and practice has further obscured attention to history. Library historians have noted an ambivalence about the past that obscures contemporary ideology at play.[65] James Carmichael argues that librarians' esteem problems stem from their lack of history. He attributes this ignorance, in part, to the prevalence of women luminaries: "Like other professions in which women predominated, librarians had been so invisible to outsiders that their work had been taken for granted, and it was therefore hard to generate interest from either without or within the profession"[66] Michael Harris and Stanley Hannah critique ahistorical approaches as a historical interpretation in itself, "heavily freighted with ideological baggage."[67] Indeed, cultural ignorance of the framing and foundational role of children's librarians suggests a larger neglect of subjects related to children and women, however prefixed or marginalized.

Increasingly, women librarians took charge. The social climate of change in late-nineteenth-century America swayed librarians toward access to the eager young audience already at the door. Reformers saw the opportunity to reach children more in school and less in the world of work as child labor became restricted and compulsory education laws enforced. The number of children with the time and interest to read stimulated a response from librarians who began offering reading rooms and lending services. Library education cooperated by offering training programs that included children's literature. The assumption was growing that a public librarian would inevitably need to know something about children's books and children's needs. Library education began in 1887 with Dewey's New York State Library School, and Caroline Hewins lectured on the history of children's books and children's reading; specialized programs followed at Pratt Institute of Brooklyn and at Carnegie Library of Pittsburgh. Through in-house training and library education, children's librarianship bore fruit through a variety of discourses involving the press, the professional association, the school, and social welfare organizations. Powerful library women were instrumental in constructing the service paradigm for children's work, which centered on *selection as prescription*: choosing books to change lives. The field of children's librarianship was officially sanctioned by the organization in 1900 of the ALA Section for Library Work for Children, and that date is considered the advent of the field.

Who were these forceful women, who in a later age could have been taken on the world with their energy and spirit, but who were drawn to the idea of conjoining literature and libraries for children? How did they shape their institutions to advocate for the best books for young readers? What difference did they make in shaping these two constructs—literature and libraries—within a selective tradition? While many names could and should be mentioned, as I argue elsewhere on the pedagogy of children's literature and librarianship,[68] I focus on the two matriarchs whose influence resounds still: Caroline Hewins and Anne Carroll Moore. Their writings were the palimpsest for the literary critics that followed. These are the "shoulders of giants" on which others stood and extended the story.

CAROLINE HEWINS

Caroline Hewins is the grand dame of the children's library cause, its first outspoken advocate, mentor, institution-builder. While Melvil Dewey was the acknowledged forefather of the library profession whose vision formulated the parameters of the field, Caroline Hewins is the rather unacknowledged foremother of children's librarianship whose vision exceeded these borders and braved new territory. Hewins was remarkable in her iconoclasm, particularly in pursuing a material and imaginative reality largely nonexistent in the late 1870s. Bright and bookish, Hewins, reared in a cultured home, was sent as a student to the Boston Athenaeum to do research for the principals of Girls' High and Normal School. Impressed by the scholarly atmosphere there, she persuaded her parents to let her work there after graduation. In 1875 she became librarian of the Young Men's Institute at Hartford, Connecticut, where she discovered few books commendable for youth, who were devouring the only stock available: books by popular writers such as Horatio Alger, Oliver Optic, Harry Castlemon, Martha Findley, and Ouida. On her own initiative she launched a campaign to improve the reading levels of children and surveyed libraries across the country asking, "What are you doing to encourage a love of reading in boys and girls?" These slim pickings, reported to the ALA conference of 1882, persuaded her to labor for the cause of children's access to libraries and good collections. Her own experience with literature, chronicled in her later biography, *A Mid-century Child and Her Books* (1926), led her to create her own selection guide, the first of its kind: *Books for the Young, a Guide for Parents and Children* (1882). In this pioneering work, which later became a selection bible and exemplar for librarians, she urged that children be given something to grow up to, rather than away from. Hewins also included a list of recommended titles, which included some controversial works, such as *The Adventures of Tom Sawyer*, frequently banned. With the publication of this work, Hewins models the role that librarians should play in this new territory: asserting authority, determining quality, and advising adults for children. And at the heart is the language of list-making as cultural prerogative and professional paradigm.

The next year Hewins began contributing a monthly column, "Literature for the Young," to the newly founded *Library Journal*, which consisted of a list of new children's books and quotations from reviews of them that had appeared in the press, as well as a section, "Notes and Suggestions," a miscellany of comments on children's reading matter and how to select it. Demonstrating that librarians should be writing in professional literature, she contributed articles to the new journal *Public Libraries*. Warning librarians not to rely on the scant notices of children's books in the press, in which "the tail of the publisher is over them all," she urged her colleagues, instead, to develop a sufficient "body of doctrine"— critical judgments, knowledge of books—so that they could guide others in the selection of literature.[69] She also sensed the importance of writing for the mainstream literary periodicals and contributed a lengthy article, "The History of Children's Books," which demonstrates a keen knowledge of the historiography of the field.[70] Here is an emphatic, learned, cultured woman claiming a high profile for her passion. Not only was Hewins the first to write a selection guide to children's books, but she also exhorted librarians to go beyond annotations and library lists toward the development of critical judgment and a more substantive knowledge of books. It was Hewins who established the "adultist" standard of selection adopted by the librarians who followed: children's books, as part of the body of literature, must be evaluated in a similar manner as adult literature and must be appreciated by adults as well as children. In 1931, Alice Jordan would write of the "Ideal Book from the Standpoint of the Children's Literature" in terms set by Hewins a half-century before: "The ideal book for a child is the one that is equally claimed by grown persons."[71] This conviction was aligned with their aspirations for similar professional stature, which Hewins sensed would come only if they were valued as critics, with knowledge of and experience with literature, a novel and unparalleled role distinguishing them from others of a more scripted position. As matriarch, Hewins failed to capture the imagination of the new generation of librarians in the same fervor as did her protégée, who followed her path with added political savvy and prolific prose.

ANNE CARROLL MOORE

Hewins's fierce faith in good books for the young materialized in the life's work of Anne Carroll Moore (1871–1961), arguably the most powerful and formative influence on books for children in the twentieth century. A towering figure, Moore is larger than life and legendary in the field. While Moore's life and influence have been honored in library history, less attention has focused on her powerful agency in a number of discourses that have shaped the field of children's librarianship as well as children's services. Do women's studies scholars explore her life and works as exemplar of the agency of women as institution-builders spanning fields? Do historians of American children's literature know of her influence on the field? While feminist library historians know of Moore and her part in making history, many in her own profession are shy on knowing what she actually wrought in this brand new field where she trudged mightily, stirring the earth with her large, long steps. Few among the academics have acknowledged the role of children's librarians in the early cultural production and reception of children's literature. Beverly Lyon Clark is unique among literary scholars in bringing to light the work of Moore and others in stimulating "a climate conducive to the nurturing of children's literature."[72] In a better world, all actors on the stage would matter, especially those who premiered the role.

Moore inherited Caroline Hewins's critical voice and pursued the written word with a similar passion for judgment and persuasion. Robert Sink, one of her later colleagues at New York Public Library, attributed her primary contribution to be helping to "develop the critical faculties of librarians so that they could identify the best of children's literature."[73] She surely mastered discernment from Caroline Hewins, whom she met on the way to her first ALA conference, where Hewins spoke on "Old and new books—what to buy," arguing for the value of older books as well as the latest literature: a policy that became practice.[74] Hewins and Moore developed a friendship of "kindred spirits," as Anne Shirley (*Anne of Green Gables*) would say, that lasted a lifetime and left children's literature a changed landscape. Moore worked in the most innovative structures for children's books: the Pratt Institute in Brooklyn from 1896 to 1906, and then the New York Public Library from 1906 to 1941. "I have spun out a long thread," she wrote.[75]

Moore's initiation into the field was under the leadership of Mary Wright Plummer (1856–1916), the library director of Pratt Institute and an impassioned advocate for children's books, who designed the first architectural space for a children's collection. Plummer was a cultured, literary woman, a linguist, a poet, and a librarian with an international reputation—quite an impressive role model for Moore.[76] She was chosen as the U.S. delegate to the International Congress of Librarians held in Paris in 1900, where she planned a graphics exhibit and delivered two papers in French: one on bibliography and the other on library and school cooperation. International visitors often visited Pratt to see the work inspired by Plummer. She, like Caroline Hewins, advocated for an active role of libraries with children's reading and upheld high standards for quality rather than quantity of books available. In an 1897 *Library Journal*, Plummer addressed the requisites for an ideal children's library, still in the drawing stages, as "suitable books, plenty of room, plenty of assistance, and thoughtful administration."[77] She succeeded in designing the first children's room especially built for that purpose with those qualities in mind.

Moore flourished under the visionary guidance of Plummer, who hand-picked Moore to be that "thoughtful administrator." In her first year report at Pratt, Moore wrote about the challenges of opening a new department for children, which "presented daily new questions of government, logic, and ethics and opened our eyes to the sociological value of all dealings with children."[78] In this report Moore expressed her interest in "the kindergarten spirit," with the reservation that the library be unique in its own character and potential for children's intellectual growth. Moore's intention at Pratt, which included kindergarten methods, was to build a children's book collection, which would be accompanied by picture and book displays as well as accompanying reading lists. She presented a landmark paper at the 1898 ALA conference, "Special training for children's librarians," in which she stated for the first time what was needed in the field, particularly in the education of picture books, still very much in its infancy as a genre: "Knowledge of children; of their books; of good pictures; and a recognition of their interrelationship, or a sense of the fitness of things."[79] Moore was arguably the first librarian to speak about children's books as art and literature, to advocate in her speeches and book reviews for an enhanced quality of children's book making, to bring literary values to the fore, above all, even knowledge of children, which became subsumed under knowledge of the literature and the judgment of the critic. Book lists became the vehicle to demonstrate that expertise.

Moore was influenced in these efforts, in part, by the appraisal movement, which gained favor in library circles around the turn of the century. The ALA sponsored a series of papers published in *Library Journal* that addressed the feasibility of a "bibliographical Utopia," where experts would contribute to a universal bibliography.[80] This project coincided with the publication of a card catalog system on a national scale by the Library of Congress. This scheme, advocated by George Iles, provided for the publication in all fields of literature of exhaustive bibliographies, with annotations "appraising" or "evaluating" the value of the title according to specialists in the field, "the consensus of the competent." Iles authored a *Guide to the Literature of American History* in 1902, which inspired consideration of parallel projects in other subject areas. Major library leaders discussed the prospects in a special symposium of separate papers published in the *Library Journal*, one of which resonated with Moore, according to scholar Sybille Jagusch in her dissertation on Moore and Hewins.[81] Moore was inspired by the objective perspective of William E. Foster, librarian at Providence Public Library, who suggested the kind of "searching" questions applicable to the evaluation of varied types of materials, such as the competence of the author, the focus of the work, utility as reference or continuous reading, and audience, among others.[82] Moore embraced the ideal of appraisal in her attempt to create a "body of sustained criticism concerning the books written and published from year to year for the children of this country and of other countries."[83] Moore's critical mettle emerged from the mentorship of Hewins and her identification with a larger movement toward bibliographic control evident in the professional association.

That her humble booklists could represent a part of the larger universe of knowledge was inspiration indeed.

In her attempts to publicize children's libraries and reading, Moore became a celebrity of sorts by her visibility in the press, in the New York cultural scene, in collaboration with book editors and publishers, and in the professional organization. If earlier discourse centered on the access to and volume of children's books, Moore shifted focus to the content of the collection, its very caliber, which seemed to her ill-formed and unsuitable. In one of her early columns in *The Bookman*, Moore railed against the current grain of children's books, echoing the prophetic fervor of mentor Hewins:

> We are tired of substitutes for realities in writing for children. The trail of the serpent has been growing more and more clearly defined in the flow of children's books from publisher to bookshop, library, home, and school—a trail strewn with patronage and propaganda, moralizing self-sufficiency and sham efficiency, mock heroics and cheap optimism—above all, with the commonplace in theme, treatment, and language—the proverbial stone in place of bread, in the name of education.[84]

Moore's tone changed as she began partnering with publishers in efforts such as Children's Book Week of 1919, the Newbery Medal of 1922, and the Caldecott Medal of 1938. With proximity to the major publishing houses situated in New York City, Moore built in the early decades of the twentieth century an empire of influence by appropriating the largesse of publishers to promote her grand designs, which necessitated a more mutually beneficial, intimate, even symbiotic relationship with publishers, who sought her counsel in their choice of books to print and reprint, or authors or artists to secure. In the book capitol of New York City and in the grand building on 42nd Street, Moore as impresario saw the possibilities of a children's library without walls, with far flung paths into literary landscapes of art and commerce, of home and abroad, a cosmopolitan nursery. Her instincts were entrepreneurial in expanding her enterprise, building branches, promoting books nationwide and internationally, and making children's books visible and valid to middlebrow culture. The communication was ever tight, interwoven, among the librarian, the schools, the creators and publishers, and the community, interpreted broadly with creative reverberations.

Moore found her milieu in the reviewing of and writing about children's books, the rhetoric introduced by Hewins. Children's books had been well covered in the mainstream literary press of the mid- to late nineteenth century, but as children's books faded from view in the lines demarcating age for literature, the coverage of children's books needed visibility once again in the new century. The periodical press seemed open to her expression of taste in books for the young. In 1918, Moore was invited to review children's books for the new literary magazine *The Bookman*, an ongoing critical column on children's books that she continued until the magazine's demise in 1926. In 1924, she began writing a children's page for the *New York Herald Tribune* under the heading, "The Three Owls," her emblem representing the critical roles of writer, artist, and critic—all considered creators of the book. In 1930, she began a column with a similar triage title in the *Horn Book*. Her commentary was always more than reviews. As a journalist and cultural critic, she debated issues confronting the children's library world far and wide, introduced authors and artists, remembered favorite books, and launched the reputation of new names like Dr. Seuss. These eclectic musings and judgment calls on children's books were collected in a multitude of volumes: *Roads to Childhood* (1920, reprinted as *My Roads to Childhood*, 1961); *New Roads to Childhood* (1923); *Crossroads to Childhood* (1926); and *The Three Owls* (1925, 1927, 1931). She also ventured into her own fictional writing in two novels for children: *Nicholas: A Manhattan Christmas* Story (1924), centered in New York City, and *Nicholas and the Golden Goose* (1932), set in France and England. This varied discourse helped to establish Moore as a formidable voice and dynamic figure in the field, with the power to canonize as professional prowess.

Moore was prolific in her writing on children's books, not only regular columns, but also lists of recommended titles, a practice she mastered from Hewins. The making of lists of best books that inaugurated with Hewins's *Books for the Young* became institutionalized with Moore as critic and bibliographer. Her first such list was a pamphlet she prepared for the Iowa Library Commission as an instructor of the Iowa Summer School in 1902: "A list of books recommended for a children's library," an ambitious project for a nascent institution. It was here she articulated her well-worn dictum that became a mantra of the profession: "To give each child the right book at the right time" and began to create her annotations, which were often considered masterful prose.[85] More booklists emerged from special library exhibits, such as "Heroism" (1914) or "Children's Books of Yesterday" (1933). The annual list, "Children's Books Suggested as Gifts," which appeared from 1918 through 1941, was a desideratum for most children's collections and commercial purposes. Her "Seven Stories High," which was written in 1932 for *Compton's Encyclopedia*, was commonly available throughout the country for years to come, an incalculable influence on intellectual thought on childhood.

The reach was panoramic. When was she was at Pratt, Moore was learning the administration of a children's room; at New York Public Library she stretched her horizons considerably by tackling outreach, writing regular book columns, public relations, branch libraries, and relations with publishers. Moore intuitively understood the need to build alliances between the library collections and its creators and producers. Her interest in networking—local, cross-institutional, international—embraced the publishing industry, just beginning to diversify into the children's book market and ripe for influence. Moore intentionally set out to shape the books appearing on library shelves. Josiah Titzell called her page in the *Herald Tribune* the "yea or nay of all children's books."[86] Editors sought her approval of manuscripts, some of which she disapproved, such as E. B. White's *Stuart Little*, as revealed in Ursula Nordstrom's collected letters.[87] Her choices for books to appear in the annual holiday exhibition—a pamphlet list published with much fanfare—were an economic impetus for publishers to listen and heed her counsel. Moore promoted a cachet for children's books that fit within her vision of the right books for the right child.

Anne Carroll Moore's zeal for quality literature for youth helped to create a synergy of activity, a network, a community, a web of influence. She made the overtures to the publishing world, which responded in kind when they realized how advantageous this collaboration could be. Franklin Matthiews of the Boy Scouts, Frederic Melcher of *Publishers Weekly*, and Anne Carroll Moore of New York Public Library, among others, collaborated in a common cause to make children's books big business for libraries, schools, homes, and bookstores. In 1929, Melcher commended librarians, with Moore as mentor, for their instrumental role in promoting reading and books as a stimulus to the trade.[88] She did not hesitate to stretch her influence to the founding of the first children's bookstore and professional journal, both ventures of Bertha Mahony Miller, inspired by Moore's children's room and booklists to create her own sense of place. Miller's Bookshop for Boys and Girls, which was founded in Boston in 1916, was indebted to Moore's use of space in making books hospitable and inviting. Above all, Mahony was influenced by Moore's prodigious selective lists. In her bookstore, which programmed activities similar to a library, she produced a series of purchase guides and booklists, which ultimately became the basis for the *Horn Book* in 1924, the first and most successful professional magazine on children's books designed for parents, educators, librarians, and the general public. Moore kept in close touch with Mahony as she began this maiden voyage, and the *Horn Book* archives hold many letters back and forth from Moore to Mahony, who sought her favor and imprimatur for her new venture in publishing.

Mahony's lists became the nucleus of the *Children's Catalog*, the ultimate selection guide reflecting the prerogatives of the children's librarian and jurisdiction. This massive tome has expressed the subjectivity of librarians and the temper of the times since 1909 to the current eighteenth edition of 2001. As a determinant of quality for buying and evaluating book collections, this collaborative collection holds enormous consumer as well as critical power. Reputations of books can be traced as to their appearance or not in the *Catalog* with its distinguishing standards and ranks; in fact, the canon of children's literature could emerge from research into its contents, an ambitious project begun by Christine Jenkins, women's library historian and scholar.[89] Jenkins has analyzed the *Catalog* over nearly a century of use to determine its canonical standards and methods of evaluation. The *Catalog* was formed as a training tool, evaluative measure, and reference guide for fledgling librarians in the new area of children's librarianship. Published by H. W. Wilson Company, the book was intended to be a compilation of authoritative lists, forty-five of which appeared in annotated form in the first volume. The lists were compiled largely by children's librarians, who served as compilers, annotators, or editors on a crusade against the onslaught of pulp fiction and sensationalism considered dangerous for youth. The *Catalog* would be an antidote to the blight of a questionable mass print culture: a salvation of sorts. The persistence of this volume over the years in its various manifestations demonstrates the library faith in such function. While designed to ensure high standards of authoritative approval, the series reveals the vagaries of reputation, subjective rather than objective truth.

These collaborative efforts toward structure—standards and bibliography—mark the fervor of these evangelistic women working in and around children's libraries. They were such doers, so dynamic in the various enterprises they formed to further their mission. And they were writers too, again following the model of Hewins with her mighty pen. They compiled bountiful lists, whole books of lists, wrote extensively in the press, the mainstream literary journals, and finally in their own professional journal, the *Horn Book*. Many in the group wrote impassioned books, a legacy that offers insight into their intentions and values. To Betsy Hearne and Christine Jenkins, in their discussion of the ethos of children's library history, this writing in the way of "psalms, proverbs, precepts, and practices" were "sacred texts," imbued with the sense of "communion and crusade" from those empowered by word, image, and ideal.[90] Hearne and Jenkins focus on a cadre of canonical writings that have made their way in the world: Anne Carroll Moore's *My Roads to Childhood*; Frances Clarke Sayers's *Summoned by Books*; Bertha Mahony Miller and Elinor Whitney Field's *Realms of Gold in Children's Books*; Annis Duff's *Bequest of Wings*; Paul Hazard's *Book, Children & Men*; Marie Shedlock's *The Art of the Storyteller*; Ruth Sawyer's *The Way of the Storyteller*; Lillian Smith's *The Unreluctant Years*; Ruth Hill Viguers's *Margin for Surprise* and *An Ample Field*; and Margaret Edwards's *The Fair Garden and the Swarm of Beasts*. These spirited humanistic texts embody the tradition of fervent criticism with suggestions of recommended titles, evaluative criteria, and discussions of classics. These writings perpetuated the children's canon, which persisted with large equanimity and little dissension until the 1940s. The ideology of reading privileged the imagination as revealed in proven classics, old and new, imprinted by the librarian.

THE PARADIGM OF SELECTION

Dee Garrison's groundbreaking and divisive history of the foundations of librarianship, *Apostles of Culture* (1979), essentialized the role of librarians as "apostles of culture."[91] This title fits those women who organized the children's room and its collections. Children's librarians were both missionaries and conservators, bent on reaching the masses and influencing the market with certain aesthetics of Romanticism: a genteel tradition of a symbolic past. Twentieth-century American children's literature derived from the experiences and presuppositions of the librarians' literary establishment: a social construction of canon formation in this small corner of the cultural world. That children's literature is intricately bound within its institutional parameters is a significant though largely unreported chapter of American intellectual history. Children's library history is also unsung. The connection between the rhetoric and regimen of children's librarians and the consequent supply of books created and produced and distributed to children in the twentieth century exemplifies how literature is cultural capital: the confluence of art and commerce, of morality and materialism, of creation and production. While adult literature emanated from diverse influences, children's literature more clearly bears the marks of the librarians who assumed this literary domain as their own.

Librarians in general are perceived as neutral intermediaries whose involvement with literature is peripheral to the creative process and product. Instead, libraries serve as "the genteel setting," in Dee Garrison's words, for the promotion and arbitration of morals and manners through a defined print culture. What a library collects is a microcosm of valued and validated literature. As an agency of cultural formation and social order, a library's principal functions are to select, save, and share its collections. What a library *is* depends on what a library *does*: its cultural work in the world, its jurisdiction in organizing knowledge, in circulating materials, in securing information and literature for its community.

Despite their perceived passivity, librarians can be defined as canon makers who reproduce social hierarchy in a systematic act of tradition bearing (also known as collection development). As civic space, the library in its actions is inherently political: Who does what with finite resources? Who is represented in collections? Who is served? These questions are highly charged when the matter is *selecting* what is included or excluded and even more potent when the issue concerns *children*. That librarians can construct standards to evaluate literature—and make choices in a commodity culture—is based on their ideology of reading that conflates professional ethics, moral idealism, and market influence.

These apostles of culture embraced the authority of cultural validation as integral to their professional paradigm. Thomas S. Kuhn's key construct in his landmark work, *Structure of Scientific Revolutions* (1962) is the idea of a paradigm, which he meant for the sciences, but which has been appropriated by the social sciences and humanities.[92] Kuhn's concept of a paradigm is based on accepted examples of actual practice, which provide models from which spring tradition. The community and commitment of a shared paradigm provide the basis for growth. A paradigm is rooted strongly enough to resist debate on foundational questions about the subject and the nature of the discipline. I believe the paradigm of librarianship that has shaped its history for a century is the ideology of reading and the librarian's place in perpetuating a selective tradition. At the core is the right to prescribe for readers via the selection process based on a discerning knowledge of the enduring from the ephemeral, the valuable from the worthless, the good from the bad. Gramsci's concept of hegemony is based on prevalent ideologies as organizing agents in promoting the status quo. The cultural studies scholar, Raymond Williams, incorporated some of Gramsci's ideas into his theory of "the selective tradition." To Williams, we can only understand a dominant culture by examining the social processes on which it depends, what he calls "the process of incorporation." For Williams, this process is founded on what he calls "the selective tradition," which is "the way in which from a whole possible area of past and present, certain meanings and practices are chosen for emphasis, certain other meanings are neglected and excluded."[93]

The meanings and practices of the American library movement reveal a selective tradition in the gospel of public culture. The product of nineteenth-century social reforms, the library movement was propagated by a cadre of new professional librarians and educators who promoted their vision of social good and social mobility through democratic access to the Book. Which books? Melvil Dewey designed a structure for the library profession by which library professionals relegated the cultural authority of choosing "the best books" to other professionals, more engrained in literary and scholarly matters. Library historian Wayne Wiegand points out that the one exception to this charge was in the area of literature for children, where he believed that cultured women had a natural talent in distinguishing "good" and "bad" reading.[94] Thus, children's librarians were granted more autonomy in shaping canons and in assuming cultural roles of guardianship over children's reading—and, by extension, the moral and intellectual life of adults, seemingly more elusive as an audience to control. In the children's realm, the genteel culture still prevailed.

Important national concerns for civic good were embodied in the library. Dee Garrison in her study of the American public library movement from 1876 to 1920 delineated these matters of cultural discourse:

> The belief that America was a radical democratic experiment in government; the sense of urban crisis and chaos; the fear of immigrant intruders; the emphasis upon the family as guarantor of tradition; the discontent of woman and labor; the hope that education would right the wrongs of poverty and crime; the hunger for education among the poor; the ambiguous paternalistic and humanitarian motives of reformers.[95]

What Garrison calls "the genteel ideology" arose from the confluence of female unrest, religious doubt, and economic insecurity: an "elite response to deep-seated fears about the drift of city life.[96] Paul Boyer's history of censorship in America traces the ambivalence of librarians in straddling professional ethics with morality. The debate over the nature of libraries concerned matters of access and selection: the quality of the books to be made available.[97] The library's efforts to promote reading as moral instruction coincided with the larger movements of philanthropy, the purity crusade and censorship, the professionalization movement, particularly for women, and the making of a middlebrow, genteel culture.

The notion of "a genteel tradition" comes from George Santayana who introduced that term in 1911 to describe the strictures of Victorian literature and philosophy, a Calvinist thread which modernism promised to break.[98] The concept of a genteel tradition generally refers to a complex of gentrified ideas from America's Gilded Age represented by economic and cultural elites. Santayana associated the tradition with philosophical idealism that dominated American religion and morals, as well as literature, with adherence to older beliefs and customs, and aligned with women's interests. As John Tomsich has observed, the genteel traditionalists sought to establish literature as a worthy vocation and to uphold standards against a perceived declining public taste. Extolling their mission to teach literary appreciation, the proponents "pictured themselves as heroes, almost missionaries, in the cause of culture."[99] The movement was often contradictory, exhibiting an abhorrence with didacticism in strident terms. Despite the attention by historians in the early decades of the twentieth century to the demise of the genteel culture, suggesting a rupture with the past, the genteel tradition lived on, as revealed in Joan Shelley Rubin's study of the making of middlebrow culture, especially through the Book-of-the-Month Club, the Great Books program, literary journalism, and historical outlines like Henrik Willem Van Loon's *The Story of Mankind*, the first Newbery Award recipient.

I hold that genteel values were transmitted through the foremothers of the children's library movement, whose Anglophilia and Romanticism preserved a sense of culture that *was* rather than *is*. While adult literature turned toward modernism and its break with the past, children's literature persisted in its glorification of America's rural childhood history and idealized family life. They privileged certain values centered on imaginative possibilities rather than realistic depiction. Their values were embedded in civic pride and the belief that books have power to shape lives, shape society. The period of 1880 through 1920 has been characterized in its thrust toward "democratic idealism," shaped by the dislocation of populations within the country and from outside and the disruption of technology and urban landscapes.[100] The literature for children tended to revere the past and prescribe values requisite for a democratic society. While the genteel tradition waned in popular consciousness, it persisted in the children's library world in its privileged sensibilities and preferences in a literature of childhood. Children's librarians assumed the role of cultural authorities—to "blow the horn for fine books," as *Horn Book* promised—in educating children, the public, and the publishing industry to their high humanistic standards.

The Selective Tradition

The developing profession of children's librarianship demonstrated a commitment to a selective tradition: a reformist belief in an ideology of reading based on transcendent spiritual values of literature. Good books from good authors bring good ends; bad books from bad authors bring bad ends. The right book for the right reader was a mantra, which was open to interpretation as to which came first. The standard for judging children's literature would be the same as judging adult literature: literary quality.[101] Implicit is the cultural imperative to make the selections necessary to further the public good and to build a collection which would serve as a blueprint for self-improvement, or in Clifford Geertz's words, "templates of experience" for the young.[102] The library's civilizing mission led to a diffusion of literacy, a phenomenal growth in book publishing, and the creation of classics as titles befitting a canon. Concurrently, alternative responses of resistance persisted, such as illiteracy, aliteracy, popular culture materials, and the devising of multiple canons, blurring what Herbert Gans calls "taste cultures."[103]

While adult librarians were entrusted with a high calling to provide appropriate reading for a community, their powers were circumscribed as passive transmitters of the canon. Children's librarians, on the other hand, were given inordinate powers by the professional mandates of Melvil Dewey, the profession's guiding spirit. According to Wayne Wiegand, Dewey's biographer, Melvil Dewey thought that librarians should select books based on reviews by experts in scholarly journals rather than make judgments themselves on literature.[104] Children's librarians, a feminized profession developing in the 1890s, were, by default, given province over children's literature, a subject considered appropriate for women, whose natural instincts were presumed to be authoritative. Thus, Dewey, as professional progenitor, unwittingly created a special status for children's librarians: the power of cultural authority, the judgment to declare the value of literature, and the autonomy to create an institutional construct to further these values. The shaping of the field in this direction led children's librarians to become singularly powerful figures in the publishing world, wielding power through writing reviews; selecting and promoted prescribed reading; training and guiding future children's book librarians, booksellers, and editors; bestowing awards; and advocating a selective tradition in books for children. Children's librarians saw their calling beyond library walls to the traffic of books in the marketplace of ideas. Their agency would contain selection as well as evaluation: readers' advisory as well as education of the field and the public. They constituted their culture-making powers broadly, appreciating the many ways texts are validated and empowered. Barbara Herrnstein Smith's insight on evaluation applies well to the canon formation of children's librarians and their special mission:

> [T]he highly individualized forms of evaluation exhibited in the more or less professional activities of scholars, teachers, and academic or journalistic critics—not only their full-dress reviews and explicit rank orderings, evaluations, and reevaluations, but also such activities as the awarding of literary prizes, the commissioning and publishing of articles about certain works, the compiling of anthologies, the writing of introductions, the construction of department curricula, and the drawing up of class reading lists.[105]

While adult librarians functioned essentially as passive transmitters of the canon, children's librarians were involved in producing and reproducing the canon by their robust agency in the high culture purviews of reviewing, literary journalism, and book publishing. Children's librarians were expected to be apostles of culture, missionaries of the word, who themselves needed to be articulate and inventive in reaching a broad audience, awaiting conversion.

The librarian ethic was rooted in the belief of the morality of reading. Indeed, the central role of libraries, as defined by revisionist historian Michael Harris, is "the preservation, transmission, and thus reproduction of the Book, and the audience for the Book."[106] As opposed to a notion of the library as primarily a producer of circulation, Harris posits the library as essentially a consumer of high culture. Part of what Dewey called "the Library Spirit" was the social ideal that the mass public would respond to the authority vested in a collection legitimated by the state and professional expertise. The librarian's knowledge would derive from the dictates of outside professional expertise on appropriate publications bearing cultural and intellectual authority. The assumptions behind library school education were "the legitimacy of the institution in which this expertise was practiced and the authority of the cultural and intellectual objects around which the expertise revolved."[107] This ethic prevailed as the dominant paradigm in the profession and became articulated through theorists on the selection process. Probably the most famous of these writers was Helen Haines, whose *Living with Books: The Art of Book Selection* (1935) was the basic text in library schools for more than a generation. Haines preached the gospel of knowing the cultural objects well and evaluating according to literary and intellectual canons, which included the role of "readers' adviser."

Librarians inherited a belief in a hierarchy of culture prevalent in the value systems traditional to the nineteenth century. Part of that belief system incorporated elements of Puritanism: ideas of having predestined and godly obligation to transmit their ideals to the world, ideas that deeply influenced founders of the country. This influence was most pronounced in New England, which was also the center of the public library movement, with Boston being Mecca. Men of letters like Ralph Waldo Emerson echoed the thoughts of Sir Frances Bacon (1561–1626), English philosopher and statesman whose essays prescribed ways of reading and values of books and libraries, some of which were inscribed on library edifices. Emerson was arguably the most articulate defender of the efficacy of the good reader and the good book. Good reading led to good behavior, while bad reading led to the opposite end. Librarians' social responsibility embraced the mission of offering the community quality reading according to established canons that excluded most new, controversial, or popular literature. In Wiegand's historical glance, "The intent of the public library in 1900 was surely equalitarian; the result surely was not."[108] While the public persisted in reading romances, French novels, and sensational fiction, librarians "willingly censored by means of selective acquisitions." Indeed, the much-touted ethic of intellectual freedom was a later development, the result of Nazi oppression of civil liberties and Library of Congress Librarian Archibald MacLeisch's impassioned rhetoric. The Library Bill of Rights (1939) represented an ideal rather than actuality throughout most of American library history.

The genteel literary code of librarians persisted in the early decades of the twentieth century. The very professionals who would argue against censorship in the later 1920s were obsessed by "bad books" around the end of the century. This concern coincided with the development of children's services and the early growth of library education; these principles of moral rectitude in collection development were embedded in the profession. One of the most articulate spokesmen of the library perspective on moral selection was Arthur Bostwick, an influential scholar-librarian who edited several texts in a "Classics of American Librarianship" series, published by H. W. Wilson. The term *classics* is defined in a preface to be the "early and standard expressions of ideas that have developed later into prominence."[109] *The Library and Society* (1920) contains essays and addresses by distinguished figures in the field on issues related to the community mission of public libraries, including "Control and Guidance of Reading." Threaded throughout the volume are warnings about reading and the dire effects of poor choices, advising cautious restraint and guidance, where without such aid, "where one will rise, a hundred, a thousand rather, will remain at the low level from which they started, or more naturally sink to still lower depths."[110] In 1908, Bostwick as ALA president organized a conference on the question, "What Shall the Libraries Do about Bad Books?" Bostwick spoke passionately against books of "immoral tendency" and warned against immigrants whose "standards of propriety are sometimes those of an earlier and grosser age." Librarians should hold the line against the "menacing tide" of dangerous books: "Thus far shalt thou go and no farther."[111] Librarians rallied to this call by sharing how they averted "doubtful fiction" in their strategies to keep certain books from the reading public: the Wisconsin Library Commission kept any book by a "modern degenerate" from its traveling libraries, and the New York Public Library reported that "immoral" classics were barred to anyone with "unworthy" reasons for such requests.[112] The gradual conversion of librarians to the censorship debates of the 1920s led to a reexamination by some of their traditional role as guardians of the middle-class values. One librarian reflected on the changes occurring. While accepting the impulse to "guide and control" the lives of others, she warned that librarians, particularly from their sheltered backgrounds, could not sustain a role as moral arbiter. She asked:

> Who, after all, are we to set ourselves up as capable of saying what will or will not harm another person? We have thought that upon us lay the heavy burden of guarding the morals of youth, 90 per cent of which could tell us things! ... And the way we tried to help our young people was to weigh them down with the same narrowing shackles of ignorance and limited experience that we ourselves were struggling with.[113]

The Gibraltar-like stance of librarians persisted. The strictures on reading were most expressed in prescriptions for children's reading. Before the specialization of children's libraries, much critical attention was paid to children's literature as largely improving works passed on from parent to child. F. J. Harvey Darton, whose definitive history *Children's Books in England* (1932) shaped library advocates like Frederic Melcher, expressed this tension as the age-old battle "between instruction and amusement, between restraint and freedom, between hesitant morality and spontaneous happiness."[114] As reflected in an historical anthology of nineteenth-century writings on children's literature, Lance Salway's *A Peculiar Gift* (1976), the precedent was set in Victorian periodicals to debate didacticism and the imagination in children's literature.[115] Serious discussions of the subject were not confined to specific children's periodicals or family magazines but were expressed in the mainstream magazines designed for a broad audience, assumed to be interested in the literature of childhood.

The earliest library mentor for children, Caroline Hewins, expressed her own concerns for the quality of children's reading, surveying pioneer library directors regarding their policies and practices toward improving children's reading. The fervor that Hewins inspired in Anne Carroll Moore, Alice Jordan, and other library leaders was a selective passion: to choose the wheat from the chaff, to privilege certain books for character development. As Betsy Hearne and Christine Jenkins point out, part of the library faith professed by early children's librarians was a passionate commitment to the social value of quality literature.[116] Equally strong was the fear of the effect of poor-quality books on impressionable youth. One of the most important library educators of the early twentieth century, Frances Jenkins Olcott, wrote the first two chapters of her text, *The Children's Reading* (1912, 1927), on "The Influence of Good Books" and "Effects of Bad Books." A prefatory chart lists classic works and famous people influenced by them. Using the metaphor of a garden for the mind, she suggests the importance of soil and seeds—and weeding—to "fill their imaginations with the noble thoughts and ideals of those great books which will help the developing men or women to resist ignoble and corroding influences."[117] Proceeding to argue for the power of books to mold character, she quotes from Plato, Plutarch, Wordsworth ("the child is father of the man"), Emerson, with references to the early reading of Milton, Gladstone, Robert Burns, and Abe Lincoln on his cabin floor reading by firelight and learning by heart the precious words of William Shakespeare and Robert Burns. To illustrate adverse effects of "weak and vicious reading," she portrayed the dangers of "false standards of life, the mock heroics, and the criminal suggestions of flashy magazines and story books."[118] These dangers are exacerbated by the evil force of motion pictures, of foreign influences, of mass-market books. The antidote is a steady diet of classics of ennobling literature. Betsy Hearne confirms the emphasis on classics pervading "the foremothers' canon," while appreciating "the struggle for balance between their certainty of 'knowing' a good book and their respect for variety."[119] Anne Carroll Moore, who became the primary voice of the formative field, resisted the litany of woes related to wrong reading and preached a messianic faith in reading and in high standards for contemporary books.

The means toward the desired ends were booklists: the time-honored practice of bibliographic control. Selection became an art and a science for librarians who believed they could distinguish quality. While most librarians looked to outside experts for authority in judging literature, children's librarians became the experts with the necessary expertise. The nature of authority is distinct in the professional parameters of children's librarianship, which has empowered the field toward greater agency in and engagement with the creators and producers of a literature of childhood. Yet children's librarians still looked to outside authorities, as was the norm in the rest of the profession. Librarians were conditioned to relinquish authority to determine the "best reading" to other authorities; others should separate the wheat from the chaff. While Dewey made children's librarians the great exception, as their cultivated womanhood is conducive to judgments for children, children's librarians were still part of a larger professional culture that privileged outside authorities whose aura would increase their perceived power.[120] And they found their inspiration all about. The foremothers of children's services were attracted to the writings of many literary figures, five of which will be explored: two Americans and three from abroad, four men and one woman: Horace E. Scudder, Mary Mapes Dodge, Sir Arthur Quiller Couch, Walter de la Mare, and Paul Hazard. These figures influenced the direction of children's literature into the first half of the twentieth century, a long reach for Horace Scudder, one of the Victorian bright lights who touched every aspect of children's literature—novels, textbooks, journals, reviewing, editorship—and was an intellectual giant to the burgeoning children's library movement, a formative influence.

MENTOR: HORACE SCUDDER

Homage to Romanticism and a humanistic spirit characterized the body of work of the first and most formative Victorian sage. A towering Victorian figure, Horace Elisha Scudder (1838–1902) excelled as editor, anthologist, reviewer, author, and critic of children's literature. His influence was huge on the early progenitors of children's services; his ideas reverberate through theirs. Anne Eaton, in covering a large expanse of Victorian history in Meigs' text, describes Scudder as "a moving force in the field of children's books for years to come."[121] His legacy was embedded in his serious treatment of children's books and his commitment to criticism and choice of books. Only the best was good enough for children, and criticism should be applied to children's books as part of the body of literature. No defining line separated children's books from the larger stock of literature; classics persisted for young and old and could be introduced to child readers in an attractive, appealing format. That he was a publisher as well as an editor and author gave him a posture of esteem and visibility. Librarians like Caroline Hewins would soon learn how they would need to pursue such a search for excellence through carefully winnowed booklists, knowledge of child life, and experience with the best in the world of literature. Alice Jordan, scholar/librarian, focused on Scudder in one chapter of her book on nineteenth-century American children's literature, *From Rollo to Tom Sawyer* (1948); she related his philosophy to Matthew Arnold's dictum of criticism as "a disinterested endeavor to learn and propagate the best that is known and thought in the world."[122] Jordan appreciated Scudder's espousal of classics, a cause she would adopt in her own career and cites his standards: "The distinction between books for children and books for their elders, so purely a creation of the last hundred years, ought to be abolished in our schools, and the better lesson taught of the common inheritance of the nation and parent country. If it is objected that this is impossible, that children cannot understand classic literature, we reply—try again."[123] Alice Jordan indeed "tries again" in her championship of children's classics: a landmark essay and booklist published in the *Horn Book* of 1947, reprinted four times, and twice edited by Helen Adams Masten (1952, 1967) and Paul Heins (1976).[124] This booklist was widely distributed and respected for its associations with Alice Jordan, preeminent scholar-librarian, and *Horn Book* magazine and shows the lingering influence of Horace Scudder. Jordan's "Classics" was the most definitive canon that children's librarians promoted, and its influence in shaping an ideology about reading for the mid-twentieth century was huge. She lists sixty children's classics, which she promises will have lifelong meaning as the best of literature. With growing attention to not only the text but the edition, she recommends certain publishers for each title. Classics were being commodified as librarians linked classics with recommended editions and publishers mentioned. Appearing in a parent-oriented guide like *Horn Book*, the list was geared as a buying guide as well as an expression of canon.

As editor of Houghton Mifflin and its predecessor Hurd and Houghton for more than thirty years and *Atlantic Monthly* for eight years, Scudder's greatest contribution is considered to be the brilliant, though short-lived, periodical, *The Riverside Magazine for Young People* (1867–1870). R. Gordon Kelly, historian of children's periodicals, regards *The Riverside* as the most distinguished literary periodical for children before the creation of Mary Mapes Dodge's *St. Nicholas* in 1873. While Dodge is well known for the quality and long life of *St. Nicholas* (1873–1940), Scudder and his esteemed magazine are largely forgotten except in the writings of children's literature scholars and librarians like Caroline Hewins, Alice Jordan, and Virginia Haviland. *The Riverside* was best known for Scudder's column "Books for Young People," which advanced progressive views on children's reading and reviewed contemporary children's fiction. He is also famous in the history as promoter, editor, and translator of Hans Christian Andersen, whose first American appearance was in this magazine. An admirer of Andersen, Scudder corresponded with him for years before the magazine was established and even learned Danish so he could properly appreciate the translations; he obtained ten new tales for the *Riverside* before they even appeared in print in Denmark or England. What an imaginative influence Hans Christian Andersen's works would be for the direction of children's literature and librarianship.

Scudder was a pioneer in articulating the cause of children's literature to the American public. In his first issue of *The Riverside* (January 1867), he began a commentary to adults to help educate them as to how to discriminate between the best books among the many; too many books and too much reading calls for selectivity by elders. Recognizing that little attention had been placed on children's books, Scudder argued for a more serious consideration of all children's books, old and new. It is imperative that adults become critics to evaluate children's literature in a way not done before; this mission becomes an epoch-making mandate for children's librarians who follow:

> A literature is forming which is destined to act powerfully on general letters; hitherto it had been little disturbed by critics, but the time must soon come, if it has not already come, when students of literature must consider the character and tendency of Children's Letters; when all who have at heart the best interest of the Kingdom of Letters must look sharply to this Principality.[125]

In his fledgling magazine, he intended to bring forth books which might seem old-fashioned but which still retain a fresh spirit—books of classic status: "names of really valuable books which are not likely soon to die and are worth reading over and over again. We shall pay no very close attention to the line which divides books written for the young from books written for the old."[126]

Scudder set about doing the discriminating reading that children's librarians would advocate when they began later to define their mission. Alice Jordan, surveying the American heritage of children's books, Scudder's sympathetic connection with children and their literature is evoked in this line from his Lowell Institute lecture Series: "it is quite safe to say that the form in which childhood is presented will still depend upon the sympathy of imaginative writers with the ideal of childhood and that the form of literature for children will be determined by the greater or less care with which society guards the sanctity of child life."[127] Scudder interpreted his calling by a popular series of stories about the Bodley family and their travels around New England, England, England, Holland, and Denmark. His editing of "The Riverside Literature Series for Young People" offered classic works as whole instead of the fragments of school readers. The right kind of reading should be chosen "to stimulate interest, rouse the imagination and fix the attention, reading at the same time healthy and sound and which shall lead to better things in the future.[128] His anthology, *The Children's Book: a collection of the best and most famous stories and poems in the English language* (1881), was praised by Caroline Hewins: "A child who has it for a companion knows the best that has been written in English for children."[129] In two articles published in *Atlantic Monthly* in 1887 on "Nursery Classics in School" and "American Classics in School," Scudder argues for whole books instead of segments in readers, that continuous reading of a classic is itself "a liberal education" that "represents the childhood of the world's mind."[130]

Scudder's last contribution was a collection of essays on children's literature, the first of its kind and an exemplar of the ubiquitous "Cult of the Child" at the turn of the century. *Childhood in Literature and Art* (1894) expressed his romanticized notion of childhood and its literature: "the essential spirit in childhood itself." Acknowledging the Romantics' christening of childhood, he looks back in history to the Greeks, the Hebrews, Early Christianity, Medieval art, English literature and art, French and German literature, Hans Christian Andersen, and concluding remarks on American literary art. I believe that Scudder best popularized the Romantics for the American literary public and library profession, especially the nascent field of children's work. Emphasizing universal qualities of childhood, Scudder finds the advent of the child in literature when a child's individualism is recognized, which he links to Wordsworth's conception of "childhood as a distinct, individual element of human life." Noting the rise of a literature designed specifically for children, he urges instead the wise selection of the best of world literature that might appeal to a child: "the books written out of minds which have not lost their childhood that are to form the body of literature which shall be classic for the young."[131] Scudder's influence was considerable in laying this foundation in the Romantic tradition of classic works.

MENTOR: MARY MAPES DODGE

Within the bound red volumes stamped in black and gold are what many see as the greatest stimulus to the growth of American children's literature and its classic core: the literary magazine *St. Nicholas*, edited by Mary Mapes Dodge (1831–1905), published monthly from November 1887 until March 1940, with sporadic issues appearing until 1943. The core years of its publication were those with Mary Mapes Dodge as editor (1873–1905). The inspiration for the magazine came from publisher Rowell Smith, a founder of *Scribner's Magazine* in 1870, who selected Dodge as editor. Dodge, the author of the popular children's fiction *Hans Brinker* (1865) and a friend of Horace Scudder, was joined by Frank R. Stockton from the *Riverside Magazine* and John T. Trowbridge of *Our Young Folk,* both eminent authors of their day and well versed in the idea of a literary magazine for children. The time was ripe for a successor to the *Riverside* and, as Alice Jordan notes, the early 1870s was an arid landscape for literature, with the exception of some New England authors.[132] Dime novels and sensational fiction were increasingly causing concern in the periodical press, so the decision to create a magazine designed for children not adults was radical and shifted the emphasis from New England to New York City. Since Scribner's acquired *Riverside*, Scudder was frequently consulted as an authority that shared Dodge's views on children's literature. *St. Nicholas* was essentially the successor to the *Riverside*, a legacy of publishing quality literature in an impressive format. In the words of R. Gordon Kelly, periodical historian, the significance lay in its high-quality entertainment value and epitomized the "style, attitudes, and values of an established, secure, upper-middle-class culture, creating a socio-intellectual pattern that touched several generations of readers"[133]—and, may I add, children's librarians.

In the heyday of periodical publishing, Dodge announced the mission of the magazine in its inaugural issue to be a different sort, not a "milk-and-water variety of the periodical for adults ... stronger, bolder, more uncompromising than the other; its cheer must be the cheer of the bird-song; it must mean freshness and heartiness, life and joy."[134] While the magazine was distinctly child-centered, its straddling of audiences and its relationship to its parent Scribner's created a certain ambiguity. Designed to parallel its adult counterpart, *St. Nicholas* was described in the November 1873 *Scribner's Monthly* as a companion publication: "Whether we shall lead the little child, or the little child shall lead us, remains to be seen."[135] What distinguished the magazine was the leadership of prominent authors, as well as her fellow editors, she secured as contributors, including many women: Louisa May Alcott, Frances Hodgson Burnett, Sarah Orne Jewett, Susan Coolidge, Laura E. Richards, Kate Douglas Wiggin, as well as Horace E. Scudder, Howard Pyle, Mark Twain, Robert Louis Stevenson, Rudyard Kipling, among many others. The magazine also encouraged young writers to contribute pieces to the magazine, which created a stimulating creative outlet for young writers like William Faulkner, Eudora Welty, E. B. White. Mary Mapes Dodge's *St. Nicholas* created a high profile for children's literature, which became part of the early background reading of aspiring children's librarians. It would be difficult to overstate the case for the importance of *St. Nicholas* as a culture bearer of the first rank. This literary magazine, comparable to *Harpers* or *The New Yorker* today, exceeded the expectations of genteel society in providing literature of good taste and quality. Frederic Melcher, in an editorial in *Publishers Weekly* of 1923 (more than a decade after Dodge retired), touted the virtues of Mary Mapes Dodge and *St. Nicholas* in bringing so many fine books to the fore that are still in active demand.[136] One of Anne Carroll Moore's most laudatory remarks on a contemporary book was that it would have pleased Mary Mapes Dodge or Horace Scudder. Moore recalls her fondly as the catalyst for quality literature for children and cross-writing of distinguished writers of the day. Attributing credit to Dodge for the golden age of writing and illustrating children's books, Moore memorialized Dodge by evoking her influence:

> Pictures of Mrs. Dodge flitted across my consciousness. I saw her seated at her busy desk, writing at top speed those charming letters which brought to the service of St. Nicholas the best writers of her time—I saw her holding up authors wherever she met them by her laughing challenge to write something "good enough for children." No author ever seemed to her too distinguished to write for children. "Are you sure you are equal to it?" was her quick reply when Kipling asked if she was not going to ask him to contribute to St. Nicholas; and a few weeks later "Rikki-Tikki" and "Toomai of the Elephants" were outlined at Mrs. Dodge's hospitable home. Thus began the *Jungle Books*.[137]

And thus perpetuated the legend of *St. Nicholas* as classic text for young children's librarians.

Mary Mapes Dodge's crusade for quality literature in her magazine included classics from the past. In the first issue of November 1873, Dodge announced her intention to preserve the tried-and-true in literature:

> It would be better to read no new books at all than to read too many of them. A man might live to be as old as Methuselah, and read a good book through every week—yes, at the end of a few centuries become really a well-read man without once looking into a new book.[138]

Advising young readers, she encouraged them to alternate new books and old books and promised features on the literary treasures of the past. A series of historical articles on classic works and literary figures by Donald G. Mitchell followed over a four-year period. The "St. Nicholas Treasure Box of Literature" was her closest adherence to a canon: selections of "standard poems, short stories, and sketches" as a way to inculcate reading habits among young readers. In her department, "Books and Reading for Young Folk," Dodge encouraged classics through biographical sketches of authors, articles on literary works and landmarks, book-lists, contests on books and reading, and reprinted selections from the past. Dodge continued Scudder's devotion to a certain caliber of literature, what constituted the canon, which she promoted through her esteemed periodical, *St. Nicholas*. She also was worthy of receiving honors in her name, although not the recipient of Frederic Melcher's largesse, reserved for the British publisher John Newbery, however ill suited for an American pioneer of children's literature. Curiously, librarians made little of her in their writings but much ado of British literati, in particular an aristocratic man of letters addressing children's reading.

MENTOR: SIR ARTHUR QUILLER-COUCH

The aristocrat of children's librarianship, to at least Anne Carroll Moore and company, was an unlikely source: a Cambridge English professor, Sir Arthur Quiller-Couch (1863–1944), whose published lectures *On the Art of Writing* (1916) and *On the Art of Reading* (1920) became scripture for their own visionary quest. While it might be thought that librarians would be more attracted to the pragmatism of an American philosopher like John Dewey or Louise Rosenblatt, they turned instead to the idealism of a British man of letters, a prolific writer, essayist, and editor, renowned for *Oxford Book of English Verse* (1900) and several other anthologies in that series, as well as for his own short stories and the retelling of fairy tales in a fine collection illustrated by Edmund Dulac. His towering intellect and grasp of spirituality implicit in the act of reading attracted librarians like Moore who were seeking to raise children's literature to new heights of spirituality and respectability. Privileging children as literature's first readers of the humanities, Quiller-Couch's words resonated: "The real battle for English lies in our Elementary Schools, and in the training of our Elementary Teachers."[139] His humanistic views on reading as a worthy art, on children's desire to learn and grow, and on education as a leading-out, a drawing-forth rather than an imposition struck a chord. His emphasis on literature reaching the spirit of the individual and connecting to a sense of universal harmony was translated into their own rhetoric on the value of the canon with children and echoed Hewins's early counsel on leading the child onward in reading.

Quiller-Couch's views informed their calling toward selection and readers advisory. Devoting several chapters to children's reading, he preached the value of reading—silently and aloud—as the door to all the avenues of knowledge. This reading should connect with a child's own eager joy to learn and to grow rather than to repress that spirit with moral tomes of Original Sin like *The Fairchild Family*, citing the infamous gallows scene of the father's object lesson for his naughty children. Instead, children needed to experience the truth of imaginative literature, which would draw out and reach a child's instinctive desires: to talk and to listen; to act in drama; to draw, paint, and model; to dance and sing; to know the why of things; to construct things. Drawing on the essence of Wordsworthian Romanticism, Quiller-Couch finds the base of all literature to be a universal truth of a simplicity accessible to a child.[140] Despite the limited opportunities of many school children for higher education, each child retains the potential to be educated through the transcendent truth of imagination and its harmony.

Espousing imaginative literature, Quiller-Couch was intentionally nonprescriptive in what readers should read. Citing a survey from his childhood, a listing by a W. T. Stead in the *Pall Mall Gazette* of the hundred best books, Quiller-Couch challenged the fallacious notion that such a numerative selection can exist: "There is in fact no positive hierarchy among the classics."[141] Asking why the Best Books be 100 or not 99 or 199, he asks also under what conditions such distinctions are made but understands the search for masterpieces as those selective few books that serve to teach through delight and as a measure of taste in developing an inner guide for lifelong reading. These masterpieces will be "the great classics of whatever Language or Literature we are handling: and these, in any language are neither enormous in number and mass, nor extraordinarily difficult to detect, nor (best of all) forbidding to the reader by reason of their difficulty."[142] While eschewing a definition of classic, he describes its essence as universality, appealing to catholic interests, and permanence, remaining significant after its time and conditions, retaining "undefaced by handling, the original noble imprint of the mind that first minted it" and ever echoing the spirit of its creator/author.[143] Believing in the power of classics to raise the reader toward the incarnation of Truth and Beauty, he challenges educators to "see what a child depends on is imagination, that which he demands of life is the wonderful, the glittering, possibility?"[144] Shakespeare's *Tempest* is cited as an example of a masterpiece accessible to the child if treated appropriately, allowing its mysteries to fascinate and allure.

Referring to Matthew Arnold's touting of masterpieces as "prophylactics of taste," Quiller-Couch finds there to be even much more: the common soul of civilization, which he connects nationalistically to postwar commitments toward Europe. Such masterpieces can shape tastes from childhood, interpret a larger cultural, civilized mind, and raise the spirit, "lift our own soul."[145]

Quiller-Couch's theoretical approach to reading shaped the sensibilities of Anne Carroll Moore. *My Roads to Childhood,* a collection of her reviews and lectures, includes a dozen references to his writings, including his literary lectures and fairy tale retellings. She found contemporary examples of progressive approaches of her mentor Margaret Wright Plummer at Pratt, which anticipated in practice his theories on reaching the hearts and minds of children and adults through imaginative literature. Moore was most eloquent on Quiller-Couch's many gifts as "this lover of French fairy tales, of English poetry, of the legends of his own Cornish hills."[146] Extolling his writings, which set his work apart from all others that treat children's reading, she reiterates his recurring themes: education as a leading out, a drawing forth of what is within the child; children's reading as part of the great body of literature; and faith in literature's civilizing power. Moore saw the beliefs of this erudite Cambridge professor, as first formulated to his university students, reincarnated in the special relationship between life and literature, as reenacted between adult and child in the sharing of classic literature. In a column directed toward teenage reading, Moore recommended his *Oxford Book of Verse* as "an anthology of the best English poetry arranged chronologically, of convenient size and attractive form to carry about," which presumably she did.[147]

Quiller-Couch's influence on Lillian Smith, who apprenticed with Moore at New York Public Library, is evident in *The Unreluctant Years*, a tribute to the universal truths of literature. In her chapter introducing her approach to criticism, Smith draws on and quotes from Quiller-Couch's concept of masterpieces as universal and permanent to build her foundation of book appraisal, whereby works are judged by the company they keep, their associative value related to established works of traditional worth. While no formulas exist to distinguish a good book from a poor one, the true support is a familiarity with books of proven value, which provide "a bedrock of reasoning and feeling" for evaluating contemporary writing for children.[148] Quiller-Couch becomes the guiding spirit for both Moore and Smith as they began to apply his aesthetics toward their principles of a selective tradition.

FORMATIVE INFLUENCE: WALTER DE LA MARE

As a poet and storyteller with visionary lines, Walter de la Mare (1873–1956) was a contemporary of Anne Carroll Moore and her favorite poet of the age. Indeed, de la Mare became poet laureate of children's librarians in the first half of the twentieth century. His first poems, *Songs of Childhood* (1902), translated Romantic themes and traces of William Blake's *Songs of Innocence* into a collection widely used in early children's libraries, just forming as a movement; the collection *Peacock Pie* (1913) established his reputation. *Collected Stories for Children*—which in their variety of theme and character included frequent references to old ladies and old houses—won the 1947 Carnegie, and *Come Hither* (1923), an anthology he edited, is regarded by many as the best children's poetry anthology of the twentieth century. Enthusiasm, love and knowledge of fanciful literature, and a heightened view of the child and the adult's responsibility toward that child are all qualities that reverberated with similar sentiments of Anne Carroll Moore and company. While a romantic by nature, de la Mare posed unanswered questions in his work, which suggest a pessimism that may have been overlooked in their ardor.[149]

Moore shared an intimacy with the poet whose works became spiritual counsel. Moore created the name "Anne Caraway" in her *Nicholas: A Manhattan Christmas Story* (1924) after reading *Peacock Pie,* which she brought back from England and touted widely. This novel for children, which she based on her own adopted wooden doll named "Nicholas" that became her ubiquitous companion and, in de la Mare's words, "her alter ego," reveals some of the imaginative leaps found in de la Mare. Biographer Sayers attributes de la Mare's influence to her invention of Nicholas and describes their close ties:

> Each acknowledged childhood as a state of being like no other, each knew the flashing insights of heightened imagination, each lived in a state of acute awareness of the mystery surrounding all that exists, including the inanimate.[150]

In a festive spirit that she associated with children's books, Moore celebrated many holidays, one of which was St. Nicholas Eve, for which in 1924 she arranged for the poet himself to appear and read from his works. She annually celebrated his birthday at New York Public Library, along with those of Kate Greenaway, Randolph Caldecott, H. C. Andersen, and L. Leslie Brooke. In 1940, after twenty years of friendship, the poet writes in a letter to Moore, "I know we share certain theories and convictions about childhood and if at any time mine seem to differ from yours, then that will be at my peril."[151] That kinship, which worked intertextually, arose from shared beliefs, in which they influenced each other. Moore, who often marked passages she admired in her reading, responded to these words in her copy of *Come Hither.*

> Words are but a *means* of conveying poetry from one imagination to another. So may a smile make lovely a plain face; or sunbeams weave a rainbow in the air. Even words themselves may be needless, for two human spirits may hold converse together (of which only the rarest poetry in words or music, paint or stone could *tell*) without one syllable of speech between them.[152]

Moore frequently quotes from de la Mare as an epigraph to her reviews and essays in *My Roads to Childhood*. In "Why Write for Children?" she draws on de la Mare's work as exemplum to an aspiring writer and to tout a new edition of *Songs of Childhood* in 1923 and quotes from another critic, who hailed de la Mare in *Peacock Pie* for "the flowering of an exquisite genius for writing quaint nursery rhymes, fairy lyrics and ballads that can fascinate the mind of a child."[153] As a respected poet who wrote for children and whose romantic rhetoric on childhood matched her own, Walter de la Mare was muse for not only Moore but a host of contemporaries, then and now, who admire his work, particularly his anthology *Come Hither*.

MENTOR: PAUL HAZARD

"Give us books, Give us wings," exclaimed Paul Hazard, another man of letters with enormous influence on the children's library movement. A member of the French Academy, Paul Hazard's (1878–1944) *Books, Children, and Men* was published and promoted by the *Horn Book* in 1944 and reprinted thereafter as a "sacred text." Hazard was an international scholar of comparative literature who was well regarded in the United States, educated at Harvard and Columbia, where he taught periodically. This book materialized on the American scene when Bertha Mahony came across the slim volume sent to her children's bookstore (The Book-shop) in 1933 along with other foreign materials sent by Esther Averill, an American expatriate living in Paris and running her own publishing house, The Domino Press. Mahony and Averill had been communicating for years over French children's books and cooperating in sharing materials for exhibits and distributing some Domino publications. Mahony arranged for its translation by Marguerite Mitchell and subsequent publishing by Mahony's new publishing firm associated with her journal enterprise. With the imprimatur of the *Horn Book* behind the publication, the book received much attention in the children's book world. Alice Jordan wrote as a pre-publication blurb, "No equally comprehensive analysis of the distinctive national traits of children's literature has been hitherto available."[154] To Anne Carroll Moore, writing in her column "The Three Owls" in the *Horn Book*, the book "has never been far from my hand since its publication" for its reminder of her literary inheritance and its eloquent defense of the Universal Republic of Childhood.[155] To Frances Clarke Sayers, writing in the *Library Quarterly*, the book articulates the lasting values in children's reading and the universal appeal of certain classics.[156]

Which international classics did Hazard herald? First, from France, fairy tales by Perrault, Beaumont, de Genlis, Berquin; from England, John Newbery's books, nursery rhymes, *Alice in Wonderland, Peter Pan*; Germany's Brothers Grimm. His standard consisted of "books that remain faithful to the very essence of art; namely, those that offer to children an intuitive and direct way of knowledge, a simple beauty capable of being perceived immediately, arousing in their souls a vibration which will endure all their lives."[157] He preferred books that teach, books of knowledge that contain a morality of certain truths and a faith in truth and justice. While adults have sought to oppress children by denying them their rightful inheritance of literature, children have defended their choices: *Robinson Crusoe, Gulliver's Travels, Don Quixote*. Of the Anglo-American classics, he mentioned a handful of great authors of children's books: Oliver Goldsmith, Charles and Mary Lamb, Walter Scott, Robert Louis Stevenson, Dickens, Ruskin, Kipling; Washington Irving, Hawthorne, Mark Twain; Pushkin, Gogol, Chekhov; only *Pinocchio* represents Southern Europe; above all, the preeminent text is Hans Christian Andersen's fairy tales. Appreciating the advances of childhood in the modern era, he singled out children's libraries in the United States as a concept with a concomitant sense of place: "an innovation that does honor to the sensibility of a people.... They are a home."[158]

The patriotism of the Allied cause, the validation of children's libraries, and the confirmation of a selective tradition in children's literature all contributed to Hazard's ascendancy. The influence of the book was huge in postwar America. In her well-cited, reprinted essay, "Children's Classics," Alice Jordan refers to Hazard's opinion of particular classics: *Robinson Crusoe, Gulliver's Travels, Don Quixote,* and *Pilgrim's Progress*. Lillian Smith's *The Unreluctant Years* acknowledges as part of her critical approach Hazard's belief in the morality implicit in children's literature: a faith in truth and justice. She draws widely from his book, supporting his conviction that writers for children must hold high standards "faithful to the very essence of art" and express "respect for universal life" and knowledge of the human heart.[159] She quotes Hazard when discussing *Alice in Wonderland* and uses a lengthy passage as epigraph to the chapter, "Books of Knowledge." Betsy Hearne's discussion of "Sacred Texts: Psalms and Proverbs" in the 75th anniversary issue of the *Horn Book* (1999) selects the work as a "sacred text" with "a masterful articulation of the spiritual and humanistic mission of children's literature;" Indeed, children's librarians were especially attached to his oft-quoted epigrammatic image, which became a kind of mantra: "'Give us books,' say the children; 'give us wings.'"[160]

Hazard's infusion of religious symbolism into his critical appraisals heightened canonical texts as secular scripture. He expressed religious inspiration from Hans Christian Andersen, found the soul in the Brothers Grimm and Perrault. In Romantic conceptions of the child, Hazard saw the child as savior, who would bring to the world new faith and hope and preserve its favorite books for all time. As mentor and muse, these formative figures made their mark on the ideology of literature for children and the cultural positioning of librarians: humanism prevailed in this perceived period of Renaissance, the self-anointed "Golden Age" of the twentieth century.

GOLDEN AGE

The confluence of children's librarianship and children's book publishing in the early decades of the twentieth century, often called the "Golden Age" or the second golden age (however contrived), contributed to a canonization of certain texts with classic status. Librarians were interested in perpetuating classics and eager to have publishers produce new editions as well as maintain a backlist of old favorites. Frederic Melcher in an editorial in *Publishers Weekly* of 1923 surveyed characteristics of contemporary children's books and acknowledged the contributions of the children's librarian movement in creating, first, the demand for new editions and reprints of the "best literature of past times," and then later the encouragement of new titles. Clearly appreciating the power of the purse, the editor notes, "Such organized opinion, backed powerfully by the practical influence of outright purchase, has had a tremendous effect on the development, and, by this new direction of their interest they are helping to build a strong foundation for a greater children's literature."[161] Librarians were edition-specific in their selection, as reflected in Anne Carroll Moore's and Alice Jordan's classic booklists. Until the 1920s children's books were more of a sideline with publishers. While crossover titles like Crane, Caldecott, and Greenaway's prompted ardent critical and commercial reception, the numbers were still low, as the data indicate from *Publishers Weekly's* records. Publication of juvenile literature was not organized as such but more a Christmas gift commodity. The inauguration of Children's Book Week in 1919 heightened interest in children's books as commodity. The first national reading initiative, the project was the creation of Franklin K. Mathiews, chief scout librarian of the Boy Scouts, Frederic Melcher, editor of *Publishers Weekly*, along with other publishers, and Anne Carroll Moore of New York Public Library, who proved to be a strong asset in her contacts and influence across the country. The success of this venture proved the viability of the alliance of librarian and publisher, which continued to produce mutually beneficial gains. Publishers could count on most of their sales (80 to 90 percent estimate) going to the newly established children's rooms in public librarians, with librarians like Anne Carroll Moore promoting books in library exhibits, booklists, and in the media. This burgeoning market for children's books stimulated publishers like Macmillan in 1919 and Doubleday in 1920 to look to the library world for editors of new divisions. The establishment of the Newbery Medal in 1922 further formalized the cozy working relationship between librarians and publishers in the sure knowledge that award recipients would determine sales indefinitely.

The "Roaring Twenties" witnessed the inauguration of children's book departments in libraries and publishing houses, children's bookstores, the first national reading initiative and book award, and a professional journal in the field, the *Horn Book*. The second White House Conference on Children and Youth, convened in 1919, recognized the role of reading in a child's recreational activities, yet missed the connecting thread of libraries to literature. The point was not lost on others who sensed that synergy. The burgeoning market for books coincided with the creation of children's rooms in public libraries; publishers sought to supply these collections with reprints and new editions of old favorites as well as occasional new titles. Attention to children's literature heightened its study, selection, and dissemination of information from and about the field: book reviews and professional literature and public promotion all coalesced as cause and commerce. The creation of the first children's book department by Macmillan in 1919 and headed by Louise Seaman Bechtel inspired rival publishers to follow suit to learn how to market appropriately. Children's librarians, such as May Massee in 1920 by Doubleday, were hired to lead these new divisions. The institution of these divisions was symbolic and substantive: children's books mattered in the economy as well as the literary culture. Children's libraries were creating a market, and children's librarians were promoting the product. With their Children's Book Week collaboration, librarians were creating a national campaign for literacy as well as a national market for book publishers in a unique and profitable partnership. No other field of publishing had its own cadre of professionals whose alleged objectivity ensured their reputation as cultural authorities of merit and promoters of the first rank.

Another boon was the prestige of awards. The innovation of an award to honor a distinguished American children's book was the creation of Frederic Melcher, *Publishers Weekly* editor and bibliophile, who instituted the Newbery Medal prize to stimulate the supply of new books by native writers. The inauguration of awards was a critical prerogative that exerted their authority in the field and established children's books as high literary fare. The award was congruent with their paradigm of a selective tradition. In 1922, the ALA through the province of children's librarians established the first of its major annual awards, the John Newbery Medal, for "the Most Distinguished Contribution to American Literature for Children." Newbery was known for his commercial energy in jump-starting the publishing of children's books in the mid-eighteenth century. A publisher honors a publisher, and in this case a British publisher, a curious choice except for its collegial commercial tie. As librarians not publishers were to make the choice, this award confirmed the reputation of children's librarians as critics, a role modeled nearly a half-century before by Caroline Hewins. The public became more familiar with the literature through the publication of the first professional journal aimed at both the public and practitioners, the *Horn Book*, founded in 1924 by Bertha Mahony Miller, who also opened the first children's bookstore. Children's librarians were spreading across the country, due to pioneer efforts of librarians like Anne Carroll Moore and library school programs like those at the Carnegie Library of Pittsburgh, Pratt Institute, and the University of Wisconsin. They began collecting their organizational work and ideological vision in "yearbooks," for volumes from 1929 to 1932. These primary sources helped to educate a larger field in their practice. By the end of 1929, *Publishers Weekly* said of children's books that they were "demanding and winning the finest talent creating today. Not only in writing is this true but in illustration and decoration, and in production. The standards are new standards."[162] Firms like Holiday House and William R. Scott began publishing books distinguished by innovative design and printing.

Although the lean years of the 1930s deflated the ranks of children's book editors as well as the output of titles and the rhythm of growth, distinguished picture books continued to appear by illustrators such as Wanda Gag, Helen and Kurt Wiese, Feodor Rojankovsky, Roger Duvoisin, Munro Leaf, Lois Lenski, Rene D'Harnoncourt, Ludwig Bemelemans, Maude and Miska Petersham, Boris Artzybashef, and Dr. Seuss (Theodor Seuss Geisel), among others. By the mid-1930s the output of books had surged again, and attention to this extraordinary talent and artistry was due. With only one award to acknowledge quality in children's books, and that quality being associated with narrative, picture books, in all their brilliance in image and design, could be easily overlooked. Melcher, with his editorship of *Publishers Weekly* and his intimate role with children's book creators and librarians, was certainly aware of the challenge, the opportunity. If another award, whose name would it bear? Who would be another John Newbery, the first who made children's book publishing a serious business in mid-eighteenth century England? Among the possibilities (Howard Pyle or Jesse Wilcox Smith or N. C. Wyatt seemed likely American candidates), Melcher chose the name and reputation of British illustrator, Randolph Caldecott, to bear the honor of this new award. He explained his reasons in this way:

> The advantage of the name "Caldecott" is not only that it has pleasant connotations for everyone, but ... his work was very definitely the kind of thing where the interest was in the pictures, yet there never was a book where the text was inconsequential. It would be my impulse to say that we should include in the wording of the final statement that we suggest that the books be judged by the pictures but that the text should be worthy of the pictures.[163]

Caldecott may have been prominent in mind because the first definitive historian of the field, F. J. Harvey Darton, had recently lauded his name. Darton's monumental study, *Children's Books in England: Five Centuries of Social Life* (1932), was the first scholarly work to be published on the subject and was widely reviewed. A book historian like Melcher would surely have read Darton's book. The announcement of the new Caldecott Medal in the *Library Journal* of July 1937 quotes from the passage from Darton's *Children's Books in England*, thus illustrating the powerful influence of Darton as authority. As no such critical book extolled the might and majesty of American children's book artists—and would not until the publication of Meigs's *Critical History* in 1953 and Barbara Bader's *American Picturebooks from Noah's Ark to the Beast Within* in 1976—the English tradition in picture books was paramount, particularly to an American book public that seemed to privilege British art and literature. And Caldecott was still a popular classic, as Michael Patrick Hearn notes:

> Kate Greenaway and Walter Crane were the rage on both sides of the Atlantic. Perhaps to gain legitimacy for the award, the American Library

Association took the name of a British illustrator, for its annual medal given to the most distinguished contribution to picture books published in the United States. Certainly Caldecott's series was then better known than any designed by American artists; already by 1920, copies of his toy books were selling better in the United States than when they were first published over fifty years before.[164]

The choice of Caldecott to bear the prize name suggests one of the inner workings of reputation making: the imprimatur of an influential authority figure (Darton) on a fashionable yet classic artist (Caldecott), conjoined by the sanction of practitioners (teachers and librarians) and the economic prowess of publishers (Melcher and publishing industry). That both awards were named for British figures in the commercial and art fields reflects a certain penchant for the Anglofied allure of history and tradition to the American breed of book. Curiously, the two awards did not commemorate famous American figures, such as Scudder, Twain, or Dodge, who were strong, memorable voices for quality in literature, particularly the classics.

The awards became contentious early on when the librarian's jurisdiction was challenged by authority figures in related fields. From the 1920s on, the field faced opposition to their evaluation standards by progressive educators. Moore's standard was to privilege the child's imaginative life over the "here and now" of lived experience. Her criterion writ large was relayed as truth through the network of her influence and remained the faith until other ideas intruded. Leonard Marcus's biography of Margaret Wise Brown—"laureate of the nursery"—illuminates this tension, exemplified in conflicts between Moore and Lucy Sprague Mitchell (1878–1967) of the Bank Street College of Education, in which Brown was inextricably linked. Mitchell's educational was rooted in principles of child development, which saw children as empirical explorers of their world. Her philosophical differences with Moore's high critical standards had much to do with the creation and constitution of the literature for children. To Marcus, these two towering figures differed in their ideas about childhood: "The librarian was a moral idealist who regarded childhood as a fixed state of innocence to be shielded from, rather than shaped by, historical change and environmental factors. Moore remained deeply suspicious of Mitchell's empirically grounded—and thus 'relativistic'—'modern' approach to literature and education. Mitchell, for her part, was convinced that people like Moore lived in a sentimental dream-world."[165] Moore's beliefs were metaphorically conveyed by her successor, Frances Clarke Sayers, who delivered a famous 1937 speech, widely reprinted, "Lose Not the Nightingale," drawing on Hans Christian Andersen's story of the bird song as saving grace. Sayers makes the connection between the real nightingale as traditional imaginative literature for children, and the mechanical bird as the reverse, exemplified in the "here and now" school of thought.

These differences were exacerbated by the award system, which reflected Moore's hierarchical approach and educational philosophy. Newbery award winners—and those behind the awards—were being challenged for their gendered, romanticized image of childhood. Were children's librarians, these gentrified book crusaders, fit to make such momentous decisions affecting what books are published, what books are read by children? The conflict intensified when a speaker at a 1937 institute organized by Sayers directly attacked their authoritative judgments. Howard Pease, a popular writer of adventure fiction for children, lambasted librarians for their closed system determined by feminist, romantic visions of the world. Their female domination of the field brought disastrous results: few male authors represented, few books for boys recognized, fewer readers period. Pease also argued for more realistic, contemporary stories instead of imaginative literature and foreign settings. His speech fueled a debate that continued in the pages of the *Elementary English Review*, a publication of a rival organization, the National Council of Teachers of English (NCTE). A strong advocate for broader book criteria, editor C. C. Certain editorialized in the fall of 1939 that the Newbery choice of Elizabeth Enright's *Thimble Summer* reflected "the faded prettiness" of a "gossamer summer bouquet" without allure to "the average tousle-headed American boy." The librarians' choices as "dear to the adult reader, but not to the child," discouraged reading among children and discouraged "vigor of thought" in children's books. The continuing saga of Newbery award contestation suggests that the surety of the paradigm was being shaken.[166] The librarians countered with a stronger conviction in their faith in the book, in the classic traditions of their calling.

THE CLASSIC

Library literature is replete with discourse on classics as the essence of tradition to transmit to the young. Classics are often distinguished from standard works, with the classic's transcendence by universality of interest. Corresponding to aesthetic standards of the adult world, classics are associated with imaginative recreations of humanistic life, an ennobling literature with spiritual resonance. The classics were of unquestioned value. In Frances Jenkins Olcott's book on children's reading, she states empatically, "It is of course unnecessary to argue here for the educational values of fine prose standards or generally accepted standards."[167] This secure consensus embodied a mystique of the child's world, a vision of the immortal child idealized from Romanticism.

The most authoritative discussion of children's classics came from Alice M. Jordan (1870–1960), legendary longtime children's librarian at the Boston Public Library and scholar in the field. Although her primary text on classics was not published until 1947, her influence in the field was felt earlier. For years she held literary discussions which drew people from far afield and organized as the New England Round Table of Children's Literature. The group was continuously evaluating books and editions for a list of classics. Jordan was also influential in guiding Bertha Mahony as she began her new children's bookstore and her journal, the *Horn Book,* both labors steeped in booklists. Jordan drew upon two sources to advise Mahony: *Books for the Young for Boys and Girls* by Caroline Hewins and *The Bookshelf for Boys and Girls,* edited by Clara Whitehill Hunt.

What ensued was a defining moment: a definitive list of classics by Jordan in the *Horn Book* of 1947, which was developing earlier and finally printed in the journal and pamphlet format. Here the classics in the field are clearly delineated as a canon. Beginning with an anecdotal allusion to *Alice in Wonderland,* Jordan sings its praises as the preeminent classic for children with lifelong appeal. Drawing on Gilbert Murray's discussion of Greek epics, she espouses "intensity of imagination" as the most important quality: the creation of a world we care about and to which we are drawn. Citing *Robinson Crusoe, Gulliver's Travels, Don Quixote,* and *Pilgrim's Progress* as four great books deserving classic status, she noted the realness of their worlds that readers long to enter. Although books must have weathered at least one generation and be received by the next, few could agree on what books would qualify. The quality of writing—what she calls "form"—is critical, as in *Andersen's Fairy Tales, A Child's Garden of Verses,* and *The Wind in the Willows.* She shares her pleasures in the fairy tale, nonsense verse, high adventure, and stories of home life, such as Twain's fiction. Howard Pyle's books are extolled for the "pleasure of spirit" he embodied in his books.

Jordan's essay is distinct in its appreciation of the importance of illustration and edition. Noting that new attractive editions of older books were being published, at affordable prices, she singles out certain ones for comment. While appreciating the illustrations of the Rhead brothers in their series for Harper of various classics, she prefers individual treatments rather than the sameness of a series. Maxfield Parrish and N. C. Wyeth are cited for the drama and richness of their interpretations of classic tales. "Old World" gems are mentioned for their evocation of a different world, such as Italy's *Pinocchio,* Germany's *Grimm Tales,* Denmark's *Andersen's Fairy Tales,* Sweden's *Nils,* and England's *Master Skylark.* The selective list of "Sixty Children's Classics" at the end of her essay includes particular illustrators and editions as recommended. The weight of Jordan's reputation, its appearance of her essay in the leading professional journal, and its reproduction and distribution all speak to the status of classics in postwar America. The foundation for this canon was built in the earlier fertile years of the century, in the labors toward raising standards and publicizing the elect to the public and the publishing industry.

Anne Carroll Moore set the bar high for quality in children's books. As Hearne and Jenkins point out in their discussion of "sacred texts," classics dominate the lists of the foremothers.[168] Anne Carroll Moore struggled with balancing best books with some variety. They quote her as saying, "I have never liked the idea of selecting 'best books' for anybody—least of all for a child who is trying out the reading habit," which seems admirable but questionable considering her insistence on quality and neglect of popular series, such as *Oz* or *Nancy Drew.* While she did commend a plentitude of books of many kinds, she was very concerned that commonplace books would deny the child an experience of art and literature of the highest caliber. The long crusade to guide children's reading to the best excluded popular culture, where lowbrow trash might adversely affect a young reader. Reading influenced a child's whole life: a powerful faith. To her enormous credit, Moore discovered many contemporary classics and actively worked to promote these books through her libraries, contacts, and publications. She created an empire that lasted long through a lineage of librarians owning that faith. Many others were just imbued with her spirit toward leadership in the field. That influence was demonstrated in the distinguished career of Zena Sutherland (1915–2002), who followed Moore's lead in writing reviews as editor of the University of Chicago's *Bulletin of the Center for Children's Books*, where she was the sole reviewer for twenty-seven years. Sutherland broadened Moore's contributions by her textbook authorship, prodigious articles, and about a dozen books. Zutherland shows in her life's work this heightened focus on the role of critic and writer.

Moore's legacy is embodied in a text that extols high culture. Lillian Smith (1887–1983), a protégée, inscribed canonical beliefs in her influential text, *The Unreluctant Reader* (1953). Here she too applied the same critical standards as adult literature, declaring: "The importance of the selective function in finding and making known the best in children's literature is the theme of this book."[169] Tolerating the mediocre mass-produced book is to misuse the purpose of book selection and the ideals of literature, which clarify distinctions between good/bad writing. In strong language, Smith states right away in her book: "A children's library of books, whether chosen for the home, the school or the public library, which has forgotten the rich inheritance of children's literature—its 'classics'— betrays the special privilege of all such libraries and becomes only a means of further distributing mediocrity."[170] The classics link the child to children's literature and so to all literature.

Or do they? Although trying to align their literature with *the* literature through a common aesthetic, the children's librarians became further separated from the shifting body of literature, as historian Anne MacLeod so convincingly shows. High minded and resolute, children's book people adhered to the selective tradition so instilled in their sense of their profession. To MacLeod, "The most basic tenet of their philosophy was the single standard to be applied to all literature, whether child's or adult.... Everyone agreed that literary quality admitted books to libraries, while lack of them kept them out."[171] This faith was shaken as children's and adult literature diverged through forces greater than their own. Modernists like Henry James kept children's literature at a distance in their desire to distinguish adult literature as anything *but* children's literature, the kind of unsophisticated reading public that adopted children's books as adult bestsellers.[172] As literary tastes veered more toward realism than romanticism, children's literature held firm in their idealistic vision as proven cultural capital: the librarians and publishers conjoined to produce a profitable market for quality art and literature for children. Children's books remained an enclave, a shelter for the literature and its shepherd. Alas, as MacLeod writes, "By about 1920, children's literature was a garden, lovingly tended by those who cared about it but isolated as well as protected by the cultural walls that surrounded it."[173] The tumultuous cultural changes of the 1960s hit those walls hard, as librarians struggled to include new images into the "all white world of children's books," as Nancy Larrick charged.[174] Difference rather than tradition might prevail. The surety of a system based on jurisdiction of best books was shaken. If librarians were losing their grip on a canon, who would assert authority? Who would inherit the power to define cultural form and value? The classics began to shift their pride of place uneasily from the library shelf to the academy, from garden walls to ivory towers.

Chapter Two

Best Books: The Scholar

"What we have loved, others will love, and we will teach them how."
—William Wordsworth, *Prelude*

The scholar of children's literature is also "Cinderella." That complex tale of trans-formation and destiny tells how the scholar in rags schemes and dreams to regain a lost patrimony, a place at the table. Alison Lurie may have been the first to use the trope in her 1984 novel *Foreign Affairs*, in which the heroine is a children's literature scholar devalued by her colleagues. Lurie writes:

> For the truth is that children's literature is a poor relation in her depart-ment—indeed, in most English departments: a step-daughter grudgingly tolerated because, as in the old tales, her words are glittering jewels of a sort that attract large if not equally brilliant masses of undergraduates. Within the departmental family she sits in the chimney-corner, while her idle, ugly siblings dine at the chairman's table—though to judge by enrollment figures, many of them would spout toads and lizards.[1]

Such sweet revenge from the author, a children's literature scholar herself who has surely endured the snubs and sneers of academia. If we take the interpreta-tion of Cinderella that Iona and Peter Opie offer, the tale is about the reclaiming of authority, the assertion of true identity: "Her story is not one of rags to riches, or of dreams come true, but of reality made evident."[2] With the rise of respectability in higher education, children's literature has become a *Bildungsroman*, coming of age.

Why such a wait for recognition? What happened between the heyday of the Golden Age of children's books and the here-and-now of children's literature struggling for a place at the table? While there are multiple social factors affecting cultural validation, I sense that their slow rise to position came through the reluc-tance of the literati to consider children's literature as art, a stature held in the height of the Victorian era in a rich, shared culture. A few scholars have pondered this mystery, which is interwoven in the history of children's librarianship and children's book publishing. One theory that bears weight is that modernists like Henry James wanted to distinguish their realism from the rampant Romanticism of a crossover literature. Relating the fate of children's literature to the rise and fall of adult fiction, Felicity Hughes argues that the status of the novel as family reading was anathema to those authors aspiring toward highbrow distinction for the novel. A serious novel would be one unread by children. Hughes states, "The consequences of this de facto segregation of children's literature from the rest can be seen in general aesthetic theory, in literary theory, in the theory and criticism of children's literature, and in the literature itself."[3] Betsy Hearne, straddling the fields of literature and library science, relates the state of research in children's literature and concludes that the field is at a crossroads. The problem as she sees it is that we ask the wrong questions. Noting a subtle persistent didacticism in the literature, she finds the focus of research to be: "What does literature do for—or to—our children? Whereas adult literature exists *ipso facto*, children's literature is still contingent on a complex set of justifications."[4]

Could some of the ambiguity be the role of children's librarians as authorities of the literature? Another scholar of children's literature and librarianship, historian Anne Scott MacLeod, reveals a relationship between the literary culture and the professional cultures at the turn of the nineteenth century. Noting the loss of a shared reading culture, she connects changes to the professionalization and specialization of children's literature, growing apart from the body of literature with "a gradual and profound effect on children's reading."[5] As specialists began to redefine the literature by their perception of audience and genre, children's books diverged from adult books with few books in common except certain classics. Adult critics turned toward realism and away from the sense and sensibilities of children's fiction, even as the children's book market burgeoned. Children's literature lost its place in the mainstream of literary culture and a common aesthetic. She attributes this loss to the inability of children's librarians to move toward realism, popular culture, and any change in the "best books" standard that had worked well for so long. They failed to recognize the loss of common culture as adult literature grew in a different direction. In MacLeod's words: "By 1920, children's literature was a garden, lovingly tended by those who cared about it but isolated as well as protected by the cultural walls that surrounded it."[6] That perception is somewhat similar to Dee Garrison's controversial history of women in librarianship, which views the children's librarians as "tender technicians," who were easy to dismiss in and out of the profession.[7]

In her recent study of the institutionalization of children's literature, Beverly Lyon Clark notes the intimacy of related fields associated with children's books in the early twentieth century but also the gulf between literature for children and literature for adults. While academia has been oblivious to the role of librarians, the perceived relationship between the literature and the librarian is suspect, with librarians seen as more "handmaidens than as fellow scholars and teachers."[8] Clark senses the resistance of academics to be subtly connected to its institutional base in what is perceived as a low-status profession. We must remember that the first scholars in the field were in departments of library science and education. I suggest that as children's librarians began to lose their locus of power in mid-century, when their authority of "best books" and philosophy of childhood were contested; this gap allowed academics to enter the field and compete for jurisdiction. Academics from humanistic fields like English and history assumed interest in the subject without acknowledging the role of librarians in establishing the field. For example, a recent study of the construction of childhood in American children's literature includes only a scant reference to children's librarians, despite its intended contextuality. Most children's literature scholarship centers on literary criticism and ignores the agents involved in making the literature happen. Peter Hunt's encyclopedia of children's literature includes a chapter on "Librarianship," written by Ray Lonsdale and Sheila Ray, who acknowledge from the beginning that librarians were the first profession to take "a systematic and knowledgeable interest in what children read."[9] Clark's *Kiddie Lit* is on the vanguard of what I hope will be a larger exploration of the contribution and role of librarianship in shaping children's literature. How could the children's librarian be missing from the picture? Their intimacy as co-creators was overlooked, rarely examined at all. There was no bridge drawn, and the two fields so interested in the same subject—childhood reading—diverged from a shared dialogue. Jack Zipes is uniquely aware of the role of teachers and librarians, trained in academic standards of evaluation, and vital to the reception and distribution of literature. His concern is with understanding the way value is accorded to particular books through a process of selection by the elect. This select group up until the mid-1940s was "in the hands of educated, white, middle-class women—a social history that has yet to be written."[10] This work intends to tell some of the story of the interstices of librarians and scholars in the privileging of texts, the making of classics.

Academic interest in children's literature is interwoven with intellectual history. Universities reflect and construct knowledge, whereby the creative process is dependent on a creative structure that transmits such knowledge. If institutions of higher education in the mid-nineteenth century had been more receptive to contemporary culture, if their canon had embraced the books extolled by the literati, ubiquitous in the press, children's literature would have flourished in Victorian ivory towers as in Victorian parlors and press. Influenced by German institutions of higher education and America's phenomenal growth in knowledge and industry, American colleges in mid-nineteenth century were evolving from an earlier monastic tradition of classical languages and textbook recitation to a broader curriculum encompassing new sciences of humankind, such as American literature, history, political science, sociology. In the slow reach of academic regard for popular culture, it would take another century for children's literature to be taken seriously by the academy. And when it was, the departments of library science and education had been faithfully teaching the subject and engaging in scholarship for at least a half century. Their contributions are vastly overlooked as *other* scholars with a different focus but a commonality of literature, which they discerned from nineteenth century culture.

In contrast to our own age, children's books were engrained in the social fiber of Victorian culture. Lawrence Levine's work on the temper of Victorian America reveals a rich, shared culture of classes and ages.[11] The literati saw the potentials of children's literature as literature, extolled by cultural authorities like William Dean Howells, the "dean of American letters," and Horace Scudder, editor of the most prestigious American literary journal, the *Atlantic Monthly*. The culture was so steeped in the literature of childhood that many famous authors wrote for children and were somehow expected to do so: "the majors writing for the minors," in Henry Steele Commanger's familiar words.[12] Discourse on children's books was a lively part of Victorian culture, represented so well in its periodicals, the mass media of the age, and its bestsellers, books read by a dual audience. Many of the best-selling novels of the nineteenth century were works we now consider children's literature: *Heidi, Treasure Island, A Child's Garden of Verses, Huckleberry Finn, Little Lord Fauntleroy*, these in just the two-year period of 1884–86. As Ann Thwaite writes in her biography of Frances Hodgson Burnett, the lines were blurred without demarcation between adult and children's literature.[13] Books were often characterized in reviews as being for grownups as well as children, a book for all ages. Jerry Griswold lists a range of bestsellers between 1865 and 1914 that were children's books read by adults, derived from Frank Mott's research on bestsellers.[14] In Beverly Lyon Clark's study of the construction of American children's literature, she considers the many children's magazines that were read by the whole family and the attention to children's books in the press.[15]

That the Victorians took children's books seriously is evident in their extensive reviewing of children's books in highbrow and middlebrow publications in England and the Unites States. Both crossed the Atlantic frequently in a cultural conversation about the literature of childhood. The two countries were inextricably connected in culture with a common language, traditions, and publishing practices that favored British publications. Lance Salway's collection of nineteenth century writing reveals the extensive commentary on children's books, as evidenced in Victorian periodicals.[16] My earlier research uncovered a large number of periodicals from 1880 to 1900 that reviewed or discussed children's books.[17] Richard Darling's research, which inspired mine, uncovered the lively critical discourse on children's books in American periodicals, 1865–1881.[18] Darling seeks to counter the impression made by several children's book commentators that little serious consideration of children's literature existed before the twentieth century, an assumption he challenges by revealing the richness of reviewing in the period, reviewing that reached more of the public books in mainstream publications than the more limited, specialized coverage today. Introducing his collection of nineteenth century writings on children's literature, *A Peculiar Gift*, Lance Salway is quick to point to the current interest in the subject in the mid-1970s through the specialist publications, organizations, and conferences in the field. Despite such flurry of activity, Salway reminds the reader that ours is *not* the golden age. Writing about the nineteenth century, Salway observes: "In many respects critical discussion of the subject was less restricted than it is now; books for the young were considered to be part of the general body of literature and writing about them was not confined to specialized journals and seasonal supplements."[19]

The last third of the nineteenth century has long been considered "The Golden Age of Children's Literature" because of its pride of place in the culture. Historian Harvey Darton, looking back from the vantage of the 1930s, revered the spirit of the Victorian era that brought so many richly imaginative works to children and adults. In the last sentence of his monumental history of "five centuries of social life," Darton writes: "It was left for the most serious of all grown-up epochs, the Victorian, to break down for good and for all, in poetry as well as in prose, the high fence that for centuries shut in the imagination of mankind at the very stage of its periodic growth when it is most naturally fixed to be free."[20] Moving from parochialism toward liberty of thought, the Victorians left a heritage of children's books as part and parcel of the culture. Noting wistfully that lost world, Jerry Griswold in his study of American classics asks if we will ever again see an age when children's books are the primary fare of publishing houses and the focus of literary giants like Mark Twain.[21] While many have noted the difference in stature between then and now, few have ventured why.

Cultural historians in other fields offer perspectives on the nineteenth century, a strategic time when disciplinary paradigms were established. Historian Lawrence Levine's work on the rise of cultural hierarchy in the Gilded Age is useful here, as he describes a culture struggling for hierarchical boundaries and in the process losing a common culture, the very culture that privileged children's books. In a quest for order amid enormous societal changes, elites began to redefine culture in the second half of the nineteenth century by establishing hierarchies and fragmenting into a multiplicity of fields and authorities over fields, thereby closing what had been a shared public culture. Extending his theories, I can see how in this shifting landscape children's books lost their hold, their centrality, only to be categorized into a cultural sphere of its own with prescribed cultural authority. While Levine does not mention children's literature or librarianship, we can see connections in how children's literature formed as a literature of classics with authorities to conserve that tradition. Levine writes: "Increasingly, in the closing decades of the nineteenth century, as public life became everywhere more fragmented, the concept of culture took on hierarchical connotations along the lines of Matthew Arnold's definition of culture—'the best that has been thought and known in the world ... the study and pursuit of perfection.'"[22] Children's librarians became the specialists with an "invented tradition" of classics possessing a cultural authority that *was* if not *is*. The thrust of New Criticism in the twentieth century represented this primacy on authoritative meaning of authoritative texts. In such a critical structure, works like children's literature would hardly matter.

Serious pursuit of children's literature has traditionally been more the realm of the bibliophile than the academic. The first of its kind, *The Child and His Book,* by Mrs. E. M. Field (1892) attempts an interpretive history of early beginnings of children's books up until 1826, which she considers the modern era. Jabbing at the rampant romanticism of the age, she sets her course toward a realistic depiction of children in books for children. Contrast these anti-romantic sentiments to the rhetoric of children's librarians of the same era:

> Children live less in their own fairy world; 'Heaven lies about them in their infancy' less than formerly; they more quickly grow up and dispel the glamour of those happy mists of childhood which in the morning of youth veil for a time the harsh realities of life. Many of our recent stories for children also have not been stories for children, but stories about children ... eminently unsuitable for the children's own reading, and, as experience proves, not interesting to them.[23]

Setting out to extend Field's scope and update children's book history into its Victorian prime, Harvey Darton's *Children's Books in England: Five Centuries of Social Life* seemed anomalous when it appeared out of context in 1932. Darton's history of children's literature was so exhaustive, so unrivalled as the definitive text that it was revised twice: by Kathleen Hines in 1960 and Brian Alderson in 1982. Widely cited in the literature, the work has been long considered the standard history and Darton the scholar of the field. The book appeared at a time, in the words of his editor Kathleen Hines, when "it stood alone, and at a time when little intelligent interest was taken in what children read or the books published for them."[24] The implication is that the era of the late 1950s was considerably different, however questionable. Darton's interpretive history is rich in publishing history and social history, but his perspectives, often idiosyncratic, were writ large in the field and took at least a half-century to challenge, as Mitzi Myers did with her revision of the women writers of the "moral tale."[25] Darton came from a long lineage of book publishers; his knowledge was acquired rather than academic; as a specialist he pursued his subject over twenty years of independent research. Historians of children's literature were largely bibliophiles, bibliographers, book collectors, book sellers, independent scholars, with minimal institutional support, but with a passion for children's books: d'Alté A. Welch's *Bibliography of American Children's Books Printed to 1821*; Margaret Moon's work on the early book trade; Iona and Peter Opie's research on nursery rhymes and fairy tales compiled in Oxford editions; Abraham Rosenbach's *Early American Children's Books, with Bibliographical Descriptions of the Books in his Private Collection*; Irvin Kerlan with his collection and gift of first editions bestowed on his alma mater; Justin Schiller as bookseller with his elegant catalogs and close connection to scholars; Michael Patrick Hearn in pursuit of Oz and the art of illustration; Brian Alderson in a long career in bibliography; John Rowe Townsend with his outline of English-language children's literature. These pioneers in their meticulous manner paved the way for the critics to follow.

A body of literature was slowly emerging, more descriptive than analytical, more survey than focus, but bearing weight as scholarship. Children's librarians assumed an ambitious project: to tell the story of the history of children's literature and children's librarianship, with particular emphasis on the American scene. Cornelia Meigs's *A Critical History of Children's Literature* may not have been particularly "critical," but it surveyed the history and chronicled the explosion of interest generated by librarians. To Frances Clark Sayers, its appearance in 1953 "shot across the sky, a brilliant exploratory satellite. No such rocket had ever been launched from an American base."[26] Including an introduction by Henry Steele Commanger, man of letters, gave a certain cachet to their efforts. The book was more in the celebratory tradition initiated by the matriarchal writings, but it succeeded in educating others to take the subject seriously and in encouraging the converted. Another precursor was Bettina Hürlimann's *Three Centuries of Children's Books in Europe* (1959, 1967), translated and edited by Brian Alderson, and Mary Thwaite's *From Primer to Pleasure in Reading* (1963), designed to teach British librarians through a broad literary survey. Scholars from related fields were borrowed, such as Philippe Aries's exploration of the history of childhood, *Centuries of Childhood* (1962), which in offering childhood as a cultural construction inspired interdisciplinary scholarship into the child.

A quickening of scholarship starting in the 1960s arose in part from the special collections of children's literature. American academic interest in children's literature as a body of knowledge is interwoven with the libraries and librarians who guide and collect for research, unlike a museum for preservation. Librarians are interested in *use* and will often promote their holdings far and wide in order to enhance knowledge of their holdings and their own university identity. After serving as a curator in a special collection of children's literature, I am aware of the dependence of scholars on those library collections built up over a lifetime. As with the history of children's librarianship, special collection librarians have been the silent partner to the researcher as well as the active partner in their collecting, cataloging, and accessing materials; they are the unsung scholar in the configuration, largely unacknowledged. Curators work individually with scholars, and their deep knowledge of the collection often turns research in a different course. Scholars turn to special collections for their unique manuscript holdings and rare book materials. They come for a physical object—a book, manuscript, or periodical—and are introduced to the contextual framework of that object. Text becomes context in the discovery of differences being related, of a larger world of knowledge extrinsic and intrinsic in meaning. The transformations of a simple children's book into studies in textual history, sociohistory, biography are the metaphorical leaps possible in scholarly collections of children's literature and with a fellow scholar-librarian.

Special collections have traditionally housed the fragile, scarce item in whatever format: old photographs and film, ephemera, maps, personal memorabilia, commercial and legal documents, as well as original manuscripts and rare books. These are the very sources now zealously sought by scholars. Literary researchers seek out original manuscript versions of a text instead of printed books, often replete with errors or omissions. Historians investigate archives for correspondence and records of political and social activity. Older publications and periodicals of the eighteenth and nineteenth centuries become vital primary sources. In the intimacy of curator and scholar, in their imaginative collaboration, academics of children's literature have a sense of place.[27]

Despite this bounty, scholars needed to be nudged in that direction. Curators in such collections work to attract scholars and keep records of what research emanates from their special library, which validates their position. The dearth of scholarship in the field is evident in historian R. Gordon Kelly's lament in 1973 on the lack of history of children's literature, noting the comparatively little serious or systematic scholarly century in the twentieth century, not only because the significance of children's books as a field for scholarly study has not been very communicated, but also because literary scholars and historians have defined the concerns of their discipline too narrowly to include the study of children's books.[28] Alternately, children's book scholars, such as educators and librarians, ignored the interdisciplinary interests that could be included in the discourse. The specialization of twigging fields of scholarly study of "the Child" needed a conjoined voice and vast crossovers of disciplinary knowledge and experience. The time was ripe for an organization of like-minded scholars to band together for legitimacy in academia.

Francelia Butler was the matriarch, the institution-builder, behind the nascent organization of scholars in the field. Teaching at the University of Connecticut, she taught a course in children's literature, which persuaded her of the validity of the subject within the discipline and the need to form a profession to support the subject in the academy. Their intent, different from the library organization of similar kind, was to promote children's literature as literature, curiously a familiar theme to the early children's library movement. These like-minded professors, sympathetic to the cause but uncertain in status, were dispersed in many types of institutions, departmental homes, and organizational affiliations, but rarely knew each other. For legitimacy in academia, they needed the heft of a tradition, a body of knowledge, their own literature. Literary academics looked to literary criticism to build a critical approach, to apply theory to their practice. As Cinderellas, the children's literature specialists had to fend against derision from colleagues, who viewed the whole affair in the spirit of Frederick Crews's *The Pooh Perplex*.[29] While Crews's mockery slowed their pace, the academicians knew the need for a body of critical scholarship and an organizational body: they needed to be centered.

Francelia Butler inaugurated a journal, *The Great Excluded: Critical Essays on Children's Literature*, compiled of essays emanating from a Modern Language Association seminar in 1969, the first session devoted to the subject. In her introduction to this vanguard effort, she relayed the sad state of children's literature in the early 1970s. Disarming the enemy, she cited why the subject was not taken seriously. Acknowledging its limitations in form and language, she rejoined by stressing the virtues of simplicity. The field was in disarray, attacked by academic politics or weakened by neophyte "experts." While the subject was regularly taught in library science and education departments, with a focus on use, what was needed was a humanities base, with a focus on art. As humanists, we needed to be concerned with the education of the young and the quality of the literature available. Soliciting fellow scholars, she stated her purpose to "stimulate the writing, teaching, and study of children's literature by humanists—to encourage humanists with the best (and open) minds to enter the field."[30] With an assortment of articles from various disciplines, some scholarly addresses, a list of recommended editions and possible topics to explore, she launched her venture. Included in the journal were two noted scholars already active in the field: historian R. Gordon Kelly and literary critic Roger Sale, who were to further their efforts into substantive criticism and scholarship.[31]

Butler's journal inspired a following. The Children's Literature Association emerged as conjoined interest in the subject. An executive board was formed to coordinate scholars in various fields by an annual conference and literary journal directed toward the grand goal of improving the climate for the academic study of children's literature. The group's first conference was held in 1978 in Cambridge and attracted scholars and specialists from a *Horn Book* editor to a Marxist scholar, from both the United States and Canada. Scholars brought a variety of critical approaches and disciplines to the conferences, the work of which appeared in two journals, *Children's Literature* and the *ChLA Newsletter*, which became the *Quarterly*. Literary analysis of landmark texts led to an interest in creating a children's literature canon, which would provide common texts for shared dialogue and curricula and presumably position the field within canonical strata of academic privilege. Jon C. Stott's 1978 presidential address to the organization called for the establishment of a canon. A committee was formed and held a panel discussion at the annual conference in 1980, "Developing a Canon of Children's Literature." The committee was composed of five professionals in the field: two from English, one from education, and two youth librarians from a public school and a public library. Committee members differed on including authors or titles, on the setting the standard as literary excellence and/or historic significance, which would include considerations of a work's impact and popularity with readers. The members of the committee differed on titles versus authors and on the idea of a canon: "a framework within which to operate;" "a rough outline map;" "a Dead Sea Scroll." Each member suggested lists, with the youth librarians promoting more popular titles. Arguing for including children's interests, a librarian urged, "The most important resource we have in the world is the children, but if we aren't paying attention to what they're reading and how they're growing, we're going to be in terrible shape,"[32] Nodelman responded to the panel in the next

Quarterly issue, an article entitled "Grand Canon Suite," in which he described the canon formation process as "an undemocratic but praiseworthy endeavor" where "some books *are* more important than others." Acknowledging that the word itself sounds so legalistic and formal and "a catalogue of saints." Relating their canon to the larger literary canon, he notes how variable canons are to literary tastes and how different each list might be depending on the principle by which choices are made. The list will never be comprehensive, but more discriminating between titles and offering a rationale for all.[33]

The canon that emerged of sixty-three titles was published in pamphlet form and distributed in 1982–83. The reception was somewhat critical, so the canon was reformed into "touchstones," drawing on Matthew Arnold's distinction of literary worth as Matthew Arnold's "touchstone"—a black stone used to test the purity of gold or silver by the streak left when rubbed with metal—metaphorically applied to the use of a literary work ("poetry") as a benchmark to evaluate other books. Arnold expressed the standard, which became a way of thinking about literary studies, then in its nascence:

> Indeed there can be no more useful help for discovering what poetry belongs to the class of the truly excellent, and can therefore do us most good, than to have always in one's mind lines and expressions of the great masters, and to apply them as a touchstone to other poetry. Of course we are not to require this other poetry to resemble them; it may be very dissimilar. But if we have any tact we shall find them, when we lodge them well in our minds, an infallible touchstone for detecting the presence or absence of high poetic quality, and also the degree of this quality, in all other poetry we may place beside them.[34]

The concept of "touchstones" was applied to the judgments of excellence in evaluating children's literature.

Perry Nodelman, who edited the project and publication of *Touchstones*—the literary criticism of the sixty-three titles chosen—defends the approach in his introduction to the first of the three volumes. Why the need for such a canon? He personalizes the need by relating his own struggles when designing his initial course, with little background in the field. Nodelman defines a touchstone variously as "a book beside which we may place other children's books in order to make judgments about their excellence," "a set of guidelines," " a shared context," agreed by all as significant, and a book that is both unconventional and representative: "A touchstone has to be unconventional enough to draw attention to itself, to cause controversy, perhaps to encourage imitators."[35] Nodelman describes these books as "the best" (in subtitle) because they are noteworthy without consideration of children's wants and needs; as titles they transcend comparison to other works by the same author. Acknowledging objections to a children's literature canon as representative alone of the academic establishment, he defends the list as dialogue, a way to open discussion and offer guidance.

The sixty-three titles included in the *Touchstone* series are represented by essays of literary criticism that seek to provide "a clearer, deeper sense of the best in children's books, and all the strength and joy to be drawn from them."[36] Each essay, written by a scholar in the field, exists to explore a specific work as a touchstone. As Nodelman's sense of the term is various, so also are the essays that follow. I have abstracted each one to reveal the discourse on canon that emerges from academia as acts of definition of greatness, of cultural validation of the field. Their criticism reveals not only canonical standards but also literary approaches that involved research, reflection, and interpretation, including feminist criticism, reader-response theory, archetypal studies, rhetorical criticism, among other perspectives. These essays are primary sources in the understanding of the role of the academic in constructing classics. The authors seek to locate canonical status—where to look for worth, significance, aesthetic value—and to determine what constitutes that worth, significance, value.[37] How do these essays inform what Deborah Stevenson calls "the canon of significance" and "the canon of sentiment?"[38] Is there hope for academic recovery of titles not popular with the public? Is the canon of significance more as a teaching canon, useful for historiography and curriculum, than as a reading list? Is the canon of sentiment more of a popular "Great Books" collection? She suggests that canonical works are those more likely read by scholars who feel capable of applying a critical apparatus to a familiar text and that popular works depend on custom and familiarity from the older generation passed on to the young.

How do these ChLA touchstones fit? In the spirit of Matthew Arnold's touchstones, how does the trajectory of these touchstones relate to Arnold's ideal of criticism as "a disinterested endeavor to learn and propagate the best that is known and thought in the world?" Does the list in its self-positioning represent the "best" in the world? What *is* the cultural function of criticism in the institution of children's literature?

These voices offer some answers. I take the time to abstract their essays because they offer such a view into canon formation in academic study and criticism: a synecdoche of the connections between the ivory tower and the nursery, the meeting ground of professionalism and disciplinary growth. The canon here represents many things internally to the organization and externally to authoritative powers that privilege classics. The list and its criticism document a process at work, where works are canonized as significant before our very eyes. The authorship itself is quite impressive: an honor roll of scholars in the field exerting their muscle for a good cause. For each title chosen as touchstone, a scholar was selected to fashion a rationale positioning the work. The abstracts, which represent essays in the three volume series, are presented in the alphabetical order in which they appear in the brochure, "Touchstones: A List of Distinguished Children's Books." In the three published volumes, the works are divided by fiction; fairy tales, fables, myths, legends, and poetry; and picture books. The time span is 1869 (*Little Women*) to 1982 (*The Borrowers Avenged*), with the majority covering the twentieth century. Curiously, no dates are given for the titles, which further decontextualizes these works. Together these "touchstones" reveal *how* and *what* scholars privilege in the continuity of a selective tradition. They reflect and construct the shifting landscape of taste and criticism of the academic elite. I offer some of my response to this canon in the epilogue.

What is the worth of creating a list of touchstones with their own accompanying defense? Do we wish to bolster the "popularity" of these books, thereby establishing more firmly their place in future canons and considerations? Is the point to create better understanding of why certain books work to foster the discussion and create better work (and possibly readers)? Will this result in a dialogue between academics and librarians (rather, did it foster that)? What are the statements about meaning implied from these abstracts? Why do some critics discuss illustration more than others? What, then, are the elements of a successful children's book? Would a librarian agree? Would a parent? Would a child? Are these valuations subject to the whims of time and fad? Has popularity positioned itself as a determinant of status or been avoided as an issue, played down and up when convenient? How useful is it to create a list as various as the opinions and experiences of those who wrote the pieces for it? All of these questions we can begin to answer better by reading the essays in abstracted form. Here are their soundings.

THE TOUCHSTONES

"*Little Women*: Who Is Still Reading Miss Alcott and Why" by Ruth K. MacDonald

Ruth MacDonald finds much that is modern in Louisa May Alcott's *Little Women*. Complex portrayals of her characters combined with an acute sensitivity to women's rights and conflicts of interest create a work grounded in realism that, despite its lack of contemporary gritty urban rhythms and panoramas, offers much to a modern reader.

Parting ways with conventionally (of the time) dogmatic characters representing Good or Evil, the March women are textured, outspoken and lively—wholly un-Victorian. They grapple with many of the same dilemmas of modern women, primarily balancing societal expectations and domestic duties with more ambitious dreams and desires to pursue financial independence and a career. MacDonald argues that herein lies Alcott's most compelling claim to her status as touchstone author of children's literature.

In remaining faithful to enduring American tendencies toward consumerism (e.g., the opening line of the book in which Jo March complains that Christmas would not be Christmas without presents) and the nationally mythologized shelter of the home (in contrast to the Civil War and other turbulent realities of the outside world), Alcott wrote a work with staying power. Her lessons and language are not didactic. She allows her story to unfold through her characters (along with any moralizing) unobtrusively. The March world is a rich one at least in description; despite ostensible hardship and poverty; Alcott's world continues to offer a

feast of visuals for readers far protracted in time. Finally, and perhaps most importantly, Alcott's progressive notions about education, women's rights, and politics
positions her heroines well to weather the changing mores of her readership's
culture.

"Alexander's *Chronicles of Prydain*: The Nature of Beginnings"
by Jon C. Scott

From humble beginnings as an Assistant Pig-Keeper to noble ending as the High
King of Prydain, Lloyd Alexander's *Chronicles of Prydain* follow young Taran
through a maze of obstacles, triumphs, and humbling defeats. With each event
comes a beginning, ripe with possibility and gleaming with worthy challenge. For
Jon C. Scott, Alexander's touchstone status begins with these beginnings. Taran's
journey is T. S. Eliot's "In my end is my beginning" and Shakespeare's "What's past
is prologue." It is the author's greatest gift to his readers: the message that their
future is one of newness and risk. He brings his readers on a wild adventure
through four books as Taran searches for his identity. Like the torment of his
adolescent readers, the plot twists and turns delineating geographies that parallel
Taran's internal search.

No reward is true unless it bears an internal revelation, unless it brings Taran
closer to a sense of himself. And because this adventure is beset with the very real
struggle of its hero to "find himself," *Prydain*'s fantasy world is firmly rooted in the
very real daily struggle of adolescents attempting to map out their own identities.
Taran is obsessed with the identity (noble or not) of his parents. By the end, when
he has finally beheld himself in the Mirror of Llunet and returned to his humble
beginnings to understand their worth for the first time, Taran is crowned High
King of Prydain—despite the unknown identity of his parents. These popular
themes of independence, possibility, and identity abound in Alexander's *Prydain*,
making it a starting place, a touchstone, for young readers and writers alike.

"Hans Christian Andersen's Fairy Tales and Stories: Secrets, Swans, and Shadows"
by Jon Cech

The poetic shadows of Hans Christian Andersen's fairy tales and stories remain as
brilliant in the canon of children's literature as his good children and graceful
swans. From his humble beginnings in a working-class family he imagined the
settings and characters of his fairy tales, which brought him great success as a
writer, complicating his affinities and adding texture to the tone of his tales.
Andersen's children's stories are a confession and transformation of his difficult life
of poverty, rejection, loss, struggle, bitterness, and vanity into beauty. He employs
and abandons the trope of happy endings and hope in his fairy tales, but always
relies on humor.

Written from the kernel of an adult concept into a story for children,
Andersen sought to and succeeded in writing for a large audience. His humor,

often class based (and sometimes sexist) and directed at adults, did not hide his dark vision of humanity. Often criticized for his pessimism, Andersen's heroes are incomplete and frequently rewarded with wholeness for being good to others and true to themselves. His stories and fairy tales are touchstones not only because they are passed on through generations, but more because of the extent to which they speak to and of our secrets. Andersen captures our hopes, fears, desires, and hidden aggressions. Because his heroes and their experiences come from his own life, there is no consistent political, social, or moral message to his work. The lessons follow life's natural path of light and dark. His writings crackle with the brilliant fire of life in all its destructive glory and illuminating resource.

"Edward Ardizzone's *Little Tim and the Brave Sea Captain*: An Art of Contrasts" by Peter Hunt

When Edward Ardizzone was a small child, he formed some of his earliest memories around his perusals of his grandfather's maritime diaries. Later, his restless mother moved them to the sea where Edward experienced more maritime adventures both charming and violent. The quaint episodes made their way into his Little Tim books; the harsh realities found their home in his paintings. An illustrator first, Ardizzone neither condescended to children nor allowed his illustrations simply to illuminate the words of a story. His talent (illustrating over 151 children's books) was and is evident in his "bold, clear" drawings that depart from simplicity in intricate lighting, positioning, composition, and gesture. In *Little Tim and the Brave Sea Captain*, Ardizzone's illustrations develop both character and story.

Far from being an illustrator content to draw simple pictures for supposedly simple minds, Ardizzone credited children for their unsentimental toughness. He tackled loneliness in every one of his *Little Tim* books (having been left at boarding school for four lonely years by his parents while they went abroad). He contrasted color with tone so that no illustration was without depth on several levels. Created as bedtime stories for his own children, *Little Tim* looks with candor and an unobtrusive nostalgia into the active, adventurous world of children. Ardizzone always said he drew not from life, but from knowledge gained from life—a broader perspective with more profound associations and the possibility for starker contrasts of reality, all of which he firmly believed in broaching (with an incurable charm and ease) in *Little Tim and the Brave Sea Captain*.

"Asbjornsen and Moe's Norwegian Folktales: Voice and Vision" by Kay Unruh DesRoches

These folktales arise from the land of fjords and avalanches, precipices and Northern Lights. The landscapes of Norway find their way into these tales not only in the settings but further in the irony of life's flourishing amidst such apparent desolation. The canonical quality of Asbjornsen and Moe's Norwegian folktales lies in their capable rendering of irony. Within the tales is always a narrator, the oral storyteller, from whence the story originated. He or she claims to have been an eyewitness, creating the irony of a fictional telling of an often-fantastic tale of ostensible "truth" from the mouth of the fictionalized teller to an ideal audience. But the page promises no ideal audience; reader and writer are as separate as two bodies in a Norwegian storm. This tension ripples throughout the folktales adding suspense, creating humor, and enriching these tales.

Their oral beginnings are apparent in the folktale's structure and style. Instead of a narrative building throughout to its inevitable conclusion as in the quest-romance of the fairy tale, these folktales simply stop, and frequently with laughable rhyming couplets. Therefore, conflict is replaced by contest, and the morality inherent in literate renditions is absent. The stories are accumulative as opposed to being the result of specific causal elements (one can almost hear the storyteller tiring of his own tale or the audience fidgeting to move on). We face our bourgeois biases, and must laugh with the stories at ourselves. Writers and illustrators place realistic detail alongside magical flourishes, approaching nightmare and grotesquerie. Privileging comedic detail over plot, these folktales are touchstones in their humor, their singular imagery, and ironic distancing of reality and ideal. Kittelsen's drawing of the cat in "The Tabby Who Was Such a Glutton" is just frightening enough to make us laugh at our own demonizing of these characters; we instead accept their connection to ourselves.

"L. Leslie Brooke's *Johnny Crow's Garden*: The Gentle Humor of Implied Stories" by Marilyn Apseloff

In *Johnny Crow's Garden*, a cat waits by Johnny Crow's front door for the mouse to leave Johnny's party. The mouse leaves by way of a backdoor, and in subsequent illustrations, the cat appears increasingly emaciated. L. Leslie Brooke captures this small story visually, without having to approach it in the written story, allowing the child reader an opportunity for discovery and renewed interest upon rereads. The ability of *Johnny Crow's Garden* to withstand the test of endurance through generations of pleased readers and furthermore to provide delight and newness to returning readers young and old makes it clearly a touchstone of children's literature.

Brooke's *Johnny Crow's Garden* stands out particularly because of the light, subtle humor and extended characterization evident in his drawings. While the written text inculcates young readers into the joy of rhyming and rhythm, it is the illustration that teaches them to read between the lines, to laugh at the mild condescension in the play between the drawings and the words, and to find messages hidden within the drawings that may not be evident to adult eyes. What better instrument, then, for creating attentive, enthusiastic readers and consumers of visual and literary culture? Adults enjoy the humor directed toward them—a book on a table in one drawing is entitled *Confuseus*—and all readers find in the rich illustrations expressive faces of these animal characters, entire stories in their gestures, comportment, and the artist's composition. Because Brooke collaborated with the most stringent and critical editors—his own children—when choosing drawings for the book, *Johnny Crow's Garden* will continue to endure with a smile.

"Frances Hodgson Burnett's *The Secret Garden*: The Organ(ic)ized World"
by Heather Murray

A complex mediation between nature and society, life and art, the voice of character and author in *The Secret Garden* inspires a continuing dialogue, according to Heather Murray, that helps set this work within the canon of children's literature. Instead of answering why the work has value, Murray broaches the subject of how it has come to be considered and considered again by readers and critics alike since its initial publication. Burnett finishes her novel with a ceding of the natural order to the social, thereby either reinforcing or simply describing the status quo. That scholars maintain the discourse is a statement about the work's ability to withstand changing critical approaches to children's literature in changing times.

Because of Burnett's frequent themes of gender confusion, the absent parent and possible psychological readings of her texts, she has been a biographer's favorite. She was prolific under financial pressures, and *The Secret Garden* rode that fine line between juvenile fiction and the sentimental romance that eventually fell entirely within the realm of the juvenile. Nevertheless, *The Secret Garden* has been popular in book and film form, and enjoyed cult status among high school and college readers of the 1970s with its disturbing characters, spiritualism, healthy eating, exercise, and positive thinking. Murray finds fascinating the inclusion of labor in this utopia, the way it has found a home in the landscape and mindscape of these children and their creative endeavors.

The Secret Garden is a text ripe for analysis. It has been adopted by feminist critics, scholars intrigued by the "liberating possibilities of folk and fairy tales," utopians, naturalists, and because of its obtuse ending (ostensibly affirming of patriarchal order) is palatable to general—and generally conservative—audiences. It has secured a strong foothold in the canon, although the columns supporting it change with time and tide.

"Randolph Caldecott's Picture Books: The Invention of a Genre"
by Ellin Greene

When Frederic Melcher donated money to begin an annual award for picture books, there was no argument that the prize would be named after Randolph Caldecott. As, according to Maurice Sendak, the inventor of the picture book, Caldecott made great strides in children's literature to move beyond the merely real or decorative to create illustrations with style, personality, and humor that speak directly to a child audience. Adults for generations have also, in turn, continued to enjoy the jokes directed toward them (a perfect example is the dish literally broken into pieces at the end of Hey, Diddle, Diddle when the parents of the spoon with whom he has run away come to fetch her and leave him all broken up, alone). Caldecott succeeded in his collaboration with Edmund Evans and later Walter Crane in creating some of the most important illustrations of children's literature history.

When Edmund Evans approached Caldecott, it was to do some drawings of nursery rhymes for small books. The illustrator proceeded to create works that have withstood the test of time and remain the most memorable renditions of nursery rhymes to date. He chose nursery rhymes specifically for children, then created a conversation between the written text and the drawings such that they enhance one another. His artistic talent captures setting, characterization, and action—at time contrapositioning these elements for humor and an unequaled richness, even in a time when attention to design and visuals is commonplace. Finally, he "immortalized the English countryside" that, along with his jokes and sensitivity toward children, will be remembered forever in the legacy of his brilliant illustrations that give and give again.

"Lewis Carroll's Alice Books: The Wonder of Wonderland"
by Beverly Lyon Clark

In an era drawn by stark oppositional conceptions of the child as either good or bad was born Alice of Lewis Carroll's Wonderland. Thoughtful, brave, imperfect, and playfully violent, Alice defied the popular models of the child as either the picture of purity and innocence or a product of original sin to be duly punished. Carroll's Alice books have withstood the test of time to prove themselves stalwarts of the children's literature canon because of their inability to remain still. These works have bountiful lives of their own that refuse resting for too long with any one reading while nevertheless being bountiful enough to satisfy many that insist upon a reductive one-to-one allegorical correlation.

Although immediately appreciated by many critics, the Alice books were also dismissed by many for their "annoying" nonsensical narratives. Carroll was able to capture the essence of childhood, devoid of moralizing pedagogy, which has endeared him with children and adults alike. He composed them orally for a real beloved Alice, and was able to live within the fancy of a child' life by escaping his life of mathematics and science. While the books offer playful games of logic and language ("Jam every other day," meaning yesterday and tomorrow, and therefore never today), they are written from the keen observations of a photographer's eye. Some twentieth century critics argue the books are more fitting for adult readers than children. However children respond well to the nonsense even if they don't completely understand the nuance. Modern and postmodern readings abound as well. Many literary critics find Carroll anticipated twentieth-century tendencies in adult fiction with fractured, self-conscious narrative.

Every possible school of critics has attempted to co-opt Alice into its symbolic system: religious, sexual, political, psychological, drug-related (the list goes on).

The books do satirize Victorian culture, but they are richer than any themed explanation. Carroll's Alice books have endured because they cannot be contained by any one totalizing explanation. So they come to us repeatedly with fresh offerings, slipping through our fingers, forever seductive and generous.

"Richard Chase's *Jack Tales*: A Trickster in the New World"
by Nina Mikkelsen

Much like his protagonist, Richard Chase achieves the impossible in his renditions of the Jack tales. Chase captures with respect and dignity the people of the Appalachian mountains of the 1930s through the language of their oral storytelling about the Jack of the Old World. Without mocking, he features dialect and idiosyncrasy to augment the humor of the tales and broaden their interest for both children and adults. Just as Jack must synthesize his emerging sexuality with his trickster nature to work toward emotional maturity, so too does Chase's version of the Jack Tales transform the Old into the New to capture a time, place, and new sensibility for posterity. The Jack of the American South reflects the approachable, kind, generous, and resourceful nature of the Ward family who told his story. He doesn't need supernatural powers; he is the trickster hero who overcomes through his own cunning and accidental brilliance.

Espousing the values of this new world, Chase finds Jack often on the road—as both the means to his victory, and end in itself. He does not accept his lot in life, and faces impossible challenges with the confidence only affordable to children or those who are somewhat dim. Both children and adults appreciate his antics: children laugh at the absurdity, and adults smile at the confluence of buffoon and trickster in Jack. Without losing their loose origins in the Grimm's fairy tales, the Jack tales are satisfying to all because of their spoken language, humor, classic themes of sexual and emotional maturation, and their inclusion of bright female characters in Jack's wily schemes. Childhood into adulthood is a transformation time-worn and rendered as fresh as it feels experienced from the perspective of one within it in Chase's Jack tales.

"Carlo Collodi's *The Adventures of Pinocchio*: A Classic Book of Choices"
by Richard Wunderlich and Thomas J. Morrissey

The Adventures of Pinocchio by Carlo Collodi is a widely adapted work that both Richard Wunderlich and Thomas Morrissey find to be at once worthy of its popularity and transcendent of its popular exegesis. The writers include Pinocchio as a touchstone because it satisfies their three criteria for a canonical text: 1) It is popular and very widely read; 2) Its stylistic texture allows for varied readings depending on reader; 3) It deals with universal human concerns. Many of the work's strengths lie in what is adapted away in the multitudinous interpretations of this Italian novel (by the likes of Disney and others) that appeared after its publication and between the world wars.

As a traditional *Bildungsroman*, the structure of *The Adventures of Pinocchio* follows the edification of this "woodenhead" as he matures into a responsible, caring young person. With humor and a tone reminiscent of oral storytelling, Pinocchio is easily read aloud to very young readers; Collodi exhibits for all a distinctive narrative voice that deftly manipulates the progression of action. With characters that make their visual mark in the imaginations of children, adults, illustrators, and filmmakers alike, Pinocchio is best understood as a character-driven novel. While the characters are delightful and memorable for young readers, adults and critics can also become intellectually engaged in the subtlety of their development. Furthermore, images abound layered with political satire, religious references, Freudian imagery, and psychological realism—despite the "magical" exaggerations of the more commercial adaptations.

Never is the novel's violence gruesome, and never are its moral lessons overly didactic. A work that "conforms to the Renaissance belief that art should teach and delight," Pinocchio studies what makes for goodness in human beings (not just in children), and lightly encourages in all readers an understanding of the worth of generosity and genuine consideration for others.

"Padraic Colum's *The Golden Fleece*: The Lost Goddesses"
by Nancy Huse

While Charlene Spretnak's revision of Homer for her daughter focuses on the powers of the goddesses, this version of Homer falls short of Padraic Colum's accomplishment in *The Golden Fleece*. Knowledge of the canon is crucial not only for the understanding of Western literary history, but also Western culture and the legacy of misogyny in which the Greek myths play an enduring role. Colum's translation is faithful to the myths in his maintenance of the tone of epic poetry and more importantly, in his rendering of the oppression of female characters. As opposed to the derision of female experience that one finds in most translations of Greek mythology, or belittling it literally within the stories to the point of non-existence, Colum allows the integration of male and female experience (e.g., Jason carries the goddess Hera over the river versus Colum's version in which Hera protects Jason, carrying him over the river and appearing to him under various guises), living in a world together, helping each other with varying strengths and weaknesses, without scorn or what is both worse and frequently found in other versions of the myths—erasure.

The Golden Fleece is deserving of its canonization because of 1) its closeness to the original texts; 2) its empathy for the female characters (gods, etc.) and their oppression; and 3) its genuine suitability for children. Colum's romanticization of Greek mythology allows for a more cohesive narrative unified in theme and imagery, in addition to making room for female characters to act with conse-quence. His un-self-conscious lyrical language is spellbinding to children, while respectful of their need for action. As Colum does not hide from Greek misogyny, nor does Pogany in his illustrations, as it was and is an important and enduring element in the Greek myths, society, culture, and legacy. Perhaps most importantly, however, Colum retains the hope of Homer's epic poem. He offers up to child readers his own "trust in poetic power to reshape the world out of the riches and shames of the past."

"Walter Crane's *The Baby's Opera*: A Commodious Dwelling"
by Patricia Demers

Walter Crane was understandably one of the most sought-after illustrators of his time, commissioned by artists of all media to do work for him, the most important, perhaps, of whom were his children to whom he was a loving, devoted father. As one of the loud admonishers of art for art's sake of his era, Crane adhered to beauty and grace in all aspects of life, as opposed to the popular and stiff morals of the Victorians. Consequently, he had a great influence on design of the period, and made an indelible mark on children's literature by seeing children's book illustrations as "the home of thought and vision." The home he created in *The Baby's Opera* captures his maturity as an artist in the complexity expressed in the harmony of decoration, design, rhyme, illustration and humor.

An adherent of "drollery and light-hearted burlesque," the illustrations of Crane's *Baby's Opera* are consistently light. Instead of the overbearing sexuality of Caldecott's milkmaid, Crane's is young, practical, attractive, but never lewd. All his women have been rounded into warm, inviting, pre-Raphaelite figures of maternal charm and romantic grace. *The Baby's Opera* was followed by *Baby's Bouquet* and *The Baby's Own Aesop*, both in the same fashion, both espousing his ideals about life and art and their comfortable confluence. By his own summation, the work of this brilliant aesthete worships: "the rich tapestry of story and picture ... , the warp of human wonder and imagination ... crossed with many colored threads of mythological lore, history and allegory, symbolism and romance."

"The Norse Myths and D'Aulaire's *Norse Gods and Giants*: Patterns of Paradox"
by Caroline R. Goforth

For the often violent and morbid Norse myths, one has to wonder if they meet C. S. Lewis's definitive requirement that myths "delight and nourish" the child reader. When considered in the larger scope of prehistoric man all the way to childhood emotional and psychological development, the challenges and conquering life forces of D'Aulaire's *Norse Gods and Giants* resound as touchstone material.

What the Norse myths accomplish for child readers is a goal infrequently set by literature for children: the lesson of life's cycles of death and life. While ostensibly pessimistic and full of injustices and paradox, these stories are fitting for older children and those concerned with fairness. Clear distinctions between good and evil, with appropriate punishments and rewards are not present in the tales. The goddess of love, Freya, weeps incessantly over the loss of her husband, Od.

Loki is a trickster villain whose clever nature often saves the gods from trouble. The poetry itself was formed from a complex, convoluted mess of violence, murder, betrayal, and loss. But in this cycle, all of life comes from destruction.

Disorder is devoured and encompassed by order, goodness. And although life on Earth is consumed with disorder, the Norse myths testify to a larger universe in which even the disorder has its proper place. These myths invoke the imagination; it is the sole refuge of hope, and of comprehending our universe, a larger schema than the one we embody in everyday, disorderly experience on Earth. What we create here on Earth is inescapably horrific, but the universe is vaster. Because we cannot know it, we are able to hope that it is more than we are.

"The Poetry of Walter de la Mare: Sweet-Tongued Words"
by Norma Bagnall

Because a child's initiation into language begins largely through riddles, rhymes, alliteration, then turns to raucous games with language, it makes sense that they have a natural ear for poetry. Walter de la Mare's poems speak to the child from the child's perspective, turning his own wealth of experience lyrical for adult readers as well. de la Mare's signature style looks closely at an object, then backs off to see it from a differing perspective, evoking the studied object through both the visual image and the sound of his language. In calling the reader to pay attention to the details both "unusual and beautiful" of our world, de la Mare teaches how to capture life before it slips away, as it will like snowflakes melting in a palm.

Walter de la Mare's poetry moves from beloved childhood nonsense to larger issues of life's cycles with a youthful ease. In "The Funeral," he affirms life by writing of the children's oblivious attentions while at a funeral. Life is fleeting and adored, death demystified and unsentimental. His language reflects the rambunctious pace of childhood and the sometimes-overwhelming fears of half-open doors and dark closets, always submitting to the rhythms and movements of childhood. His lullabies hush children with magical renderings of the night and the luxuriously awaiting world of dreams. Change, aging, and loss find their proper home in de la Mare's poems. Replete with linguistic delicacies foreign enough to seduce the imagination and tongue of the child reader—names like, "haggis," and "Cheshire cheese"—they soothe fears and delight child and adult alike: "Elf-bells, steeple bells—sweet-tongued words."

"Dunning, Lueders, and Smith's *Reflections on a Gift of Watermelon Pickle*: Watershed in Poetry for the Young"
by Aletha K. Helbig

Reflections on a Gift of Watermelon Pickle is a dynamic anthology of poems that speaks of the concerns and obsessions of twentieth-century youth. At its first printing the anthology was an instant hit with critics, youth, and the public at large. Humor of animals, delight of spring, the loss in shaving, apartment buildings, missed loved ones, war, from the minutiae of life to its bigger issues and back again to one's head. With the majority of the poems focusing on "memorable moments" laden with irony befitting the era, *Watermelon Pickle* gives its readers credit for intelligence and a rapacious curiosity desiring aesthetic (albeit loose) form. These 114 poems spring from the pens of both unknown authors and those highly acclaimed (Pound, St. Vincent Millay, Cummings). The strongest message of *Watermelon Pickle* concerns poetry itself. Like the lives of the child readers, it is wide open, a terrain of possibility, replete with objects worthy of study—and in a playful, not necessarily studious, manner. Most of the pieces focus on "memorable moments" laden with irony befitting the era of the anthology. *Watermelon Pickle* espouses no specific morality, no politesse, and no didacticism; the content of this book is as tough as the kids who read it. Not all poems are of enduring significance, but the imaginative ordering of the anthology consistently invites associative thinking and imaginative play. Black-and-white photographs accompany a modern typeface to make the whole work have cohesion and an air of modernity.

The unifying thread of these disparate works is that all are appropriate for the young reader. This anthology paved the way for others, set a trend, and began a new consideration of the literary intelligence of children. Today's standards are tighter regarding thematic and imagistic unity. *Watermelon Pickle* stands out among them nevertheless because it was first of its kind to open the minds and imaginations of children to a poetry they can call their own, unencumbered by the weight of outdated language, custom, and moralities, educating the joy of language and life.

"Eleonor Estes's *The Moffats*: Through Colored Glass" by Louisa Smith

Many authors of children's literature, like Eleonor Estes, offer honest, real portrayals of family life peopled with well-developed characters. What elevates Eleonor Estes's *The Moffats* to the status of touchstone work is her rendering of the very peculiar and particular perspective of a child, Jane Moffat. Estes's portrayal of Jane's childhood is one sheltered during a time of war, one separate from the adult world, as experienced by a child, with a child's sense of time and attention. From studying her street with her head hanging between her legs to looking at the day through colored glass or backwards through binoculars, we see what Jane sees. Adult readers are able to recall their own childhood, at once strange and familiar.

Jane sees strangeness of familiar objects as she takes time to contemplate life's objects and situations as a child. Estes too finds this slow, leisurely attention of use as a writer. *The Moffats* serves as a call to review the world dulled through familiarity with the fresh eyes of a child. In addition to freeing Jane from the mundane, her childlike vision includes a healthy imagination that helps her escape from the difficulty of life in a "poor," single-parent family (Jane's mother insists on calling them "poor" over "poverty stricken" when Jane inquires). Her imagination shapes her individualism. Estes manages to balance that individualism with an American reinforcement of the family unit as the central force of power in the life of the Moffats. *The Moffats* satisfies our need to slow down, sit down, and look at life's kaleidoscopic offerings through the eyes of a child.

"Esther Forbes's *Johnny Tremain*: Authentic History, Classic Fiction"
by M. Sarah Smedman

In *Johnny Tremain*, author Esther Forbes manages to capture the conflict of a historical era through a central character whose struggles to grow from the rash bravado of adolescence into humble adulthood transcend time. From her Pulitzer Prize–winning research into the American Revolution, Forbes draws from her historical knowledge of the apprentices of this era to create Johnny. In so doing, Forbes accomplishes the necessary requisites for a successful historical novel. She blends the personal with the political, connecting the reader to a central character through universal themes and experiences; she presents that character in a public sphere and accurately renders social events and circumstances. Finally, Smedman finds *Johnny Tremain* to satisfy T. S. Eliot's definition of a classic as a work that expresses and embodies maturity, making it a touchstone work.

Adolescents strongly relate to *Johnny Tremain*; the book is wildly popular with them. Johnny himself moves from arrogance through an accident harming his hand and altering his fate. In the Revolution, his handicap is rendered virtually unimportant, and situates him to begin to see others as more than mere extensions of himself. Through his interactions in this "struggle for independence," Forbes weaves all sides of the issues at hand, carefully allowing for humanity to rise above difference, diminishing it, and leading to mature realization, resignation, and growth in her title character.

The backdrop of the American Revolution serves as an ideal setting for young readers who favor stories in which an adolescent is thrown into an impossible situation and must find a reasonable escape. Forbes uses environment as well to express emotion with restraint instead of resorting to simple sentimentality. Her language is succinct and replete with memorable images. Above all, Forbes's novel is a success because of her ability to blend contemporary concerns with historical and universal concerns while delighting in the development of her characters and readers.

"Louise Fitzhugh's *Harriet the Spy*: Nonsense and Sense"
by Hamida Bosmajian

Hamida Bosmajian posits that literature for a child should capture life's absurdities, finding sense in nonsense without oversimplifying the difficulties and pain of existence. Author Louise Fitzhugh accomplished this juggling act of existential angst, growth, and laughter in her novel, *Harriet the Spy*. Offering a world of obstacles and dubious rewards, she follows Harriet's alienation and eventual integration into a world of textured, albeit at times dissonant, connection. By beginning with loss, Fitzhugh sets the reader on Harriet's course of growth through shedding layers of her youth (like the onion she portrays) for her uncharted complexities of an empathetic experience of reality.

Fitzhugh connects sense and non-sense through nonsense. For example, the author embeds Harriet's Nietzschean loss of her nanny, Ole Golly ("God is dead"), in a joint recitation of Lewis Carroll's violently absurd (or absurdly violent) "The Walrus and the Carpenter," an apparently humorous poem that ends in the devouring of several of its characters. Ole Golly's wisdom stays with Harriet, although even her wise Nanny cannot explain the connection between her literary quotes and life. Harriet must un-anesthetize her heart herself as part of the maturation process. Through her life as a spy, Harriet struggles with distance and alienation, emblematized in the grotesque characters of the novel. When Harriet's peers find her notebook of observations whose indictments include nasty ones of them as well, she is the satirical focus. By the novel's close, Harriet has learned the difficult life lessons that allow for proper integration of the self into the social.

The satire, the pain, the angst, the detachment never reach beyond humor in *Harriet the Spy*, keeping the novel one for children with nuance and a satire embedded with morality for all readers. Fitzhugh's novel is genuine literature for children. Like other canonical texts, it refuses to offer didactic messages. Her characters demonstrate a means for sensing connection through an empathetic life. Growing up is difficult. Existence is painful and full of loss. By the novel's end, Harriet has grown into a comfortable closeness to the people in that world, no longer needing the distance of her life as a spy.

"Wanda Gág's *Millions of Cats*: Unity through Repetition"
by Mary Kissel

It is widely agreed among critics and fans of picture books that had the Caldecott Award been existence at the time of its publication, Wanda Gág's *Millions of Cats* would have earned that along with the Newbery—the first of many more to come for Wanda Gág. As a formally trained artist and solid storyteller, Gág's artistic integrity was such that *Millions of Cats* was not only hailed as an immediate classic, but also was the only children's book featured at the annual show at the American Institute of Graphic Arts. The repetition of theme, motif, and mood through the book's visuals make this book human and of high aesthetic standards, warm and real.

Gág used all the devices available to advance the book-making form. An expert lithographer, she insisted on the highest-quality prints and claimed the work she put into her picture books was never any less in quality than a piece she would be happy to turn over to a gallery. She relied on the journey structure of folklore in *Millions of Cats*, and the long, thin format of the book reiterates the journey's length. After the millions of cats kill each other in the contest to decide which is the most beautiful, and which, then, is allowed to return with the simple man (another mainstay of folklore), the only cat remaining is the weakest, scrawniest one, surrounded by white space to emphasize his diminution and loneliness. The happy ending is reinforced with a warm, domestic image full of circles and curved lines. Gág described her work as always striving to be "warmly human, imaginative or humorous—not coldly decorative." (Scott 174) *Millions of Cats* crosses the real with the avant-garde, turning ordinary life into art.

"Kenneth Grahame's *The Wind in the Willows*: A Companionable Vitality"
by Neil Philip

Despite Kenneth Grahame's conservative career as Great Britain's Secretary of the Treasury and a life without many close friends, *The Wind in the Willows* is a touchstone work of enduring vitality about the gift of friendship. Grahame's Mole and Toad live in an odd world of make-believe with a logic all its own. This make-believe world is not one of utter nonsense, however; Grahame's idyllic life by the riverside for these small animals mocks adulthood and sketches a version of nature as refuge from the onerous adult world of unattractive authority and tiresome responsibility.

Drawing from the work of R. L. Stevenson and Richard Jefferies, *The Wind in the Willows* balances between the perspective of child and adult, providing delight for both, with a heavy dose of Pan in the middle chapters, "A Piper at the Gates of Dawn," and "Wayfarers All." Like many children's books, this one began as stories Grahame told to his son, Alastair. He continued the tales through letters that served as the seedbed for the novel. While much of the intimacy and accessibility to children is lost in the translation from letters to novel, what Grahame achieves in its place is a satisfying synthesis clearly drawing from his crystalline memories of being a boy between five and seven years of age. He discards narrative lines and details as would a child who found them superfluous to the story's exciting heart.

While country life is praised as an escape, the author does not hail from a provincial background, and imbues his narrative with his classist, urban outsider perspective. The narrative transcends these political shortcomings, however, in the strength of the bonds between the characters. Readers young and old exult in *The Wind in the Willows*. It is a classic according to Ezra Pound's definition, because it possesses "an eternal and irrepressible freshness."

"Kate Greenaway's *A Apple Pie*: An Atmosphere of Sober Joy"
by Patricia Dooley

While the whimsical, popular Kate Greenaway may be a controversial candidate for the touchstones list because of the very source of her popularity—a sentimental view of childhood—her restraint, control, and abiding influence mark her in this territory. In Greenaway's *A Apple Pie,* children dance, cavort, frolic, and strive through the alphabet for the object of their desire: an apple pie. Because her drawings are larger and free of her usual ornamentation, gardens, flowers, and frivolous costuming, this work lands her a place in the canon. Conversely, because of those missing characteristic elements, *A Apple Pie* could not be considered an accurate representation of her work.

Separated in time and space from the adult world and adult concerns of politics, war, economics, and aggression (all "male" here in her highly feminized world of children), these children are free to inhabit their own space in two dimensions, without imposing horizons, and within plenty of white space. They are allowed to be subjects, not objects, a noteworthy advance in the consideration of children both in art and life. These children occupy themselves only with play. Their graceful garments and dancing figures support them slightly above the ground, released too as they are from gravity. Time, obligation, ill manners, and worry have no place in this garden of Eden. Greenaway's idealization of childhood still carries charm and desirability today. Her influence reached far beyond clothing styles for children and into the very fabric of the creation of childhood, a garden of happiness, freedom, and protection from all that is sullied and worn, and within time.

"The Tales of the Brothers Grimm: In the Black Forest"
by Joyce Thomas

Arguably the whole of children's literature originates with the fairy tale. And although the Grimm fairy tales have been censored, re-visioned, and rewritten to expunge improper behavior, morality, and violence, they endure as the cornerstone not only of children's literature, but also of narrative structure in Western literature. Inside (and interpreted from) fairy tales we find writ large our social fears, explanations for nature, sexual repressions, patterns, and proclivities, the traumas of birth and death, rituals, rites of passage, sexual and political power struggles, and moral systems of ordering our world. But their mere existence overshadows any interpretation. With beginnings ripe with simple possibility, and endings we can predict, but journeys full of surprise and wonder, the *Volksmarchen* of Grimm etch a humanistic meaning into the lives of all their readers.

With basic characterization, the tales begin, "Once upon a time" with someone in a place, encompassing in one line the entirety of humanity, situated in place and a subject of time—Life. The close relationship between the word and the world it creates in the Grimm fairy tales attaches child readers to language early. With setting, ensuing conflict, then its resolution (often with the bond of love), children learn a pattern of synthesizing meaning. Their own lives become stories, and stories within their control. Basic desires, virtues, and sins are all present here in a balancing act, with a lesson about disequilibria (conflict) as integral to life itself. In the integral connection between fantasy and reality, with one begetting the other or standing in as one and the same, readers are invited to greet the world with wonder and joy, an openness that connects human to human, human to nature, human to beast, and all of life to mystery.

"Joel Chandler Harris's *Tales of Uncle Remus:* For Mixed Audiences"
by Hugh Keenan

In spite of the controversial dialect of Joel Chandler Harris's *Tales of Uncle Remus*, their enduring popularity and place in the canon of children's literature cannot be disputed. However authentic and correct these tales may be, as evaluated by contemporary scholars of African American culture and literature, the dialect fell out of favor, only to be brought back more recently by the use of dialect by acclaimed writers such as Alice Walker and Toni Morrison. Fortunately, these folktales are imminently enjoyable by both children and adults, enabling their translation through the adult reader as mediator, deciding whether to render them as written or speak them in plain English to avoid miscommunication and offense. Harris's tales were so popular around the turn of the century, he wrote a total of nine books of *Uncle Remus*, many of which remain in print. And although that may be evidence enough of worth, it is Harris's ability to render the real struggles of growing up from apparent innocence into the adult world of competition and struggle for power, with the weak oftentimes at a loss. What Uncle Remus teaches Little Boy, however, is that wit can win over brute strength.

No other children's book as ably captures both a lighter, more encouraging view of humanity (in the relationship between Uncle and Boy), alongside the bellicose one of the animals. Humanist and humorous, Uncle Remus continues to teach valuable lessons of humility, hard work, and honesty without alienating either the child or adult reader with heavy-handed moralizing. No wonder his public and publisher pressured Harris into nine books—some of the later necessarily straying from the authentic ones of the black South, borrowing from other folktales of the Old World (France and England) and the New.

"Padraic Colum's *The Children's Homer:* The Myth Reborn"
by Yancy Barton

The heroes of Patraic Colum's *The Children's Homer* loom large enough to tell of humanity. With Colum's able translation that combines both the *Iliad* and the *Odyssey*, they attain mythic proportions—at once fantastically powerful and fatally flawed. Their corporeity makes them real for child readers; Colum's poetic language allows them to exist as heroes on quests among gods, monsters, war, and love.

Colum moves with seamless transitions between the two tales, retaining their integrity while nevertheless altering some plot points to facilitate narrative. He does not attempt to translate the epic poem, but translates Homer as a story for children, comprehensible by them but always leading their imaginations to new, ancient stomping grounds. From his omissions rises a myth that retains cultural values of Greek society: the importance of hospitality toward guests and paying homage to the gods. Because these characters still resemble "us," their downfalls resulting from their falls resonate, and children have the opportunity to learn from them (for example, Achilles loses Patroclus from his pride, realizes it, and stubbornly remains vain all the same). Stylistically, Colum's prose is poetic. He renders the characters and details of the places with all the weapons of poetry: alliteration, imagery, simile, personification, and a brilliantly evocative vocabulary. He mimics Homer's structure and tone to stay "true" to the texts. Finally, Will Pogany's illustrations etch the odysseys of these mythic characters in children's imaginations with simple black lines that reference the Greek drawings of life and humanity on pottery for posterity, collaborating with Colum to make what Yancy Barton deems truly "high art."

"Irene Hunt's *Across Five Aprils*: Let Your Conscience Be Your Guide"
by Janice M. Alberghene

Not only does the Civil War represent the quintessential American drama for Irene Hunt's *Across Five Aprils*, it serves as a metaphor for a body divided, seeking unification. While this transpires on a literal level with the novel's linear progression through this war, the notion is synthesized and studied more carefully through young Jethro—in both his family and his developing mind. Because of Hunt's privileging of discourse surrounding historical events of violence, the novel has been referred to as a "conversation piece." Because Hunt also follows event and circumstance, it is a strong piece of historical fiction. But Hunt's novel is as much a tale of the American formation of a moral conscience as it is one of a family divided by the Civil War.

From the youthful bravado of admiring elders who make brash, bold, aggressive decisions to a more considered contemplation of the ethical dilemmas inherent in any important choice, Jethro becomes an empathetic young adult. His pattern of growth follows the challenge to his ignorant assumptions with conversation with an adult, then reconsideration of his position, and eventually a change of heart and mind. Hunt posits this at the core of the formation of the American ethos, from the Puritans to contemporary society.

Eventually claiming this contemplative pattern as his own, Jethro takes responsibility for his growth and seeks advice outside the home, sparing his ill father the trouble of worry when Jethro is faced with the dilemma concerning what to do about his deserter cousin, Eb. In consulting President Lincoln, Jethro puts himself at risk for aiding a fugitive. Jethro sees Abe Lincoln as someone who understands consequence and complexity. When he counsels mercy, the central message of *Across Five Aprils* emerges again: mature strength comes from empathy and forgiveness. Hunt's novel is a touchstone work because of its embodiment of what she demonstrates of the reflective American character: considered, mature, and unafraid to grapple with complexity. Jethro is the American mind under construction, beset by social and familial conflict, emerging empathetic all the same.

"Joseph Jacob's *English Fairy Tales*: A Legacy for Today"
by John Warren Stewig

In collecting the forty-three tales that comprise *English Fairy Tales* at the end of the nineteenth century, Joseph Jacobs made a significant mark on the field of folklore study whose brilliant coloration is evident to this day. Not only did Jacobs save these tales from the natural wear of time on an oral phenomenon, but he also transformed a portion of folk culture (compiling tales from England as well as the British Isles, Australia, and the United States) into such a pleasurable text that its color has bled into subsequent literature, language, advertising, film—its reach continues beyond. These tales he captures have been retold and rewritten in so many variants for both children and adults that their importance in the imaginations of children cannot be ignored. As Bruno Bettelheim would argue, they can offer solace to a child's fears, or—as Jack Zipes finds—serve as a template for the multitudinous contemporary versions that speak more directly to modern child consciousness and concerns. In either analysis, their pedagogic worth is rich and generously rewarding.

The original collection joins forces with its offspring to bring riches to the classroom. Through the comparisons and contrasts that beg themselves into existence through the many variations on the English fairy tales, child readers enjoy an opportunity to explore story (structurally and stylistically), heighten their visual acuity, and increase cultural awareness and understanding. The advanced vocabulary and complex sentence structure of Jacob's version credits young readers with an intelligence and attention they do not find in many other books written for them. Early familiarity with Jacobs' legacy stands to be an invaluable gift that keeps giving through a lifetime of reading and cultural consumption.

"Ezra Jack Keats's *The Snowy Day*: The Wisdom of a Pure Heart"
by Kenneth A. Marantz

Ezra Jack Keats's amazing strength is in helping readers see themselves as part of an inclusive humanity. He said, "If we all could really see ('see' as perceive, understand, discover) each other exactly as the other is, this would be a different world. But first I think we have to begin to see each other." Incorporating the humanism of Judaism, he grew up in Brooklyn with parents who escaped from Poland because of persecution. What Keats calls honesty in his work enables him to see beyond race to the human spirit, to a young child's heart, regardless of color; in *The Snowy Day*, he takes us on a blissful journey through the snow, led by a black pre-schooler. The bright, curious boy is on an adventure, a quest to touch the snow, play with it, manipulate and understand it, then share that adventure with his friend the following day with a fresh layer offered from the sky.

Despite lukewarm reviews upon publication, the book was awarded the Caldecott in 1962 and retains its beating heart even today. While some reviewers might have complained of a lack of story, the story is the process of discovery, and taking joy in nature. On an allegorical level (if one insists), it is the story of searching for meaning through interaction with nature, then through sharing information and experience with another (a friend). But because the book itself bears such truth in its simplicity and illustrations, such imposition is unnecessary. The images and words cannot be separated; neither was conceived or achieved completion alone. There is room in the collage of large shapes for the reader's imagination to fill in shadow and space. This abstraction of the object world plays across demarcations of gender, race, time, and age. The discovery of snow, the play with nature, and the communion between friends are part of the human experience that can and do remain through time. Thanks to Keats for his acknowledgment, aiding ours.

"Kipling's Mowgli and *Just So Stories*: The Vine of Fact and Fantasy"
by Celia Catlett Anderson

From abandonment and abuse in childhood Rudyard Kipling culled memories of language, fantasy, and light to create his *Just So Stories* and tales of Mowgli. And while some have criticized these stories for their lack of scientific fact, generations have understood these myths to be powerful, joyful adventures into the natural and social worlds. These works are touchstones as great reads. Kipling's linguistic play encourages reading aloud to young readers, creating an environment for edification and exchange. *The Jungle Book* is much more of a romantic epic; its moral message is correspondingly more substantial. Man is not at home in nature, but in society; nevertheless, his brilliance derives from its manipulation and his ability to form society through language.

While the *Just So Stories* delight in nonsensical play with their only morality resting in the success of animals that employ perseverance and cleverness, Mowgli must accomplish the heavy task of becoming part of a human community—a theme common in classics. He is at times vindictive and individualistic, but the family unit consistently grounds him. Kipling finds Man's home to be in a social order, providing the moral mooring to his existence. Thus, *The Jungle Book* is a positive socializing tool for children. Like all mythology, Kipling's works create a connection between the world of human and animal, rejoicing in the colorful strangeness of the animal kingdom, while drawing on its shapes to understand our own odd creations. Kipling is enamored with language, lending his talents to spirited works that have much to say about humanity, mythology, and our exotic, jungle world.

"Andrew Lang's *The Blue Fairy Book*: Changing the Course of History"
by Glenn S. Burne

Reared in Scotland, the land of fairies, goblins, and princesses, Andrew Lang, and
his contribution to children's literature, fell not far from the tree. In *The Blue
Fairy Book*, followed the next year with *The Red Fairy Book*—and then ten other
volumes of fairy tales, so popular were the first two—Lang collects tales from
Scotland, England, France, Northern Europe, and more "distant" locales. He
adapted *The Arabian Nights*, Grimm, *Gulliver's Travels*, and even some Greek
mythology into fairy tales. With his wife closely editing his language and sentence
structure to be appropriate for young readers, Lang succeeded in quickly establishing himself as an important folklorist and social critic. What Lang found to be
remarkable in folktales was their similarity across cultures. Perhaps they resonate
still today because (as Lang demonstrated in subsequent collections of folktales
from all corners of the world) the same stories emerge repeatedly *independently* in
varying cultures, and often expounding similar virtues.

While Lang promotes no specific morality in *The Blue Fairy Book*, disparate
cultures tend to espouse similar beliefs and concerns. Heroes and heroines succeed
as a result of both outside help and, more importantly, their own initiative. Characters are often extremes—caricatures of themselves. Lang's pleasure in these
thirty-seven tales is consistently evident in their rendering. Intended to transport
children to a world where their imaginations might roam more freely, Lang's
collection does not always deliver happy endings. But Lang's collection and its
multitude of imitations do prove that we all wish to transport ourselves to distant
lands of magic wherein the details of our world become nonsense and our deepest
beliefs more real in their vivid validation through the "symbolic realism" of these
seductive tales of Faery Land.

"Robert Lawson's *The Story of Ferdinand*:
Death in the Afternoon or Life under the Cork Tree?"
by Jean Streufert Patrick

The Story of Ferdinand by Robert Lawson is a bizarre illustrated story of a bull
from Spain named Ferdinand who defied all expectations, and behavioral prece-
dents, and simply loved to smell flowers. Ferdinand is a victim of irony,
introducing a central element in contemporary literature to young readers. By
chance when he happened to jump about frantically from a surprise encounter
with a bee in a patch of flowers, he was chosen for a bullfight. Ferdinand, the
most physically impressive bull around, of course sat down in the ring and
happily inhaled the scent from all the flowers adorning the women at the fight.
He is no fighter whatsoever. Lawson skillfully allows readers to understand the
characters at times better than they understand each other, further startles the
reader with unexpected results, and then subverts again to the reader's thrill and
satisfaction.

Many of Lawson's images invite the reader to fill in the blanks with their imagination—engaging them on a noteworthy level with the text and crediting young readers with a perception usually reserved for adults. There is even a bit of play with Hemingway's *Death in the Afternoon* that treats bull fighting with an air of hero worship, rendering Lawson's light humor, equivalent attention to detail, and abnormal bull a veritable parody. By following the "iceberg theory" Hemingway posits in this very work, Lawson rejects Hemingway's values of "combat, bravery, and death" in imagery, portrayals of masculinity, and his subversion of a "noble" death that never occurs. He makes a strong statement for individuality and adherence to free-thinking. Touché.

"Edward Lear's *The Book of Nonsense*: A Scroobious Classic"
by Mark I. West

When Lord Derby hired Edward Lear, aged twenty, in 1932 to draw his menagerie of birds and animals, Lear managed to stretch the task into a four-year job, escaping the poverty brought to him by his bankrupt father and neglectful parents. Little did he know that it would not be these drawings, but rather the limericks and accompanying drawings he produced to entertain Derby's children in the nursery that would bring him lasting fortune and his work a firm standing among the best of children's literature. *The Book of Nonsense* was a landmark because of its child-centric humor and absurd illustrations that made no attempt at realism.

At a time when any humor in children's books was purely for the benefit of the adult reader, and every work was necessarily edifying, Lear did not moralize. He allayed the anxieties and fears of children with absurdity and humor. His illustrations, often drawn in a room full of children for their immediate enjoyment, addressed directly children's sensibilities and perspectives. Expounding on the eccentric characters and events of the nonsense poems, they exaggerated, distorted, and remained always simple—a style not even imitated until the twentieth century.

Later in life, Lear finally followed *The Book of Nonsense* with several other volumes of nonsense poems. But these works were longer poems whose content dealt (albeit symbolically) more with the difficulty of being homosexual instead of displaying the nonconformist zest of his youth, and are thus more for adult readers. Like his contemporary (and fellow nonsense-poet) Lewis Carroll, Lear had no children and an uncanny brilliance for speaking directly to them in language and concepts they can appreciate. *The Book of Nonsense* remains in print, adored by readers, writers, artists, eccentrics, misfits, kids, and dreamers alike.

"Madeleine L'Engle's *A Wrinkle in Time*: Seeking the Original Face"
by William Blackburn

The external search through time and worlds is a journey representative of the contemporary tendencies in literature toward the interior and has been undertaken in adventure stories and children's literature to an increasing extent. In Madeleine L'Engle's *A Wrinkle in Time*, she adds to this tradition through Meg Murry, in search of her identity, and dealing with the also common theme of alienation. Although Blackburn sees L'Engle's novel as a success in its depiction of fantasy, he concludes that its status as a touchstone is meta-textual and rests in its ability to speak about moral didacticism in children's literature.

With a story of struggling with evil, Comazotz's "IT," it is love that conquers both fear and conformity. As a rarely fear-inducing (because of its trite depiction in *Wrinkle*) embodiment of evil, IT is an enlarged, red, disembodied brain. Instead of dealing with evil as part of the human psyche, as this image implies, L'Engle instead invokes pat Christian notion of good and evil without any substantive exploration. Purporting revelatory treasures about the human psyche, *Wrinkle* fails miserably at the task L'Engle sets for herself. Relying on an external allegorical structure (Christianity), L'Engle does not integrate any complex treatment of evil into the development of her characters and story. Furthermore, the references to Christian imagery are gratuitous. When combined with her thinly veiled political indictment of the U.S.S.R. (in the form of the evil IT who demands conformity) climaxing with Meg defeating IT through her recitation of the Declaration of Independence, *Wrinkle*'s message seem dated and self-righteous and lacking in the complex analysis of human psyche's relationship to evil. Finally, defeating IT by loving her brother—a victim of enforced evil not of his choice—Meg's victory is once again facile. *A Wrinkle in Time* lacks the textural complexity and narrative integrity necessary to communicate more than a self-congratulatory cheerleading session for Christian Americans.

"C. S. Lewis's Narnia Books: The Reader in the Myth"
by Murray J. Evans

Although the Narnia books are laden with Christian metaphor and imagery, C. S. Lewis claims to have begun them with singular images without external meaning, rich unto themselves. However, he admits his goal of communicating the empathic experience of feeling the loss in Christ's death. Lewis transforms the Christian stories children usually learn from obligation—and with a great distance—into felt experience, bringing them closer to the reality of Christ's sacrifice (and he has been accused of creating Christian propaganda). Myth is the union between abstraction and "fact"; in Narnia, Lewis communicates his belief in their confluence in Christianity. For Lewis, thinking takes us away from feeling. With the otherworldliness of Narnia, we can enter and lose ourselves in an emotional and sensual reality, beyond rational description and therefore closer to God.

Playing with the union between worlds is at the imaginative core of Narnia, a place of desire for the ephemeral, for its beauty is ultimately beyond description. Doors and windows open our curiosity, hint at connection between rational reality and the other world. Lewis posits the imagination at the base of transcendence from our world of facades into one of truth and meaning—the spiritual. Thinking takes us away from feeling. With the otherworldliness of Narnia, we can enter and lose ourselves in sensual reality, beyond rational description.

Lewis's Narnia books follow the pattern of attempt, expectation, disappointment, and failure. The series begins with endings and follows one after another—all false until the ultimate one, ultimately inexpressible by the narrator. While the series contains the rich imagery and characterization necessary to stand on its own, understanding Lewis's Christianity is crucial to comprehending the resonating power of his Narnia. Aslan's country is Narnia within Narnia, a world within a world where perceptions are unhinged from reality and combined with an incomparable clarity of vision. Lewis found the power of Christian doctrine resided in its ability to unsettle certainties and create longing for our home and ending. Without obligation, he invites and seduces children into this imagined reality, one whose sensual delight is beyond words and leaves a taste for more.

"Leo Lionni's *Swimmy*: Undetailed Depth"
by Mary-Agnes Taylor

Leo Lionni's work expands in breadth and depth when considered in terms of his biography and the literary tradition to which his books spoke. Beginning with elaborate terrariums he designed and created for small pet animals in his youth (that became aquariums in *Swimmy*), Lionni's formative years in Amsterdam were ensconced in art. It was there that he taught himself to draw by attending the various museums, if he was only to return to drawing later after earning his doctorate in economics. For *Swimmy*, Lionni wrote the text first, and this dependence on the story—an original one—as the backbone of this tale is clear. His language is literary. He quickly establishes his setting, characters, and central conflict; his conclusion follows the same efficiency. But betwixt these two logical localities is a world of poetry, where the precision of his poetic language tells a profoundly rich tale in fewer than three hundred words.

Through Swimmy's eyes, the reader experiences "marvel to marvel" underwater. While continuing nevertheless in the concise tradition of Aesop's fables, Lionni has managed to imbue a straightforward fable with literary excellence and texture, adding to and expanding the tradition—and all within reason given the attention span of a young reader. In creating a work that is non-referential (regarding the history of children's literature, and unlike some of his other works), Lionni has created an exceptional tale that invites readers to see the world anew (as an artist does), filling in the blanks of his compositions with meaning and imaginative creations of their own, further adding to his own oeuvre on the worth of the individual—even the very small.

"George MacDonald's *Princess* Books: High Seriousness"
by Roderick McGillis

According to Matthew Arnold's conception of classic texts, touchstone works are at once deeply serious in theme and purpose, while being profoundly enjoyable. The combination of these contrary forces is what lies too at the heart of George MacDonald's *Princess* books (*The Princess and the Goblin, The Princess and Curdie*), alongside his thematic Hegelian chorus of achieving unity through the synthesis of oppositional forces. From Irene, the independent, adventurous, and intelligent heroine at the tale's core, to Curdie of the male/phenomenal, to Irene's great-grandmother, Irene, who symbolizes the ultimate reconciliation of opposites, there is a tug of war between Thinking and Feeling. Along with the Romantics, MacDonald believed that feeling precedes and enables thought. MacDonald employs language, imagery, and all literary devices to communicate this poetic truth.

While *The Princess and the Goblin* is a gentle fairy tale, *The Princess and Curdie* is a romantic quest, stern, austere, and intent in its seriousness. Biblical images abound, even ending in an apocalyptic river that invokes Novalis, Shelley, and Blake. Both tales are written with humor and comedy, however, with textured themes, exciting adventures, and developed characters to satisfy young readers. These touchstones are rich and subtle enough to engage adult readers—-particularly with the political, social, and religious satire of *The Princess and Curdie*. In searching for a synthesis greater than the sum of its parts, MacDonald emphasizes vision as pivotal to understanding. Skeptical of social and religious "truths," MacDonald propounds an immediate, personal comprehension resulting after much searching.

"Robert McCloskey's *Make Way for Ducklings*: The Art of Regional Storytelling"
by Anthony L. Manna

The recipient of a slew of arts awards and recognized within the establishment for his work, Robert McCloskey prided himself in doing work that was seen, that served a purpose, that entered people's everyday lives, as opposed to being cloistered and coddled within the white walls of galleries. He spoke within the recently created tradition of having both written and visual storytelling advance the narrative of the picture book, thanks in large part to advances in printing processes and the subsequently growing market in publishing for children's books. Learning early to use humor and folk tradition in his visuals, he also learned to tell of the places he was familiar with (Ohio) so that setting would emerge from inside a story, as opposed to being a structural backbone, an enforced exoskeleton.

Make Way for Ducklings is doubly successful because McCloskey builds on his previous theme of the importunity of increased industrialization and a technologized existence and the common, overwhelming affection felt by proud parents for their children. The reader follows this family of mallards around an impossible Boston looking for a home. Using well-scaled visuals and perspective, McCloskey has underscored the miracle of their eventual safe arrival at a public gardens. As with many other powerful picture books, these visuals illustrate the narrative, driving it forward. By shifting perspective in his illustrations of *Make Way for Ducklings*, he achieves a oneness with the birds that unites reader with flight and family, security and freedom. McCloskey's accessible work begs to be loved by the imagination, and succeeds.

"David McCord's Poems: Something behind the Door"
by Myra Cohn Livingston

There is mystery there. There, behind the door, is the duality of existence. The mysterious Something could be either monstrous or delicious. "Something behind the door," a line from the poem "One at a Time" by David McCord embodies the sense of McCord's poems: pregnant with the mystery of life, open to interpretation, optimism, cynicism, or an apathetic shrug. His poems succeed as poems for children because they do not shy away from reality; McCord is a realist. Like a wide-eyed child looking closer and closer at a caterpillar coming out of silk, asking *why*, and listening to the answer—which leads to further questions—McCord inhabits the wonder of a child, without sentimentality.

McCord grounds his poems in the world of a child, allowing for the nonsense expected of the genre and a gravity children possess despite adult misconceptions. McCord does not believe children live in a wonderland of protected bliss. There is joy, disappointment, mystery, pain, thrills, risks, and always the presence of supportive adult figures that scold at times and hold close at others. His poems work because he never posits joy without tempering it with life's omnipresent complexity. His poems swing between dark pools reflecting light and bright sunlight with its sharp shadows, connected by ropes of hope, possibility, and choice. In "One at a Time" a swing hangs from a walnut tree and transports "the backward No to the forward Yes / That the world begins in the sweep of eye, / With wonder of all of it more or less."

"A. A. Milne's Pooh Books: The Benevolent Forest"
by Anita Wilson

From *Winnie-the-Pooh* to *The House at Pooh Corner*, A. A. Milne's inhabitants of the forest charm and charm again child and adult readers alike. Milne's Pooh books could easily be categorized among the touchstones merely for their far-reaching cultural influence through countless reprintings, into consumer and even academic cultural products. But it is Milne's succinct, apt characterizations of the inhabitants of the forest that has fixed Winnie-the-Pooh as a seminal presence in the imaginations of children and in the arena of children's literature.

Following the fleeting whimsy of early childhood, nothing in the Pooh books is stiff. Appearance, character, and action are naturally linked; anthropomorphized animals do not follow any animistic rules of behavior, but act as their humorous personalities dictate. The light satire of his characterizations allows for adult enjoyment. But no indictments are made in the Pooh books. Winnie is lovingly clumsy, dim, hungry, generous, and proud. His misadventures do not lead to important lessons learned—never are the books didactic, there is no clear progress or change, which is satisfying to young readers.

Milne ably captures frivolity and freedom from responsibility. His inventive structuring allows children to play at once audience and participant in the character of Christopher Robin. He is the ultimate authority of the forest, mirroring the imaginative play that occurs in real playrooms of children, and based on the real relationship between Milne's son and his stuffed animals. *The House at Pooh Corner* remains untarnished by the adult, outside world, a benign, fun-filled phase through which to grow and eventually leave, and always love.

"A. A. Milne's *When We Were Very Young* and *Now We Are Six*:
A Small World of Everyday Pleasures"
by Anita Wilson

Unlike his predecessors R. L. Stevenson and Christina Rossetti, A. A. Milne writes of and about children without sentimentality and moralizing. Far from offering then a pained portrayal of the tribulations of growing up, his poems in *When We Were Very Young* and *Now We Are Six* accomplish the very opposite: they sing with the exuberance of early childhood. And although Milne was not as close to his son Christopher (Christopher Robin) when he was a toddler, he captures all the same an effervescent lyricism that renders with realism and light humor childish proclivities and personality traits—and always without supercil-iousness or a patronizing tone.

If all of his characters are not children, they all act as if they were—and never without dire consequences. In "The Knight Whose Armor Didn't Squeak," a knight is acclaimed because he can write all his letters and multiply up to four; a fickle king grants and withdraws his affection with a caprice practiced by children. His effortless, uncomplicated poems tell small, funny stories of the everyday life of a child.

While Milne's poems miss the interactions of the schoolyard, they excel in capturing the interior life of a child. Usually befriended by animals real and stuffed, the characters of these poems are confounded by the desires, demands, and values of the adult world. Milne found children to be heartless, selfish egotists, and faulted them not one bit for their nature. Their universe of playing in sandboxes, walking in the woods, mildly misbehaving, and role playing as they search out identity is charming and replete with a lyrical humor that employs a child's speech patterns (for example, doubling plurals and repeating words). Milne does not capture the whole of childhood; as one reviewer, Thomas Burnett Swann, wrote: "He has perfect vision out of a small window."

"Maud Montgomery's *Anne of Green Gables*: The Architect of Adolescence"
by Mary Rubio

Anne Shirley of *Anne of Green Gables* is tortured with desire and adolescent indignation. This imaginative force inspires a life dedicated to beauty. Praised by children and adults alike, *Anne of Green Gables* has claimed iconic status through several films, plays, musicals, and countless tourists who visit Cavendish, the model for mythical Avonlea, on Prince Edward Island, in search of more clues to the beauty of Anne's world. Drawn from her own real experiences as a child, Maud Montgomery created in Anne a model for the artist in society. In the indomitable spirit of Anne, her feisty behavior, love of beauty and language, and her humorous conflicts with the adult world is a psychological portrait of the artist as a young woman. In spite of themselves, with their grim, Protestant hypocrisies and pious poses, members of Anne's community cannot help but allow themselves to review their reflection in the once-stilled waters she stirs with her exuberant love of life.

Montgomery's mild satire and comedic conflicts delight adult readers while conceding to the substantial thematic messages inherent in the book's texture. Anne must confront and grow through stages of development shared by all children: first with her immediate family and neighbors, then with Avonlea, and eventually the world outside picturesque Avonlea. Bookish children and creative adults resonate with Anne's impulsive, imperfect, vivacious, and disruptive personality. As all children must, Anne becomes a whole adult who gives back to those who have given to her (even if her decision to stay with Marilla is problematic in contemporary feminist politics). The arc of Anne's growth is psychologically astute and involved. Her lush world is one Montgomery renders palpable with each repeated read.

"The Nursery Rhymes of Mother Goose: A World without Glasses"
by Perry Nodelman

The involved attempts at giving Mother Goose a face and body parallel the useless searching for sense in the absurd tuffet of "Little Miss Muffet." This hasn't stopped "scholars" for the past several centuries. But Mother Goose's nursery rhymes are so steadfastly anonymous and resilient to the tumult of explication that their "canon" even co-opts the satirical works of their harsh critics (for example, from Samuel Johnson to Samuel Griswold Goodrich's "Higglety Pigglety Pop"). It is therefore because of the pleasure they elicit when remembered that Mother Goose's nursery rhymes (sometimes counted at more than 800 in number), and because of the flexibility and creativity of memory that they have been transformed through time into the exuberant bits of addictive poetry they are even today.

Pre-media, the rhymes were created to be spoken, and their delight lies therein. Far from their meaning resting hidden within their absurd content, the meaning of Mother Goose resides in the significant role of their nonsense in our lives. Precisely because of the lack of coherence in the small tales they tell are we able to instead focus on the pattern, rhythm, rhyme, and repetition of the nursery rhymes, and enjoy them to their maximum capacity. For even when we understand the secret of the riddles, we are sent back inside the absurd imagery and language for the way it distorts reality. Mother Goose makes strange the mundane, as does all good poetry and literature. No wonder, then, that they are such a touchstone experience within the reading life of children. Their odd phrasing is alluring and intoxicating enough to remain in the mind, on the edge of memory.

"E. Nesbit's *The Story of the Treasure Seekers*: The Idiom of Childhood"
by Anita Moss

With the refreshing narrative voice of a child, E. Nesbit's *The Story of the Treasure Seekers* was a groundbreaking touchstone for children's literature of the twentieth century. By merging fairy tale with reality, the bohemian Nesbit wrote an iconoclastic tale matched in anarchy perhaps only by her own personality. The narrator, Oswald Bastable, tries to conceal his identity, which slips out whenever he accidentally recounts his tale in the first person or praises the character Oswald Bastable. Nesbit harmonizes the prior dissonance between the child-audience and adult-writer of children's literature through the "voice" of Oswald. For Nesbit he is a dramatized device both in chorus with herself and humorously manipulated against the action to create light irony and develop character. Furthermore, this was Nesbit's first serious book for children, and she herself was searching for a narrative voice to call her own.

The adventures of these treasure seekers focus around saving their father from financial ruin. As they search for treasure (trying to sell liquor, using divining rods, etc.), Nesbit satirizes religion, piety, and adult hypocrisy. With a deceased mother (following the fairy tale structure), their activities are those of holiday, away from adults, and end consistently in comedic catastrophe. All ends well (as in Dickens, notes the reader *and* Oswald) with Albert's uncle taking them in to his grand mansion and sharing his wealth with their wayward family. The freedom of the seven children is not one of adult neglect, as evidenced by their ability to enjoy it. Were they dealing with abandonment, the *Treasure Seekers* would not have the light, humorous tone Nesbit sustains even in some of the narrative's grave situations. Adults are not the enemy, but they are of a separate world, until the Treasure Seekers are forced away from imaginative, inventive adventure of childhood toward the often-stale "grown-upness" at the book's end.

"Mary Norton's *The Borrowers*: Diaspora in Miniature"
by Lois R. Kuznets

The Borrowers series by Mary Norton is a close-up gaze into the meticulous imagination. As opposed to a world seen through a magnifying glass, it is the perspective of Norton as a child, placing these works within the tradition of the *Bildungsroman*. Poised to pounce into young adulthood is fourteen-year-old

Arrietta Clock, one of the remaining few survivors of the Borrower "race." Her friendship with the young boy of the house where the Borrowers reside comfortably is the catalyst for the book's movement, and the Clocks eventual disappearance. The structure also works in layers, paralleling the world within worlds. It is Norton's mastery of craftsmanship, however, in constructing this fantastic diaspora that makes this work a touchstone.

Perhaps drawn directly from Norton's experience of fleeing Great Britain for the United States with her children during World War II, *The Borrowers* is an able rendering of immigrant family living on the fringe of society and may even serve as an analogy to the German Jews during the Holocaust. Like many youth, Arrietta longs to explore beyond the safe confines of her parents' protection. Her friendship with the boy enables her to communicate with relatives, live well "borrowing" from the humans in the house, in exchange for reading stories to him. The Nazi-reminiscent housekeeper, Mrs. Driver, longs to exterminate the Borrowers, to see them "laid out in sizes on a clean piece of paper" (163). Norton displays further her technical adroitness in descriptive passages that build suspense or setting, although she is sloppy with her political jabs at the welfare state. When Mrs. Driver gasses the Clocks out of the house, the boy enables the Clocks' possible escape, although their fate is never revealed in the story. Instead, Norton finishes *The Borrowers* from the distance of the humans (Mrs. May to the young girl), leaving the miniature small and intact within the imagination.

"Robert C. O'Brien's *Mrs. Frisby and the Rats of NIMH*:
Through the Eyes of Small Animals"
by Althea K. Helbig

After engrossing themselves in the realistic microcosms of these rats and mice, readers are not surprised that, along with making the National Book Award and *Boston Globe–Horn Book* lists, Robert C. O'Brien's *Mrs. Frisby and the Rats of NIMH* was awarded the prestigious Newbery Medal. *Mrs. Frisby's* enduring popularity rests in O'Brien's stylistic accomplishment of rendering an unknown world both plausible and intimately compelling. From the details of the cotton and dirt that form the walls of their tiny homes to the ferocious power of the farm cat Dragon, O'Brien renders the lives of these tiny animals relevant and real.

Mrs. Frisby and the Rats of NIMH is the first science fiction novel that works for children. Although ostensibly about Mrs. Frisby's plight to move her house and family across the field to avoid being plowed, it is the story of the rats that help her that forms the narrative momentum. Herein lies the fault of the novel: O'Brien never reveals the fate of the rats, whether they are able to escape extermination and create a self-sufficient utopia across the river. Coupled with this narrative indecisiveness is a lack of character development or depth. Flat and predictable, these characters (the efficient, heroic, generous widow, Mrs. Frisby; the rat's leader, Nicodemus, a compassionate, cosmopolitan idealist; the wise, forgiving owl) do not distract, however, from the adventure and excitement of the tale.

O'Brien's is primarily a stylistic achievement. He fashions a believable make-believe from the perspective of these tiny animals. Without anthropomorphizing them entirely, he explores the details of their lives carefully and lovingly with images that appeal to the senses. It is not hard to reenter the world of the rats of NIMH and imagine them in prosperous safety.

"Philippa Pearce's *Tom's Midnight Garden*: Finding and Losing Eden"
by Raymond E. Jones

Phillipa Pearce leaves no cobbled stone on the pathway to an empathic life uncovered in her imaginative *Tom's Midnight Garden*. By turning over and over our sense of time, space, and linear progress, the author artfully crafts her profound masterpiece about continuity and change in life's painful landscape. When young Tom is "exiled" to the Kitson's for a summer to escape his brother's measles, he invents a garden in his dreams as a restorative escape from the lack of wilderness and Nature in the daytime of the Kitson's grim apartment. In and around the dream of this edenic garden, Pearce uses the pastoral romance to challenge the sovereignty of logic and rationality not only in the adult world, but also in the developing mind of Tom.

Pearce constructs her fantastic novel around drama that gently uncovers metaphor and leads the reader closer to her themes. In his midnight garden, Tom is invisible to all except a girl, Hattie, with whom he acquiesces into friendship out of necessity. He allows their relationship to grow, but she proceeds to grow through her protected childhood while Tom remains stagnant until he becomes invisible to her and has literally and metaphorically fallen from the garden. He must leave the garden to grow up and into a deeper understanding of people and himself in the world. When Tom understands that Hattie is the elderly neighbor Mrs. Batholomew (whose dreams of her childhood overlapped with Tom's, placing them in the same midnight Eden), his dreamed life has integrated with his waking one, and his growth is afoot.

Pearce's illuminates her complex portrait of the pain of growing up in her irony, juxtaposition, and drama. Ironic reversals in time point out the role of imagination in altering reality. Readers finish the novel with Tom's sense that the imagined/felt universe is sometimes even more real than reality.

"The Fairy Tales of Charles Perrault: Acute Logic and Gallic Wit"
by James Gellert

In the late seventeenth century, fairy tales were very much in vogue in all the finest French salons. Charles Perrault, although in his late sixties, was a literary man about town (Paris). The publication and immediate success in 1697 of his *Histoires ou Contes de ma mere l'oye*, a series of prose renderings of fairy tales and Mother Goose nursery rhymes, solidified his place in history as one of the most influential figures of children's literature. Reprinted *ad infinitum* in many languages, and adored still today by children (and adults), his prose versions of the fairy tales running rampant around Paris in the late 1600s had clear morals and characters, tidy (and often re-worked) endings, memorable settings, and a light, sardonic humor that has endured through three centuries of reading.

Justice takes the back seat to kindness, generosity, and forgiveness in Perrault's *Histoires*, often cleaning up the grim details of Grimm fairy tales to represent and gently deride courtly manners, behaviors, and personages. Owed in part to French classicism, Perrault's witty, concise dialogue carried the essence of the characterizations. Male characters are rendered as the French like to think of themselves, sharp and rational, with quick, strong minds that get them and others out of trouble; the women are graceful, kind, beautiful, humble, and hard-working—establishing for future generations sexual stereotypes upheld by Disney today. While logic is always preferred in his fairy tales, one can find almost the full range of human emotions present. The "morally coherent universe" of Charles Perrault's adored fairy tales satisfies the Lockean goal of entertaining and instructing (yes, "didacticism" is the word) while providing children's literature the invaluable service of inscribing these fairy tales into Western consciousness for centuries past and centuries to come.

"Beatrix Potter's *The Tale of Peter Rabbit*: A Small Masterpiece" by Jackie F. Eastman

The first of Beatrix Potter's Peter tales, *The Tale of Peter Rabbit,* is a touchstone simply and unequivocally because of its hero ensnared in innocence, its captivating story, and its balanced composition. While first rejected by publisher Frederick Warne & Co., her self-published first edition sold well enough to pay for a second edition, at which point the publisher relented, providing she would reillustrate the text in color. With this entire artistic universe in proportion—small characters in a small world captured in a small book held by small hands—Potter has created a satisfying classic that helped define childhood adventure as being entirely possible within the confines of one's home.

Peter too is tiny, smaller even than a rabbit, and the scale of his adventure matches his stature, but lacks not one lick in excitement for the child reader. He acts as a child: at times disobedient, awkward, and the victim of his own risky behavior. He gets in trouble and out again, with one picture per page, and only a couple of sentences beneath each—everything scaled to a child. Potter plays with our knowledge of Peter's ultimate security by putting him increasingly impossible binds, baffling and then rewarding the reader with Peter's reliable victory.

Peter "has become a major figure of our culture" from children's literature to the Easter bunny. His youthful ebullience is at once attractive and the very thing that gets him into his difficult situations. Structurally, then, Potter has maximized the impact of her child hero in allowing him to be imminently childish and exuberantly satisfying as a subject of adventure and joy for generations of readers, past and to come.

"Howard Pyle's *The Merry Adventures of Robin Hood*:
The Quintessential Children's Story"
by Taimi M. Ranta

Who does not know the tale of Robin Hood? While immortalized within American memory more recently through Disney, it was first and more importantly the American illustrator and writer Howard Pyle who wrote the definitive version of this legendary story in 1883. Robin Hood, as rendered by Pyle, is the quintessential hero, whose story is told within an episodic book from the time Robin Hood became an outlaw to his death. The book is ideal children's literature as it is highly entertaining while being instructive. Robin Hood dedicates himself early to narrowing the gap between legal and social justice; he is a hero whose life is both full of adventures and directed by his conscience. The legend presumes a renegade approach to justice and a distrust of authority—themes popular in American consciousness at the very least. Pyle draws (both literally and figuratively) Robin Hood from a multitude of characters from Sir Lancelot to Cyrano de Bergerac to Jesse James or Billy the Kid.

As an attractive hero made even more so by Pyle's visual writing and illustrations that further elaborate both Robin Hood's person and his setting in Medieval Europe. Engraving-type black-and-white illustrations and elaborate lettering join force with a rich prosaic style that both challenges young readers and renders the setting and era as visceral as another of Pyle's "round characters" (to quote E. M. Forester). Pyle keeps readers enthralled by speaking to them at their particular phase(s) in life while serving as a solid and beloved foundation for later study of the heroes of classical literature from Odysseus to Beowolf and beyond.

"Howard Pyle's *The Story of King Arthur and His Knights*:
A Backwards Look at Chivalry"
by Jill P. May

In *The Story of King Arthur and His Knights*, author Howard Pyle shows the unmarried Guinevere having a marvelous time at the expense of her gardener's lowly assistant. When King Arthur later introduces himself as such, Guinevere is horrified and stricken with fear. King Arthur, however, is the picture of chivalry and gentlemanly behavior—forgiving, warm, and large-hearted about that matter and in general about his respect for her as a member of the fairer sex. Pyle's King Arthur not only captured his own modern sensibilities, but also set the precedent for all renditions of subsequent Arthurian tales and theatrical productions (in addition to forming the basis for the popular game, Dungeons and Dragons). Pyle's *King Arthur* established the notions of the noble knight, the code of honor, the glories of battle, the questing hero, and did much to reinforce a "healthy" distrust of women. A sought-after illustrator, Pyle built on the success of his *Robin Hood* in reworking Arthurian legend from English and German versions to transmit notions of the American romance much in the style of his previous work and the work—quite popular at the time of publication—of Sir Walter Scott.

That he did not pay mind to Celtic myth is clear in his solid message about the goodness of domesticated women in opposition to their evil, troublemaking behavior out in the countryside. Men at home are wise; in the field they are courageous and noble.

So successful was Pyle's *King Arthur* that characters modeled after King Arthur and his noble knights have appeared in countless books of children's literature. Pyle passed on the tradition of the aristocracy to readers, both in terms of how they viewed themselves as purveyors of justice, protecting the weak (women), and acting with nobility and wisdom at other times (unless under the influence of a treacherous woman's black magic). The legacy of Pyle's *King Arthur* clearly reaches beyond children's literature and into the social fabric of class, race, and gender constructions in Western culture today.

"Arthur Rackham's *Fairy Book*: A Confrontation with the Marvelous"
by Gillian Adams

Confronting the fantastic is the focus of the Arthur Rackham *Fairy Book,* which Rackham composed of illustrations he produced in the last years of his life. Despite his working-class background, Rackham became a formally trained artist while working as a clerk, but retained his hard-working, down-to-earth sensibilities and values. In this collection of illustrations of fairy tales, Rackham includes all his various styles and proclivities, with works ranging from impressionistic watercolors to elaborate woodcuts. Wildly imaginative, with a strong sense of satire, composition, versatility, the grotesque, adaptation, and an ability to create intricate and superior work while remaining organic to a story, his work is widely recognized and admired. By nodding both to the masters of visual art and his contemporaries in visual art and illustration, Rackham was able to bridge worlds and create new ones—all the while focusing on humanity's psychological relationship to fantasy.

Because Rackham additionally was an able businessman, he used all the latest technological advances in his work, thereby aligning himself with the likes of Edward Evans (and consequently the tradition begun with Greenaway, Caldecott, and Crane). He adopted their style of strong lines filled in with color, even altering some former works to fit this practical vision. Ironic though it may seem, Rackham's pragmatic worldview found voice in his work on fantasy. He realistically rendered transformed worlds in terms of our psychological need for them and allowed humans to profit in "our confrontations with the marvelous."

"Arthur Ransome's *Swallows and Amazons*: Escape to a Lost Paradise"
by Peter Hunt

For England's children and adults, the Lake Country is a beloved idyllic landscape whose history is present alongside its rapid disintegration. Like the transforming setting of childhood, the lake adventures of Arthur Ransome's *Swallows and Amazons* reside in the nostalgia of adult readers and the expansive imaginings of child readers, brimming with possibility. Widely imitated, still available in paperback, adapted both for television and successfully as a film, Ransome's series of lake adventures with the Wallace and Blackett children have entered the British imagination as thoroughly as the lake poets or Beatrix Potter. Ransome's continuing presence passed through from the hands of adults to their children through generations attests to his works' genuine status as touchstones.

At the center of these books is the negotiated freedom between children and adults—an abiding arbitration. The children's liberty is self-regulated with an adult presence, reinforcing the centrality of family both in the values it espouses and as a valued structure in itself. The reality of his characters and setting attest to their origins in things familiar to and beloved by the author. Although Ransome has been criticized for writing adventures with character types—many of whom are stagnant and remain at an awkward distance—this solidity could be a much-needed respite from the pervasive psychological novels in the current literary scene for children, and a comfort to adult readers.

Ransome is more subtle than these critics allow, however. He surpasses the wooden prose he often employs in the detailing of their sailing adventures with vivid, evocative images of the lakes. Perhaps this series transcends time because of its rendering of a specific (bygone) era coupled with a healthy life of fantasy. As sailboats have anchors, these imagined adventures are real enough to offer a moored aura of possibility and a lake country for exhilarating growth.

"Maurice Sendak's *Where the Wild Things Are*: Picture Book Poetry"
by Raymond E. Jones

Maurice Sendak likened the picture book to a complex poetic form. This form requires an exacting diligence and commitment to balancing text and visual and capturing truth: "Truthfulness to life—both fantasy life and factual life—is the basis of all great art." In *Where the Wild Things Are*, Sendak created a touchstone work by accomplishing three crucial feats. The content and form both have literary significance. As the text must harmonize with the illustrations, so too must the graphic form resonate with the genre's form and book's content—and does. Finally, these elements combine with Sendak's brilliant detailing (written and visual) to complement the graphics and the literary model.

Max's journey is the mythical sort, but experienced psychologically (in a dream) rather than physically. Nevertheless, it has real-life consequences in helping his relationship with his mother. Because the content is true to both reality and the fairy tale structure, and furthermore to the stuff of child fantasy, *Where the Wild Things Are* sings with truth. Max's place in his journey is rendered through visuals that move from his destructive misbehavior at home (hence his punishment) to the epic journey (away from mother), and finally through his test in taming the wild things that enables his safe return: the sturdy circle so familiar in literature. Furthermore, graphically, Sendak mirrors Max's growth—pictures enlarge with his progress, borderless images entirely of his fantasy world, double-paged expanses within his expanding imagination. Once returned to reality, the border image of before is gone. Max does not feel the same need to escape. Colors evolve to follow Max's story. Sendak repeats language and images to bring Max, and his readers, full circle. This wild, poetic picture book thrills with fantastic truth, so real.

"Dr. Seuss's *The 500 Hats of Bartholomew Cubbins*: Of Hats and Kings"
by Mavis Reimer

Theodore Geisel, who as Dr. Seuss created *The 500 Hats of Bartholomew Cubbins*, has been said by Selma Lane to have a "subversive alliance with the child's free spirit against all forms of authoritarianism." A perennial professional, Geisel created children's classics—*500 Hats* among them—unburdened by double meanings and personal demons. His books teach children to read without being didactic; Dr. Seuss is simply fun. But *The 500 Hats of Bartholomew Cubbins* exceeds its own categorization in recounting a complex, original fairy tale of wish fulfillment. Irony, humor, and suspense all collaborate to create a fantastic tale of the mysteriously reproducing hats.

The feudal setting is familiar to the fairy tale. Although Geisel does nothing didactic to subvert this power structure in *The 500 Hats*, he does set the reader to considering its verity in illustrating the vast differences of perspective between King Derwin and Bartholomew; the king's perspective in no way overshadows any other. Geisel plays with color and composition to support a worldview in which Bartholomew's fatal flaw—his reproducing hats—is alluringly red and omnipresent, while the king's elaborate entourage is depicted in black and white. The reader is allowed to root for Bartholomew even while he fails to root for himself, thereby creating a more complex reader–text relationship. Finally, Bartholomew's materialist ending is in somber black and white. The childhood independence and imagination have been exchanged for something cold, lumpy, and meaningless in comparison with the richly red, malleable, inviting hats.

Adult versus child, arbitrary containment versus imaginative freedom, framed arches versus open road: the promise life holds to a child. Derwin has come to appreciate the now finite hats, observing them in a case of nostalgia. Bartholomew is glum, but with a homecoming illustrated on a page with a meandering road alongside—a possibility. Geisel has created a vastly complex kingdom here of childhood, its losses, pains, and exuberance. Let us appreciate it and *The 500 Hats of Bartholomew Cubbins*.

"Johanna Spyri's *Heidi*: The Conversion of a Byronic Hero"
by Malcolm Usrey

As one of the singularly most attractive, memorable, and delightful characters of children's literature, Heidi exudes nature's restorative powers. Heidi is ecstatic with nature's beauty. One of the recipients of her healthy joy is her grandfather, a

Byronic hero recluse who has retreated from a society that cannot understand his past and rejects his alternative lifestyle. Pure in her kind innocence, Heidi does not fear him or his life in the mountains outside Dorfi. In *Heidi*, Spyri created a "convert-and-reform" novel that was not a breakthrough at its time of publication, but whose compelling Heidi has been copied in countless successive novels. While in Frankfurt, Heidi's decline in health is paralleled by her learning to read and her religious education that eventually provides for her grandfather's conversion. Arguably predictable in structure, her alienation while in Frankfurt did establish a theme to be explored in later works of children's literature.

Although *Heidi* is often criticized for its religious didacticism, the Christian pedagogy tends not to ruffle child readers. Obviously, the book remains popular (along with Christianity) among adults. The more pervasive theme of Spyri's *Heidi* is the transformative possibilities of the spirit immersed in nature—appetite for life, ailments, handicaps, and heart sickness all find cure with Heidi and in the vigorous mountain air. Nature and religion are connected thusly.

Heidi is widely read almost 150 years after its publication because Spyri's nature pleases the senses and brims with potential for change. Grandfather's tears at the story of the prodigal son say as much about forgiveness as they do about connection between old and young, ill and strong, marginal and mainstream. There is hope for us all in the clean air of Swiss mountains.

"Robert Louis Stevenson's *Treasure Island*: The Ideal Fable"
by Susan Gannon

In the novel *Treasure Island*, an incontestable touchstone work of children's literature, Robert Louis Stevenson exhibits not only his brilliance with storytelling, but also his sensitivity to the narrative needs of his young audience. Balancing his quest romance between two equally adept and differently complex narrators (the young Jim and the adult), Stevenson fills in the gaps for child readers while carefully building the novel's suspense. Both Jims add to the depth of *Treasure Island*. The elder Jim projects his adult flaws and knowledge onto his young self, without spoiling the narrative's slow build. When young Jim lacks the maturity to understand a conversation or character or even his own feelings about an event, the narrator or an intelligent character enunciates for the child reader. Often Stevenson externalizes emotion that Jim is too young to understand—as children are wont to do.

Stevenson never loses sight of his young reader. Because of dearth of experience in children, Stevenson must be simple and straightforward when describing characters, He trains his reader to read characters, and often through their appearance. The author guards both his reader and Jim from excessive violence. Even when Jim shoots Hands, it is more of a reflex than a conscious act.

Jim understands the blood that has accompanied the treasure, so his success is not unencumbered. Although a happy ending is requisite of the genre, Stevenson tempers it by finishing *Treasure Island* with the grave, stiff, adult Jim, suggesting an ambiguity to Jim's fate. The thrills of the monetary treasure are further reduced with the Christian morals intoned throughout the novel, hinting at a higher judgment, and throwing even Jim's character into question by likening him most closely with the unprincipled and captivating pirate, Long John Silver. With such an attentive eye to the vision of a child in a world in which he must eventually become an adult with all the rights and responsibilities that entails, a child has much instructive excitement to gain from the rewarding *Treasure Island.*

"J. R. R. Tolkein's *The Hobbit*: The Magic of Words"
by C. W. Sullivan III

To judge J. R. R. Tolkein's *The Hobbit* against his more popular *Lord of the Rings* is to miss the particular strengths of this first novel by misunderstanding entirely its intended audience. Although Tolkein has become a cult favorite among fantasy enthusiasts and subcultural movements, *The Hobbit* was written for children. True, it served as a foundation on which Tolkein constructed the *Lord of the Rings*, but it should not be seen merely as a precursor to that larger work. When considered as a novel by a philologist that culls language, structure, and story from European myths and legends, *The Hobbit's* worth emerges. Tolkein borrowed linguistic and narrative strategies of works such as *Beowulf* and *Sir Gawain and the Green Knight* to draw Middle Earth. His linguistic play with song and riddles, his solid story of growing up, and the intruding narrative voice all clearly mark *The Hobbit* as a children's story.

It is Tolkein's play with words that defines his particular fantasy world and elevates the book to the level of a touchstone work. Images in Tolkein's own words imprint themselves in the reader's memory. The author presents advanced semiotic concepts in a manner familiar to children, following their own discovery of the power of words, songs, naming, and language games. Word and action combine forces in *The Hobbit* to move Bilbo Baggins through his necessary growth stages. Because the novel was created for children, it really is a solid story first and foremost. The book requires viewing within the tradition of the legends and myths—a tradition from which Tolkein learned that the great ancient tales are retellings of the same story, in the voice of different storyteller. Tolkein surely claimed through language a fantastic and compelling world of his own in *The Hobbit.*

"E. B. White's *Charlotte's Web*: Caught in the Web"
by Sonia Landes

The genius of E. B. White's *Charlotte's Web* is in its seamless confluence of reality and fantasy. Transformations such as that of Charlotte's "SOME PIG" to "ZUCK-ERMAN'S FAMOUS PIG" attest to this fluid continuum between human and animal, fact and dream. Wilbur the pig is saved twice: first by young Fern in the first two chapters, second by the spider, Charlotte. In each world it is words that save him (Fern's plea: "This is the most terrible case of injustice I ever heard of"; Charlotte's woven words). From the plot to the last paragraph, language is at the heart of *Charlotte's Web*. With White's powerful instrument, the magic of nature enters lives of the characters, and love just might triumph over rationality.

White's careful construction of content and style demarcates his child audience. With Wilbur saved in the first two chapters by a human, the possibility of his second salvation is real, thereby calming the fears of his young readers. In his edenic barn, White drew his characters from his own farm, and wrote country life as more sane than urban, that the food chain cannot be avoided, and that it's all part of life's cycles of change and growth. At the farm, females are more caring than males, and irony abounds amidst the oppositional forces of life and death. *Charlotte's Web* is a celebration of life in lists, repetitions, song, and naming—always within the grasp of his child audience. Details down to the apt names of White's anthropomorphized animals and the measurement of ingredients in Wilbur's slop or Templeton's ton of junk attach children to this farm world and some adult humor as well. *Charlotte's Web* is a gripping story, ripe with the tension of life, of what we want and cannot have, of what we must fight for because of its magic: love.

"T. H. White's *The Sword in the Stone*: Education and the Child Reader"
by Adrienne Kertzer

The dark view of humanity pervading the revised version of T. H. White's *The Sword in the Stone*, published in a 1958 edition with the other novels of the series, departs from the original legend. *The Sword in the Stone* published in 1938 is a paean to learning written for a child audience. White couples his story of Wart's learning to learn with his construction (and deconstruction) of the farcical medieval romance for his child reader. As Wart learns about life, so too does the reader learn about this fantasy world. In line with his pedagogical approach, White tosses the reader into the largely foreign territory of allusions, Latin, and ironic humor that gives credit to the capacity of his reader to learn along with the story. In confronting romanticized notions of the past, realism versus fantasy (i.e., nostalgia), and larger issues of humanity and self in terms of literature, White wrote a rewarding work that continues to challenge and child and adult reader alike.

White succeeds in capturing the complexity of existence and one's relationship with literary conventions. Borrowing largely from Malory, White sought to "write of an imaginary world imagined in the fifteenth century"—imagined by White in the twentieth century. Where Malory finds tragedy in the disconnect between a knight's long-term, committed quest and the unattainability of that goal in reality (and out of fantasy), White finds comedy. While clearly evoking the particularities of this specific era, he challenges assumptions about the past, disallowing historic tourism or preciousness in his novel, and simultaneously arguing for the sameness of life in any period. Amid White's dark conception of humanity as brute, excessively violent, and wrong-headed, he allows for possible change through children. In *The Sword in the Stone*, he leads them to water, but he can't make them drink.

"Laura Ingalls Wilder's Little House Books: A Personal Story"
by Virginia L. Wolf

That Ronald Reagan's favorite television show in 1980 was "Little House on the Prairie" highlights the nexus of critical debate over Laura Ingalls Wilder's Little House books. Is Laura more of Ma's child or Pa's? Is Wilder frighteningly conservative, sexist, racist? These critics often forget that these books are romances written for children. Wilder's series is more personal than these debates acknowledge, with answers to those questions that contradict and lead simply and calmly inside. Amidst the tension around pioneer and farm life, home life and community is a resounding message that the only real control possible is within. Along with Laura's growth, the Little House books stylistically progress from the myth of the pioneer life to the realism of internal growth.

Wilder's Laura must move away from the sanctuary of home toward a bolder independent self in a larger world. Wilder posits a value system of freedom, hard work, and compassion—both individually and institutionally—but no clear political position. The directly contradictory arguments formed around the series attest to both their touchstone quality and the author's privileging of the specificity of circumstance over any totalizing perspective. The adventure of the Little House books positions humanity against nature, but Laura must learn to become at peace with the forces of the world (natural and social); this is maturity. Wilder's books are about responsibility and peace, about ambition and collaboration with others. Because the Little House books speak to abiding issues of moving toward maturity, the calm they achieve endures.

BEYOND TOUCHSTONES

That the logic of such consensus provoked controversy is self-evident. A canon chosen by a committee (or any canon?) is ripe for attacks, some of which were recorded in the *Quarterly* and some presumably behind the scenes, which Nodelman addresses in the final volume, explaining why some influential works did not receive touchstone status and others appeared on a list "worth watching." Nodelman defended the omissions of such favorites as *Wizard of Oz*, *Peter Pan*, and *Mary Poppins* by articulating why they exhibited weaknesses in format or quality that disqualified them from greatness. The omissions and slights were contested by some readers, who objected to the absences of certain titles presumed to belong, by the relegation of some distinguished authors and artists to the margins, and by the slight representation of other cultures. One scholar found the whole notion of an official canon to be "a travesty of authoritative scholarship" and urged its withdrawal.[39] One member of the committee objected to the frame of a canon, which suggests "a sacredness and authority and inevitability" few would wish to claim; the secondary list of "worth watching" was condescending and the choice of titles or editions arbitrary; and the lack of diversity on the committee revealed a larger "parochial myopia."[40] Nodelman then changed the focus and terminology to be "touchstones" rather than "canon." While Nodelman intended the canonical project as dialogue and curriculum, the discourse came at a critical point for the field as institution and body of knowledge. At a time when Anglo-centric canons were being challenged, when the field was awakening to new voices and new disciplines, the concept of a canon was problematic indeed.

One organizational goal for which there was more unanimity was affiliation with the larger parent organization, the Modern Language Association (MLA). Francelia Butler's initial journal of *Children's Literature: The Great Excluded* (1972) included on the title page the provenance: "Journal of the Modern Language Association Seminar on Children's Literature," alluding to tentative ties with MLA, which was critical to the viability of the field, and finalized by 1980 as an official division. The journal *Children's Literature* emerged in 1975 as the most scholarly venue for critical work. Interdisciplinary work on children's literature began to appear in mainstream journals, such as *PMLA, Critical Inquiry, Nineteenth-Century Literature*, among others. Twenty years after that fledgling journal of 1972, where Francelia Butler staked a claim, the MLA published a volume, *Teaching Children's Literature*, with essays on pedagogy, collections, and curricula, edited by Glenn Sadler and introduced by U. C. Knoeflmacher. To have such growth in two decades is phenomenal for children's literature in academia, a conservative institution to say the least.

All is not rosy, of course. U. C. Knoeflmacher in his introduction to this volume in the "Options for Teaching" series rails against the isolation of the field and references "kiddie lit" as waning but still around. We look in the mirror as well. Peter Hunt finds academia too interested in what *was* rather than what *is*. He questions the standard of judging children's books by the same value systems used for adult books—a heretical position considering the persistence of that belief from the early librarians on through the touchstone critics. Looking over contemporary scholarship, Hunt challenges us to explore the critical questions: "Why are we reading? What are books *for*? (with emphasis on *for*).[41] Drawing on cultural studies, others question if aesthetics should be considered apart from culture or politics. The delicate balance between children's literature and the child raises problems in a body of literature with "children" in the title and as intended audience. As Margaret Meek reminds us: "Children's literature creates too many paradoxes in too many places."[42] The child as reader is a complex consideration, largely neglected, but kept in view by scholars like Margaret Meek, Peter Hunt, and John Rowe Townsend. Beverly Lyon Clark's provocative discussion of "kiddie lit" explores some of the ambivalence in cultural discourse on children and their literature: its rhetorical power and nostalgic appeal, its commodification, its uncertain status as "literature." She ponders why feminist scholars, like Jane Tompkins, quoted so much in this book, ignore children's literature as part of an argument against patriarchal dominance and its effects on women writers. Women's studies scholars seem reluctant to embrace a field with traditional mother–child overtones. While both breathe in the same culture, academia is slow to integrate children's books into the body of literature. In short, Clark states: "Children's literature has low status in literary criticism," despite its fertile potential for interdisciplinary scholarship.[43] Even scholars studying marginality, who embrace issues of race, gender, and class, ignore age, particularly youth. Clark's affirmation of the child as *child* is a healthy antidote to efforts to overcome that condition in search of greater glory in the ivory tower. Underlying all the gloss is the child as reader, the ultimate creator of meaning.

Chapter 3

Best Books: The Reader

"Books swept me away, one after the other, this way and that; I made endless vows according to their lights, for I believed them."
—Annie Dillard, *An American Childhood*

From the first cautionary advice by Dr. Spock, read by an anxious mother holding in her hand an anguished infant, to the giddy goose rhymes, "Pat-the-Bunnies," or moon melodies read at bedtime, to the cereal boxes of champions on the breakfast table, to the scout manuals memorized, the fugitive diaries, the Peanuts cartoons, and to those first chapter books, a child is raised by arms of print. Those who survive in one-, two-, and three-syllable words travel beyond the rearing borders of home and school through the agency of literature, the fictional journey of the mind. We fall in love with language.

Books swept me away, and I believed them. I have a fervent relation with formative books of my childhood as the ground of my being, the word made flesh. While cultural authorities may marginalize the reader's romance as beyond the cultural forum, these early books matter deeply. Reflecting on his own childhood reading, Graham Greene writes, "Perhaps it is only in childhood that books have any deep influence on our lives.... But in childhood all books are books of divination, telling us about the future, and like the fortune teller who sees a long journey in the cards or death by water, they influence the future."[1] To Eudora Welty her early reading was, as she exquisitely writes, "a sweet devouring," in which she learned the bare bones of language from a love of the alphabet.[2] After creating the image of literature as a "City of Invention," author Fay Weldon writes to her niece: "Truly, Alice, books are wonderful things: to sit alone in a room and laugh and cry, because you are reading, and still be safe when you close the book; and having finished it, discover you are changed, yet unchanged! To be able to visit the City of Invention at will, depart at will—that is all, really, education is about, should be about."[3] Perhaps this is what our own classics are about: a City of Invention whereby we construct meaning and make a life.

Invention evokes Frye's "educated imagination," but the "City" offers more than an education into classics. What we rarely acknowledge is the subtext of why we choose particular texts as our own: romance, intimacy, desire. Catherine Stimpson in "Reading for Love" introduces the concept of the "paracanon": the value of a work depending on its power to inspire love. Stretching the criteria of "good" to encompass "love," she believes that any text can belong to this canon as long as beloved by many. Speaking of the effects of passionate reading, she evokes its powers.

> In our gratitude, we treasure the books we love. We may even become addicted to them. For they provide some of love's relational and terri-fying thrills: its ecstasies; turning with a different being; the threat of the loss, the closure, of those ecstasies; the sensation of inhabiting a world apart from the world that normally inhibits one; an oscillation between control and self-abandonment; a dance with the partners of amusement and consolation; the gratification of needs that a reader has concealed.[4]

This romance simulates coupled love between a text and a reader. More than just a private relationship, paracanonical love involves social and cultural forces at play in the construction of subjectivity in a collectivity of readers. The commu-nity of textual lovers keeps the work alive and, in turn, is enlivened by the text. Surpassing Wayne Booth's sense of an ethical community of readers, she distin-guishes between "the text that provokes official respect and the text that provokes unofficial love."[5] Stimpson draws in Victor Nell as well, appreciating his concept of "ludic reading" as playful and private but departing from his sense that the ludic reader distinguishes between pleasure and merit. Such division, to Stimpson, severs "authority from dearness" and perpetuates the practice of "middle managers of culture" who have "edited feeling from criticism." This dichotomy reveals the greater divide between a more masculine, critical, public realm and the more femi-nine, emotional, private domain. The paracanon reconnects readers and texts in a process whereby autobiography enters literary studies and fuses "reader" and "self." And such union offers a model for institutions as distant as librarians and academicians to find common ground. She writes: "Mapping a paracanon is a historiographical project that can lead to narratives about a period that tell of the connections among its emotions, its libraries and classrooms, its literacies and illiteracies."[6] Oppositions between "canonical" and noncanonical" only intensify the larger division between excluded and included social groups. In a principle of inclusion, Stimpson's vision encompasses the canon and the paracanon, much in the way of feminists who celebrate elite women authors and the popular fare they may have despised. The paracanon subverts the canon in its otherworldly way and hovers about, disturbing the peace. Her first love was *Little Women*; mine was Nancy Drew and *The Secret Garden*. Through my own romance with these texts, I have learned my pedagogy, whereby I explore such dynamics and invite reader response.

Reading is both social practice and private experience, a powerfully transformative experience. Textual power—the performance of text and reader—is the subject of Louise Rosenblatt's instrumental writings. In her 1938 landmark work, *Literature as Exploration*, she presents the act of reading as anything but passive. When a text is successful with a reader, success comes from the fact that the reader brings to it all that she is and has experienced. From the merger of text and reader comes a new creation that is as singular as the reader. As she says:

> The process of understanding a work implies a recreation of it, an attempt to grasp completely all the sensations and concepts through which the author seeks to convey the qualities of his sense of life. Each of us makes a new synthesis of these elements with her own nature, but it is essential that she assimilate those elements of experience which the author has actually presented.[7]

Pursuing the nature of literary experience, Rosenblatt sees this syntheses—an "evocation"—resulting in the "aesthetic object" or "poem." Her goal is to understand literature as a cultural activity of "the living work of art" in the lives of real readers. As Rosenblatt so dramatically states, a text is a performance, a kind of poem composed of the reader's interaction with a particular literary work.

As the role of the reader emerges behind the curtains of the literary stage, cultural notions of greatness evolve. The reader indeed matters in the grand scheme of things Terry Eagleton views the history of modern literary theory as passing through three major stages: a Romantic absorption with the author, a New Critical focus on the text, and a shift of attention to the reader.[8] Reader response criticism as a critical approach focuses on the act of reading as a dynamic process in which the reader is not a passive recipient, but an active producer of meaning. It is in the ways that readers receive and use texts that people exert far more control over their lives than ever before acknowledged. Reader response criticism calls into question the idea of the canon as an elite cultural club, to which readers will belong as they differentially evaluate certain works as classics. Despite the supposed objectivity of the canon, the ways in which readers attribute value and meaning to a text are shaped by the social, cultural, and political background they bring to their reading. Rather than an absolute standard of literary value, there are multiple centers of value from which to assess a text. A reader judges quality not through a pure analysis of immutable text but through cultural tools, which continuously evolve and differ according to gender, class, race, ethnicity, geography, and time. My tools have come as I envision classics as cultural work: the power of text as *landscape;* the power of text as *ethic;* the power of text as *myth*.

Perspectives change with the reader re-visioned as a creative maker of meaning. Reader response theorists view the reader as significant to literature as are the cultural contexts that affect what authors write and how we read. Stanley Fish argues that all texts exist in the reader and within certain "interpretive communities."[9] Reading is not merely the transfer of information from author to reader, but also a dynamic process of making meaning. The search for meaning in a text is shaped by a "horizon of expectations," in Hans Robert Jauss's terms.[10] This framework of sociocultural contexts, both contemporary and historical, creates the interpretive communities that receive texts. Jane Tompkins's study of the reception of popular American fiction in the nineteenth century recovers the historical response of contemporary readers to "sensational designs," a desired social and political order, "not in relation to unchanging formal, psychological, or philosophical standards of complexity, or truth, or correctness."[11] Ethnographies of reading explore the social bases of reading within particular contexts, or "historically specific conditions." Janice Radway and John Fiske are notable for their studies of popular culture audiences, in which they argue that texts become popular by offering to readers constructions that appeal to their psychological and social needs. In her study of romance readers, Radway suggests that readers choose texts that offer ways of reading their own experiences. She argues: "By focusing on social process—that is, on what people do with texts and objects rather than on those texts and objects themselves, we should begin to see that people do not ingest mass culture whole but often remake it into something they can use."[12] These texts are called "producerly" in their construction of familiar motifs and multiple meanings. Fiske suggests that audiences make choices based on the textual appropriation of relevant contemporary images and issues.[13] Cultural studies that consider literature as re-creative do not require a repudiation of elite cultural forms, but seek the representation of what gives these particular forms agency in specific contexts: how the texts of books enter the texts of lives. I envision these texts as cultural work: the power of texts as *place*; the power of texts as *ethics*; the power of texts as *myth*. In the rest of the chapter, I explore this cultural work through landscapes and inscapes of literature made classic through a social process. Seeking to connect not isolate texts, I use intertextual tools to read classic landscapes, personal and public, for their value and meaning as interior space and social order. As Gerald Graff reminds us: "No text is an island."[14] In presenting an autobiography of reading, my own intellectual history, I wish to restore pleasure to the drama between text and reader. My pleasure, your pleasure: a paracanon. I offer my own frame of sense making: the ways of seeing and contexts of literature by which I play a role as librarian, scholar, and reader, romancing landscapes of childhood, "the heart's field."

TEXT AS PLACE: LANDSCAPES OF CHILDREN'S CLASSIC

The image of "the heart's field" is from Eudora Welty, who writes in her essay "Place in Fiction" that "[l]ocation is the proving ground of 'what happened? who's here? who's coming'—that is the heart's field."[15] Fiction depends on place for the simple truth that feelings are bound up in the land, in homeland, that most contested real estate. Environments imprint themselves on our physicality and spirit, and we respond in war and peace, young and old.

I am struck by the meanings of places I have known, houses where I have lived, locales that continue to form my own sense of inner and outer reality. The vacant lot on the corner of Castleman Street in Pittsburgh where I romped at will with the street kids on our pirate isle, the earth under our nails. The summer place at Lake Chautauqua, New York, which was my own Victoriana preserve and my first experience of perfect freedom. My grandparent's stucco house strewn with ivy in the idyllic village of Mendham, New Jersey, which was where I always wanted to live, and which I try to re-create in a symbolic way every place I live. The speckled islands off the coast of Penobscot Bay, Maine, which recall for me a line from the poet Yeats who said that for each of us there is an image that if we were but to know it, it could direct our lives. The Cornish coast where I have walked, its northern reaches of black headlands and stormy sea reminiscent of Maine, the softer southern edges whose cliffs are steep meadows speckled in heather and golden gorse. Is it piney woods or piney islands in the sea, or perhaps, in the words of the wandering Odysseus, "the honey lights of home"? Landscapes are personal for they answer the basic questions—who we are, where we came from, and where we are going. Landscapes are also cultural myths of sense-making that exist at a deep, unconscious layer.

Think of the places of your childhood. The paths you walked in the woods and found remnants of bird nests. An old swimming hole that smelled like leaves. A pier where you caught fish with your brother, or the dock where you sat in the summer—on one of those limitless blue afternoons—to have your picture taken in the new tank suit. The July night camping out in a pup tent and gazing at the vista of an endless sky of stars. Or open, rolling fields of wildflowers now crowded with new developments, euphemistically called "Devonshire" or "Canterbury Hills." The pastoral idyll just in the far horizon of memory, twenty, thirty, or more years back.

The landscape contains our stories, and we find a passionate attachment to the places of childhood, real and imagined, what Eleanor Cameron calls "the country of the mind." Readers take pilgrimages to fabled birthplaces and literary homes of favorite authors, hoping to capture in Stratford or Hilltop Farm an aura or shadow of the author's muse. Writers often return to their own vanished worlds, looking for remains or re-creations. We recall Thomas Hardy's Wessex or William Faulkner's Yoknapatawpha County, Misssissippi, which he called his "own postage stamp of native soil," now forever part of the American myth of the New South. To writer Virginia Woolf, the coastal landscape of Cornwall became the setting for her novel, *To the Lighthouse*. Twain's riverboat days on what he described as "the great Mississippi, the magnificent Mississippi, rolling its mile-wide tide along"— became not only his preferred narrative settings but also his name, his pseudonym the old river term, a lead-man's call, meaning safe water. Or Kenneth Grahame's revered Thames country, Cookham Dene in Berkshire. Hans Christian Andersen's Denmark, where his fairy tales evoke the meadows and canals and waysides of his own land. Heidi's Alps. Lucy Boston's manor house at Hemingford Grey whose gabled, towering walls became transformed timelessly. Frances Hodgson Burnett's garden. Maurice Sendak's dreamscape. Robinson Crusoe vision. Russell Hoban's notion of territory. Eric Carle's creaturely skyscape. Ezra Jack Keats's Brooklyn with its snowy days and billboard art.

Literature itself is a kind of atlas, an imaginative map of the universe, a guide-book. Culturally, we read the landscape, romance our remembrances at holidays, and even attempt to make our technology familial with terms like "home pages" and "visiting sites." I think the attraction of landscape is its rhythms—an ebb and flow that, as Margaret Drabble writes, "represents at once the changing and the unchanging."[16] In Annie Dillard's *Pilgrim at Tinker Creek*, she sees the yearning for landscape to be just this: "to explore neighborhood, view the land-scape, and discover at least *where* it is that we have been so startlingly set down, if we can't learn why."[17]

You may wonder how I am using the term *landscape*. It is just as uncertain and elusive a term as "text" or "literature," or, surely, "children's literature." Like Proteus, it can take a number of shapes, making its central features and conti-nuity difficult to recognize. The concept of landscape is a bit of a mystery drawn from various sources, a complex, multilayered palimpsest of geography, history, and myth. There is a sense of extension and depth, spatial and temporal. The word originated at the end of the sixteenth century from *landschaft*, which meant a way to organize space and a place for habitation. The word *scenery* is even more recent, dating from the late eighteenth century. *Topography* means the writing of a place. The words we used to describe locale are continually interpreted, as writers, painters, historians, archaeologists, and geologists have demonstrated. To poet and naturalist writer Annie Dillard, the essence of landscape is "the texture of intricacy," in which the texture allows for " a beauty inexhaustible in its complexity."[18] The landscape historian J. B. Jackson, who was perhaps the first, in the early 1950s, to use the phrase "to read a landscape," defines it as "a concrete, three-dimensional, shared reality."[19] The emphasis, for me, is the phrase "shared reality," a conjoined existence in a topsy-turvy universe. Our landscapes are, as Barry Lopez reminds us, always dual: the one outside the self, the other within. The external landscape is the one we see—the topology of the land as well as its natural inhabitants, the weather, seasons, and evolution all about. The second landscape is interior—a projection within a person of a part of the exterior land-scape—in Welty's words, "the heart's field." Our patterns of thought are influenced by the patterns of nature in the particular place we inhabit.

Geographers suggest that this "human enhancement" of place is cultural, a network of patterns and templates through which we make sense of our experi-ence. Landscape is socially constructed, a concept predicated on the values and ideals of its own time. We envision natural and domesticated structures in terms of cultural values relating to our very model of society itself. Historian J. B. Jackson speculates that the typical farm scene—with its barn, shed, outbuildings, and nearby town—is symbolic of a parent surrounded by offspring.[20] The British geographer Denis Cosgrove sees the idea of landscape not only as "a way of seeing" but as a profoundly ideological concept that reveals the way classes portray them-selves and their world through an imagined relationship with nature. Some have begun to refer to the "biography" of a landscape or use the metaphor of the land-scape as a text, as a book. Anthropologist Clifford Geertz has long advocated looking at culture as text. To him, culture is something that is "read" as one might read written material. The use of the term "to read a landscape" reinforces the connections between landscape and literature.

Associated with the concept "text" is intertextuality, the textual context of a literary work. Originating in literary criticism, the term has stirred interest among historians, anthropologists, and cultural geographers. I teach my children's liter-ature course in terms of intertextuality: the way texts draw upon other texts, that themselves are based on yet different texts, and so on. Umberto Eco perhaps best describes it in his extraordinary novel, *The Name of the Rose*, when Brother William suggests the conversations that take place in a medieval library, where "books speak of other books," and the narrator Adso recognizes the library as "the place of a long, centuries-old murmuring, an imperceptible dialogue between one parchment and another, a living thing, a receptacle of powers not to be ruled by a human mind, a treasure of secrets emanated by many minds, surviving the death of those who had produced them or had been their conveyors."[21]

I want to suggest that books not only speak of other books as a common land-scape, but also of other places, lived, remembered, read, re-created. We see these places through our earliest vision of them, shaped by our minds, which are contin-ually sketching, illustrating, filling in the gaps. J. R. R. Tolkien suggests this power when he writes:

> If a story says "he climbed a hill and saw a river in the valley below," the illustrator may catch, or nearly catch, his own vision of such a scene, but every hearer of the words will have his own picture, and it will be made out of all the hills and rivers and dales he has ever seen but specially out of The Hill, The River, The Valley which were for him the first embodi-ment of the word.[22]

Landscape, then, may be the construction of stories that we tell ourselves about ourselves, which arise from frameworks of national identity, ideology, narrative tradition, and the imagination.

Landscapes remembered from childhood are continually remade in literature as well as in our lives. This is essentially Romanticism: the idea that childhood is the foundation of later human experience. The poet reaches back into childhood spent in a particular landscape in a quest for the wholeness of the self. William Blake evokes the magical purity of childhood perception, where children live without labeling or dividing the world into abstract categories and thus feel a natural kinship with all that they behold. William Wordsworth writes in "Ode: Intimations of Immortality": "So was it when my life began. / So it is now I am a man. / So be it when I grow old. / Or let me die!" So was, So is, So be—past, present, and future. These are not always sanguine possibilities. John Clare suffered from the loss of the familiars in his own beloved Northamptonshire countryside, where his family had farmed for generations, now in the eighteenth century transforming common open fields into private holdings. Clare poignantly speaks of every exile when he writes: "I've left mine own old home of homes / Green fields and every pleasant place." The Romantics straddle these kinds of contraries of place, this uprooted land. In Blakean terms, we carry the vision of Innocence forward into the years of Experience.

Our first landscapes remain a prism through which actual landscapes are and will be viewed. Piaget's developmental studies confirm the creativity of children in making intentional worlds that help to confront meaninglessness and chaos. Edith Cobb's *The Ecology of the Imagination in Childhood* is a classic study of a child's innate connection with the natural world. Imagination is the ecological field that connects outer and inner worlds. This animated, dynamic, and interactive universe is captured in the words of Walt Whitman's "Leaves of Grass":

> There was a child went forth every day
> And the first object he looked upon, he became,
> And that object became part of him for the day or a certain part
> of the day,
> Or for many years or stretching cycles of years.
> The early lilacs became part of this child,
> And grass and white and red morning glories, and white and
> red clover, and the song of the phoebe-bird,
> And the Third-month lambs and the sow's pink-faint litter, and
> the mare's foal and the cow's calf.

And not only a light and airy Spring appealed, but also "the noisy brood of the barnyard" and "the mire by the roadside." This is the geography the child wishes to explore—that of life itself, its spacious country of hills and vales and the spaces between.

Children's books are the site of adult re-creation of an earlier geography. The locales of many children's books are the enshrouded landscapes of childhood, remade, re-visioned. The backward glance is borne by the surety that what "I was" is part of what "I am." Such nostalgia thrives in moments of transition, in which the gaps and slippages quicken a longing for continuity. Novelist and historian Gillian Avery writes a brief remembrance of being eight years old and including in her birthday card for her mother, along with her usual threepenny bunch of violets, a most unusual two lines from a favorite childhood hymn, "Time, like an ever-rolling stream, bears all its sons away" (words written by Isaac Watts, noted Puritan hymnist and juvenile poet), which suggests, to me, that these thoughts are not confined to jaded adults. The author as traveler holds memories of the past while, paradoxically, knows the past is gone. The tension is centrifugal—outgoing, away—as well as centripetal, indwelling, homebound. Such utopian as well as nostalgic tension makes children's books a site for the confluence of time and place, which Virginia Hamilton calls "hopescape." Books are tethered to physical places in which we are where we lived, and we are what we have read. A story maps roads traveled and less traveled, and landscape reveals, in every sense of the word, a "point of view."

I would like to explore this broad topography through a glance at just a few of the children's books, mostly from the Victorian and Edwardian period, whose landscapes strike me, shape me, intertextually. I surveyed a vast panorama of titles in which the locales or wilderness, rural, and urban are evocative, indeed essential, in the co-mingled genres of folklore, fiction, and memoir. I winnowed down the sites to but a few titles with brief commentary, just a sampling to stir the imagination about the place of place in our lives and in the books we read, write, and share with children—in William Blake's words "the Echoing Green." So many of the titles openly proclaim *place*: the Emerald City of Oz, a garden, a land where wild things are (not just the wild things), a house on the prairies, a river chattering stories, as well as the other designations that come to mind suggesting a willowed wonderland, the Wild Woods, or even Neverland. My concern is with the ideas of space, or place, that ground these works intertextually in the mapping of a literary landscape of childhood.

I begin with the fairy tale, whose wilderness haunts our dreams, our psyche, our shadow selves, in Jungean terms, or, in Joseph Campbell's mythic words, "the primer of the picture-language of the soul." Joyce Thomas considers the setting of stories we take for granted as the grounding of other narrative fiction. In her piece, "Woods and Castles, Towers and Huts," Thomas discusses the heightened significance of setting in providing the atmosphere for a tale's action and theme, which is often a dialectic between matter and magic, internal and tangible. The forest is a threshold to the supernatural, a separate peace between humanity and nature, an enchanted place where words cast spells, children once lost become found, and identities of worldly power are blurred. This is the perilous "faerie" realm. The castle, a bastion of material mass, is impervious to the animations within, while, at the same time, creating its own exotic enchantment. The tower, as a small part of the whole, is akin to the attic in its associations (I am reminded here of Gilbert and Gubar's Victorian study, *The Madwoman in the Attic*). The tower, like a trunk, suggests treasures waiting to be found; the tower, as a symbolic construct of vertical space, rises rather unnaturally in the landscape as focus and locus. The hut, however, stands alone, a different kind of life, more akin to nature than not. Thomas suggests that these points be much more than occupied space but teach about the uses of setting, the importance of place. She writes: "We flutter away from one landscape to another, changing locales like disoriented migratory fowl, yet whenever, wherever, we temporarily settle, we reconstruct our personal nests, delimiting a tiny patch of earth or woods for our own castle, tower, hut."[23] Who is not such a homesteader? For particularity, in a tale like Cinderella, we have the cemetery, the garden, the hearth, the palace—all resonant of nestlike settings that confine and liberate. This is the wisdom of folklore, the message taken to heart by writers as diverse as Lewis Carroll, Rudyard Kipling, L. Frank Baum, Beatrix Potter, J. M. Barrie, Kenneth Grahame, and so many other architects of children's native land and Neverland.

In fiction, these well-worn threads and bits of straw are transformed, spun into gold. While the role of landscape in fiction is larger than the square foot of any writing, I wish to explore a few such places, ways of seeing. Several texts come to mind related to "faerie": Lewis Carroll's *Alice in Wonderland* and its American kin, L. Frank Baum's *The Wizard of Oz*. Both reflect a surrealistic setting that fits. Carroll's original title—"Alice Among the Elves"—suggests his own recognition of that connection: that a small child is set out into a magical world. Alice's world, as in so much folklore, is a place to visit but not to live. While she is there, she wonders if she will ever experience a natural life again, which to her means an ordered and civilized world. Clearly, she feels distant from the setting of the garden, which is an artificial one at that. The story begins with a riverbank setting, a pastoral picnic, but one where the protagonist tires of such reverie, is put off by books without pictures or conversations, and wanders off, in a true folkloric way, on to adventure, away from home. As Carroll describes in his introductory verse:

> The dream-child moving through a land
> Of wonders wild and new,
> In friendly chat with bird or beast,
> And half believe it true.

This dream child wanders, however, without a map, without guidance or formula. What is left is the sheer grit of a heroine determined to make sense without social, spatial, temporal, or moral structure. While folkloric backgrounds are often as threatening, Alice's adventures are unique in her control of the environment, in the sense of entrance and exit. The real setting she faces is anthropomorphic, what has been described as "a post-Darwinian tent." John Fowles's suggestion in *The French Lieutenant's Woman* that *Dr. Jekyll and Mr. Hyde* is a psychological guidebook to Victorian literature seems to apply here to Alice's quest to understand "self" and the "other."

L. Frank Baum's *The Wizard of Oz* is meant to be an American Alice, with less excess. As Baum writes in his preface, this story will be "a modernized fairy tale, in which the wonderment and joy are retained and the heartaches and nightmares are left out." Whether this intention is realized is problematic. But the landscape is clearly the most distinctive aspect of the story. Readers clamor for stories about Oz, not about Dorothy as such. And the yellow brick road to the Emerald City is just as real as any map and destination. And this destination is just as elusive as

Alice's garden, both quests, but Dorothy and her friends are in search of the Wizard and the American Dream. This dream, as Mary McCarthy notes in *The Stones of Florence*, is not the typical quest for treasure, which seemed close enough to most American readers, but, rather, for courage, knowledge, heart, adventure, or, simply, home.

Home is the abiding landscape in the tale, and this is no pastoral. Kansas is described as:

> [A] great grey prairie on every side. Not a tree nor a house broke the broad sweep of flat country that reached the edge of the sky in all directions. The sun had baked the plowed land into a gray mass, with little cracks running through it. Even the grass was not green, for the sun had burned the tops of the long blades until they were the same gray color as to be seen everywhere. Once the house had been painted, but the sun blistered the paint and the rains washed it away, and now the house was as dull and gray as everything else."[24]

From this poor dirt farm, Dorothy moves to a land of milk and honey, a world ripe with fruit, flowers, birds, and streams, what is described as "the Garden of the World set in the midst of the Great American Desert."[25] One critic has described Oz as "a kind of secular paradise ... an Eden before the fall, and that this, in turn, is a mirror of the American dream if an unspoilt land of opportunity."[26] America writ large becomes the landscape of Oz, a life promising more than a fairy tale because here no magical solutions are required, just an endless plain of possibilities.

Other books that struggle with the representation of the prairies—as fantasy and reality—are the Laura Ingalls Wilder series, Pam Conrad's *Prairie Songs,* and Patricia MacLachlan's *Sarah, Plain and Tall.* "The Little House" series begins with the suggestion of fairy tale: "Once upon a time, sixty years ago, a little girl lived in the Big Woods of Wisconsin, in a little gray house made of logs," and the series closes with her entering a little gray house on the prairie, which she describes as "so wide and sweet and clear. In *Prairie Songs,* the story begins with a different image: "The prairie was like a giant plate, stretching all the way to the sky at the edges. And we were like two tiny peas left over from dinner, Lester and me. We couldn't even see the soddy from out there—just nothing, nothing in a big circle all around us." *Sarah, Plain and Tall* turns on the conflict between two symbolic and very real landscapes: the prairie and the sea. The prairie is described when Sarah arrives, as "green grass fields that bloomed with Indian paintbrush, red and orange, and blue-eyed grass"; and Maine as "rock cliffs that rise up at the edge of the sea ... hills covered with pine and spruce trees, green with needles." The crucible in this novel is the choice between terrains. This short novel for young readers powerfully conveys the correlation of landscape to mindscape.

Transported from the vast plains to the more intimate English countryside, Beatrix Potter's tiny compass portrays the farmlands, gardens, and villages of Westmorland remembered from childhood's slow accrual of summers. Potter's picture books are rooted in the Lake Country, which she frequented with her family on holiday and where she finally settled as a sheep farmer and preservationist. Many of the tales are set in her home of Hill Top, a picturesque beamed cottage built around 1690 along with a 212-acre working farm, situated near Winderemere in the Lake District, or in the stunning landscapes of the region. Potter set her stories in actual locales, which she sketched with meticulous detail. The beautiful lakes and hills near Hill Top are seen in the tales of *Mrs. Tiggy-Winkle, Jemima Puddle-Duck, Squirrel Nutkin, Mr. Tod,* and others. The interior of the farmhouse is depicted in *Samuel Whiskers,* and the garden is evident in *Tom Kitten.* The nearby village of Sawrey is the setting of *The Pie and the Patty Pan* and *Ginger and Pickles.* The street scenes in *The Tailor of Gloucester* are Gloucester. Always a serious student of the natural world, Potter's expeditions with her brother through the forests and fields of Scottish highlands prompted her interest in natural history studies, where nothing in or on the ground escaped her attention. Peter Rabbit and his sisters "lived with their Mother in a sand-bank, underneath the root of a very big fir-tree." This humble sandbank is one of the most famous addresses in children's literature, and her beloved Lake District, a perfect splotch of a hamlet with its whitewashed shops, slate-roofed shops, winding lanes hemmed in by towering stone walls, and rolling green hills, attracts more than 80,000 visitors a year, many of them from the opposite side of the globe. And many more enter this geography through her small books, big words, and accomplished watercolors. Potter's picture books present a delicate balance—in critic Fred Inglis's words, between "a colonized, accomplished horticulture and agriculture, and the stable but mysterious Nature which lies untamed beyond the garden wall."[27] Many classic children's books continue this dialectic.

Kenneth Grahame's *Wind in the Willows* is about home as well, an autobiography of feelings toward nature: river, field, and moor. Grahame re-creates here the landscapes Grahame remembered from his years with his maternal grandmother in Cookham Dene, a village near the Thames in Berkshire, where he later in life returned to live while writing this novel. The Cornish town of Fowey is also interwoven, a place of retreat with friends like Arthur Quiller-Couch and Edward Atkinson, a place that he describes in the book as "the little grey sea town that clings along one side of the harbour." Grahame's seasons: the passing of summer in the willow herb, comfrey, and meadowsweet. The winter where Mole "was glad that he liked the country undecorated, hard, and stripped of its finery. He had got down to the bare bones of it, and they were fine and strong and simple." The swallows explain their migration and their return home: "The call of lush meadow grass, wet orchards, warm, insect-haunted ponds, of browsing cattle, of haymaking, and all the farm buildings clustering around the House of the perfect Eaves." The animal creatures, so familiar to the fable and fairy tale, the woods in the winter, the long days of summer, picnic feasts on the river, "messing about in boats," afternoon tea, *dulce domum*—all these images are potent pastoral dreams. As biographer Peter Green writes, this is a book that stops the clock, that presents old England, the nostalgic rolling hills and enchanted riverbank of Kate Greenaway and Randolph Caldecott. As in Wordsworth's "Prelude" or in Mark Twain's Mississippi, the river dominates as narrative and shapes our relationship to the phenomenological world. The river in *The Wind in the Willows* is described as a "sleek, sensuous, full-bodied animal" and as a storyteller. The opening chapter's paean to the river resounds in the Rat's ninth chapter dream of the sea: "What seas lay beyond, green, leaping, and crested! What sun-bathed coasts.... What quiet harbours, thronged with gallant shipping bound for purple islands of wine and spice, islands set long in languorous waters." This is also a text that is often examined for its signification of classes and social roles with respect to external nature: the civilized and the wild, the gendered world of male camaraderie, the Old England and the New.

Another book of contested landscape is *The Secret Garden,* a treasured childhood text. No book has ever stirred such a feeling for the land as lived, with all of its rich metaphorical texture. With my deep affinity for this book, I lose the critical eye, wanting to preserve the place as stable, as it was and remains for me. To others, the layers of colonial India, English gentility, and country Yorkshire disrupt the ground of their reading. Mary Lennox comes to Misselthwaite Manor, her uncle's Yorkshire home in the moors, "where nothing grows on but heather and gorse, and nothing lives in but wild ponies and sheep." She learns to play in this new landscape: to run, to skip rope, to plant seeds, to make things come alive from the ground, "daffodils and snowdrops and lilies and iris working their way out of the dark." The fertile ground for this play is the secret garden. With the help of Dickon and the robin, a spade, seeds, and a bit of earth, the garden comes to life as she does. As this once-pale creature blossoms, she reaches out to share her green patch of life. Burnett relates how she was inspired by the neighborhood in Manchester, where she lived as a young girl before moving to America, and where she wondered what was behind a locked fence of an abandoned house and by using her imagination turned the soil into a flowering garden of roses, violets, and hyacinths. Burnett spoke of her experience in Manchester as being an exile and found the thickets, woods, and mountains of Tennessee to be her home. But it was the abandoned garden of her childhood that was her formative landscape experience of the pastoral. At the end of her life, Burnett wrote an essay on the experience of gardening, where she says: "As long as one has a garden one has a future; and as long as one has a future one is alive."[28]

In approaching such a representation of nature in children's books of the late Victorian and Edwardian period, it is important to consider both a real as well as a mythical element. Raymond Williams argues in *The Country and the City* that despite the tendency of each generation to cite the mythical lost Golden Age in the previous generation, there are those who "lived" that history, and to whom any change was very real. *The Secret Garden,* like *The Wind in the Willows,* derives much of its strength from the Romantic tradition's representation of childhood and nature. Both works, however, are far from idyllic in the worlds they represent. In *The Secret Garden,* Mary travels across the moors to her new home, in a bleak midwinter that captures her emotional state:

> On and on they drove through the darkness, and although the rain stopped, the wind rushed by and made strange sounds. The road went up and down, and several times the carriage passed over a little bridge beneath which water rushed very fast with a great deal of noise. Mary felt as if the drive would never come to an end, and that the wide, bleak moor was a vast expanse of black ocean through which she was passing on a strip of dry land.

Mary's experience with the land—part domestic, part wild—is a movement to interior space as well as social order. Burnett, I believe, is suggesting the transformative power of the imagination—as part and parcel of nature—to effect changes in the external as well as internal worlds. This is the belief that Fred Inglis holds for a children's book: its potential of "radical innocence." In this story, I sense the redemptive power of nature, of a deep love for the world that can come from its earth, of the communion we share in searching for what is on the other side of the wall, for what is the magic beneath the surface. This book was my beginning, my adventure into a world still revealing its mysteries, where what was lost is found, where what was dead is "wick."

Another book that holds this promise for me is E. B. White's *Charlotte's Web.* Talk about lost causes—trying to keep a pig from the slaughterhouse, from being the holiday feast. This is a story about the sweetness of life, tempered by the nearness of death, and set in a quintessential American landscape: a New England farm.

In a letter to a fifth grade student in Larchmont, New York, White writes:

> It is true that I have a farm. My barn is big and old, and I have ten sheep, eighteen hens, a goose, a gander, a bull calf, a rat, a chipmunk, and many spiders. In the woods near the barn are red squirrels, crows, thrushes, owls, porcupines, woodchucks, foxes, rabbits, and deer. In the pasture pond are frogs, polliwogs, and salamanders. Sometimes a Great Blue Heron comes to the pond and catches frogs. At the shore of the sea are sandpipers, gulls, plovers, and kingfishers. In the mud at low tide are clams. Seven seals live on nearby rocks and in the sea, and they swim close to my boat when I row. Barn swallows nest in the barn, and I have a skunk that lives under the garage. I didn't like spiders at first, but then I began watching one of them, and soon saw what a wonderful creature she was and what a skillful weaver. I named her Charlotte, and now I like spiders along with everything else in nature.[29]

That speaks eloquently to me about the power of this book—and other such landscapes—to engender such love. While there are many levels to this book, which could be called a treatise on parenting, friendship, and writing, there is always the barn. As I cannot do justice to White's words, this is my favorite passage from the book, which in all its oppositions suggests a kind of utopia where I could reside:

> It was the best place to be, thought Wilbur, this warm delicious cellar, with the garrulous geese, the changing seasons, the heat of the sun, the passage of swallows, the nearness of rats, the sameness of sheep, the love of spiders, the smell of manure, and the glory of everything.

E. B. White's sense of melancholy sentiment here fits my own sensibility better than any other book. Frances Hodgson Burnett believes a bit more in magic than I, and while that book may have been the touchstone of my childhood, White's barnyard world is more who I am now, as I contemplate the place of friends and writers in my life, as I make a litany of the things I really love, including many a spinewy weave.

A peaceable kingdom exists for me in these childhood and children's narratives, which recall and remake origins, where as T. S. Eliot writes, "home is where one starts from." Locales are important to the text of the book and the text of our lives from the density and tactile "feel" of specificity. Writers, whether grounded in the countryside or in the city, resemble the mythical figure of Antaeus, the giant whose strength came from having at least one foot on a specific patch of ground. Good writing, to me, is the ability to imagine fully the place one knows, and my knowledge of the world is surely fuller, richer. Such narratives shape a child's sense of identity, one that is both private and public, a spatial sense of being "home" in the world.

I am left with a sense of how the world inside a book changes the world outside the book, how the text of a book enters the text of a life. And this is where I fold the map, close the guidebook. Annie Dillard begins her book, *An American Childhood,* at a point where I end. She writes:

> When everything else has gone from my brain—the President's name, the state capitals, the neighborhood where I lived, and then my own name and what it was on earth I sought, and then at length the faces of my friends, and finally the faces of my family—when all this has dissolved, what will be left, I believe is topology: the dreaming memory of land as it lay this way and that.[30]

I believe that this dreamy land is the landscape of childhood and a storied literature, lying this way and that, in the thorny paradise about. On that landscape was another text in my paracanon, one annexed from series fiction, and offering a singular education.

TEXT AS ETHIC

When I was thirteen years old, and lived at 43 Lenox Avenue in Ridgewood, New Jersey, I was given a diary called *My Private Life: A Personal Record for the Teen Years*, written by Polly Webster. The author introduced the book by a letter to "Dear Teener," and followed with advice on developmental changes in adolescence, described as "the BIG FOUR sides to your nature": physical, emotional, intellectual, and social. The author encouraged the reader to write about herself and emphasized this line with italics: "*The more you write about yourself the better you will come to understand the teen years of adolescence.*" Unfortunately, I didn't heed that advice very well; the book is only sparsely filled with my musings. For someone who thought of herself at one time as a writer and wrote stories based on Nanny in *Eloise* ("Madame Oushaw" I named her), I gradually lost the connection between the text on the page and the text of my life. However, *My Private Life* documents the dreamy, idealistic self I was at age thirteen and reveals the influence of books like Nancy Drew on a ripe, receptive reader. On the page entitled "Inside You," I wrote on the blank space provided:

> I like to pretend I am "Nancy Drew" girl detective. I have always made up imaginary characters all my life (so far!). I love to make up stories and hope I can write a book. I hate predjudice [*sic*] people and I hope I won't ever be! I hate jokes and tricks at the expense of another person.

As I reread that passage, I see a connection, unconscious at the time, that a literary character like Nancy Drew inspired my imagination, literary ambitions, and an ethical conscience: a certain vulnerability—something needing defense—that I detected in myself and in others. Nancy Drew belonged in the same breath as civil rights and the golden commandment of do-unto-others. In short, I sense a pilgrim progressing the hills and vales of mid-1950s America—an "Everygirl." To understand that form against the landscape, I wish to explore the anatomy of allegory, the genre of mystery, and the feminist relational theories that help to illuminate for me the Nancy Drew I knew.

What literature frames this confluence of mystery and justice, of might and right? The late-fifteenth-century allegory *Everyman* includes characters that could come from such a sharply defined moral universe; the cast includes God, a Messenger, Death, Everyman, Fellowship, Good Deeds, Goods, Knowledge, Beauty, and Strength. Everyman is summoned by Death and finds that no one will go with him except Good Deeds. As a late medieval genre grounded in sermon literature, exempla, romances, and works of spiritual edification, the Morality Play dramatized the battle between the forces of good and evil on the pilgrimage through life to death. Such dramas served as a repository of allegorical instruction to shape the individual to the larger community.

The genre retains a palimpsest role in a contemporary form of mystery, miracle, and morality. Traces of the drama are inscribed under layers and embedded inter-textually. P. D. James, the grande dame of contemporary detective fiction, has described mystery fiction as "a kind of modern morality play." Distinguishing the British detective story from the crime novel, James grounds detection's roots within the larger British literary traditions of pastoral, which affirm the moral norm: "the assumption that we live in an intelligible and benevolent universe; the assumption that law and order, peace and tranquillity are the norm; that crime and violence are the aberration; and that the proper preoccupation of man is to bring order out of chaos."[31] Mystery stories offer a solution, an exorcism of sorts, where the agency is most human, natural.

While some regard *mystery* as a commodious term, with antecedents in the Old Testament as well as in Greek drama, the modern *female* detective story owes its origins largely to the gothic novels and sensational fiction of the late eighteenth and mid-nineteenth century. These predominantly female authors—women such as Maria Edgeworth, Anne Radcliff, Mrs. Henry Wood, and Mary Elizabeth Braddon—aggrandized the narrative possibilities of secrets, sensational crimes, investigation, or, in the words of Jane Tompkins, "sensational designs." These authors held "designs" in the sense of presenting an alternative view of woman-hood, one that idealized woman's social sphere of domesticity and revealed subversive possibilities of female agency. What is revealed is what Maureen Reddy describes as "women's position in society[:] ... the terrifying underbelly of the apparently placid domestic haven idealized by official culture."[32] Elaine Showalter, in *A Literature of Their Own*, argues that the sensationalists spoke the fantasies of their middle-class female readers: "The sensationalists made crime and violence domestic, modern, and suburban; but their secrets were not simply solutions to mysteries and crimes; they were the secrets of women's dislike of their roles as daughters, wives, and mothers."[33] This insight supports Janice Radway's position in *Reading the Romance*, in which she suggests the oppositional reading of romance fiction by its readers. The interpretation is a feminist endeavor, as defined by Nancy Miller: "to articulate a self-consciousness about women's identity both as inherited cultural fact and as a process of social construction" and "to protest against the available fiction of female becoming."[34] The agency of female detec-tive fiction reinforces the notion of power, a force defined by Carolyn Heilbrun as "the ability to take one's place in whatever discourse is essential to action and the right to have one's part matter."[35]

The "mattering" resonates with sea changes in modern epistemology, a new paradigm that seeks meaning apart from universalism and autonomy toward particularity and community. Carol Gilligan's studies of the moral reasoning of women and girls are grounded on a definition of morality in terms of relationships and the value of affiliations, reinforcing the notion that women read the world differently. *In a Different Voice*, the author deconstructs the traditional view of women's moral thinking as too relativistic and thus inferior to the absolutes of male moral principles; she offers instead "an alternative concept of maturity" and a "new perspective" on relationships that expand the moral domain.[36] To Gilligan, selfhood and morality are intimately connected. As opposed to the separate and autonomous selves envisioned by Piaget and Kohlberg, Gilligan proposes the relational self, formed through relationships with others, particularly in the critical years of childhood. The self based on relationship, care, and connection is different from the self considered separate and autonomous.

The self that emerges from Gilligan's vision is a storyteller, not truthteller. Stories imply interpretation and multiple voices rather than facts and evidence. By making the connection between narrative and selfhood, Gilligan suggests that women make sense of their lives by constructing stories about themselves that reveal a moral voice. I find Gilligan's caring voice to be a counterpoint to the ethic of justice, a distinction that contributes a certain context to the act of writing mysteries, the agency of female detectives, and the response of girls reading stories of female detection Carolyn Heilbrun, in her book *Writing a Woman's Life*, writes, "I suspect that female narratives will be found where women exchange stories, where they read and talk collectively of ambitions, and possibilities, and accomplishments."[37] These ambitions, possibilities, and accomplishments are often centered on the business of peacemaking, of righting wrongs, of solving the insolvable: the genre of female mystery fiction and its own particular intimacy—a citizenship—in the reader's moral universe.

What of the discourse of *juvenile* female mystery fiction? To what extent does this genre evoke the intentionality of the morality play? The counter-tradition of women mystery writers who created female protagonists of moral authority? How does this particular feminist literary form, designed for young female readers, represent "sensational designs" that seek to reshape the social order through relational ethics of care and justice? Where does Nancy Drew fit into my own mysterious quest as a young detective in search of clues to the meaning of the small universe on which I dwelled? These are the questions that intrigue me in the recent renaissance of interest in the Nancy Drew fiction series, which mentored my own sense of imagination, creation, and morality. The School of Journalism at the University of Iowa was the catalyst for scholarly interest—and reader response—into Nancy Drew. This conference, held on April 16–18, 1993, demonstrated the multiple literary locales interested in the character and the series. It would be difficult to exaggerate the significance of this event for privileging popular culture and the particular, personal meanings of readers toward the books. Just as Janice Radway's pioneering *Reading the Romance* was instrumental in attracting respectful attention to genre fiction and its readers, so also did this conference—and its subsequent publications, *Rediscovering Nancy Drew* by Carolyn Dyer, Nancy Romalov, and a special issue of the journal, *The Lion and the Unicorn*—inspire a re-vision of Nancy Drew as feminist mentor to many young readers. The surge of critical and popular works that follow examine her persistent and serial appeal, the stereotyping of characters and its implicit ideology, feminist and anti-feminist croppings, enigmatic motifs, and other constructs of our own mysterious identification with this character. Their insights illuminate the power of popular culture in its reflection and construction of culture, including gender and socialization, and inform my sense of a literature that lets the mystery be.

My own peculiar questions arise from an intellectual as well as personal (and gendered) slant of light. I am interested in how Nancy Drew fiction resonates with the way young female readers *read*: the role that mysteries may play in their imaginative landscape, in their moral development, in their necessary life-task of resolving the conflict of good and evil. Nancy Drew as detective heroine exemplifies heroic qualities—often attributed to males—of independence, self-confidence, intelligence, and physical courage. These characteristics come to bear not through her own aggressive ambition to solve the mystery but largely through her heroic efforts for others: in allegorical terms of *Everyman*, her embodiment of "Good Deeds." The contribution of the serial character Nancy Drew to the art of the juvenile mystery is complex, but lies somehow in the emphasis on a character's explanation of a mystery—the great Mystery of life—through her own powerful agency and generous affiliations with others. Cases are solved because Nancy becomes involved in a larger context of individuals whose situations have been adversely affected by the injustice she seeks to redress. Unlike the hard-boiled private investigator or the cerebral Sherlock Holmes, Nancy Drew engages her inquiries as a form of peacemaking. The crime that has been perpetrated has disturbed the balance of the world, at least as it is known in the microcosm of River Heights. Nancy Drew's benevolence toward the circle of victims leads her to unravel the mystery through the providence of Good Deeds, the knight errant of Mid West law and order, with its concomitant rewards and punishments. Nancy Drew is, in the words of one earlier critic, "a gothic girl scout."[38]

Nancy Drew's cultural work—a kind of community service—resonates with the developmental reading roles of the age group of juvenile mystery-series readers. In his study of the psychological and literary development of child readers, Nicholas Tucker characterizes the mid-years of childhood as "the constant tension between their still surviving infantile fantasies and their increasingly accurate perceptions of the demands of reality."[39] Tucker also traces the child's growing sense of natural justice, from an expiatory form of justice to harsh moral judgments to an idea of reciprocity, where the punishment logically fits the offense, and finally toward a more relativistic sense of restitution and reform.[40] J. A. Appleyard in his study of the reading process of fiction, *Becoming a Reader*, describes the school-age child (roughly the ages of 7 to 12) as "the Reader as Hero and Heroine." He views this period as one whereby the child reader "is the central figure of a romance that is constantly being rewritten," as the child's schema of the world expands in romantic ideals, which are unconscious analogues of inner selves. The child's sense of self is being shaped by a new sense of mastery—what Robert Kegan calls "agency" and Erikson calls "industry" or "competence."[41]

Paradoxically, this growing sense of self-possession includes an awareness of having private feelings, a secret life. As Margaret Meek wisely observes: "Reading is an anti-social activity for most eleven-year olds."[42] Reading assumes aspects of identity, in the image of a hero or heroine who, as an archetype, satisfies the need of the child reader to be, in Appleyard's words, "the central figure who by competence and initiative can solve the problems of a disordered world."[43] That the Nancy Drew series and *The Secret Garden* were my classics, the inspiration of my imagination, suggests the deep resonance of revelation for prepubescent readers. In a world of encroaching doubt and danger, the Nancy Drew novels offer some reassurance that all will be well, and that I, as a young female reader, will play a part in that brave new world.

The formulaic adventures of Nancy Drew appeal by their consistent and concrete enactment of the defeat of evil by good. Cognitively and affectively, the child is testing whether the world is a place to be trusted, to be the arena of growing competence and deliverance against threatening forces of evil. Northrop Frye reminds us that romance—the backbone of adventure fiction—is the nearest of all literary forms to the wish-fulfillment dream. Romance is, to Frye, "the search of the libido or desiring self for a fulfillment that will deliver it from the anxieties of reality but will still contain that reality."[44] Romance suits the way the child reader wishes to see the world: a landscape of larger-than-life figures who embody the mythic representations of human life. Happy endings are assured as Right battles Might, as the youthful protagonist rebounds from knocks and restores rightful order. As a young female reader, the endings of the mysteries resonate with what seems fit. While boys often construct story endings that stage confrontation and conquest, girls often seek alliance and mediation.[45] To Alison Lurie, the fictional works that re-create this balance, referring to Nancy Drew among others, are "the sacred texts of childhood, whose authors have not forgotten what it was like to be a child. To read then was to feel a shock of recognition, a rush of liberating energy."[46] Nancy's resolutions help to restore a stable and harmonious family.

An examination of Nancy Drew's heroics reveals some of this energy and self-knowledge. Titian-haired Nancy with her blue roadster is empowered to do things that matter, that remedy wrongs, that exemplify the idealism of youth. In the very first book of the series, *The Secret of the Old Clock*, on the very first page, Nancy performs one of her rescues of the innocent that characterize her adventures. She saves Judy, a little girl who has toppled over a bridge into the water below, due to the erratic speed of a moving van, which, we learn, contains some goods stolen from her house. Judy is the ward of the Turner sisters, who struggle with modest means to raise the rather wayward child. Nancy's overture introduces her to the larger mystery involving the estate of Josiah Crowley, an eccentric who befriended many needy relatives and presumably provided for them in his will. Alas, that will is missing, and the only extant one benefits one avaricious side of the family. In seeking to uncover the missing document, Nancy becomes involved in the lives of the Crowley family and, in her own way, brings justice and prosperity to those who were wronged.

This first book establishes the moral geography of Nancy Drew mysteries and its tutelage. Vice and virtue are articulated through Nancy's engagement in the misfortunes of others, which she seeks to ameliorate. The resolution of the mystery is possible through Nancy's heightened charge toward good deeds and engagement with place, a social-moral landscape that involves the reader emotionally. The settings are romanticized, with the pastoral the most privileged. In the first book, *The Secret of the Old Clock*, the author imbues the countryside with moral value:

> Selecting a recently constructed highway, Nancy rode along, glancing occasionally at the newly planted fields on either side. Beyond were rolling hills. "Pretty," she commented to herself. "Oh, why can't all people be nice like this scenery and not make trouble?"

Such rapture can be disturbed by the wilds, the vagaries of the weather. Just pages later from the previous passage, the wilderness breaks through the pastoral kingdom—nature managed and mild:

> About halfway to River Heights, while enjoying the pastoral scenes of cows standing knee-high in shallow sections of the stream, and sheep grazing on flower-dotted hillsides, Nancy suddenly realized the sun had been blotted out. Vivid forked lightning streaked across the sky. It was followed by an earth-shaking clap of thunder. The rain came down harder.[47]

The peaceable kingdom can be threatened by the perils of the unknown, creating a wilderness, as ominous as the Dark Forest of the Grimm tales. In other Drew adventures, a sudden storm disrupts a boating outing, a dangerous cloudburst disturbs the peace on an Arizona ranch, and dense vegetation cloaks the enemy. While cities are suspect, some with more historic resonance, such as the Old South of New Orleans and Richmond, are favored. The settings in the series must be congenial to heroic activity from a redolent past or in their own present natural—but tamed—environment.

Nancy Drew's heroics are shaped by moral geography as well as gender, particularly the fate of women and children, often replete with pastoral. In *The Clue on the Crumbling Wall*, Nancy assists an eight-year-old girl and her mother who live in a dilapidated neighborhood but with a yard "a mass of colorful flowers, . . . and vines half-covered the unpainted, weatherbeaten porch."[48] In *The Bungalow Mystery*, Nancy rescues her friend Helen at the beginning of the story when their boat is rammed by a log, towing her to the shore in turbulent waters. From this adventure she meets Laura, a penniless girl who has been robbed of jewelry and securities. At one point Nancy almost shies from the challenge. Finding a trap door in the cellar of the bungalow, she contemplates retreat from the danger ahead, "but the fear that some person was in distress gave her the courage to open the trap door."[49] In *The Clue in the Diary*, Nancy rescues the inhabitants of a burning house, takes five-year-old Holly Swenson under her wing, and stocks Mrs. Swenson's empty pantry with food, among other good deeds, which serendipitously lead her closer to the resolution of a mysterious code. In *The Mystery of the Ivory Charm*, Nancy befriends a small boy from India who has escaped from a cruel circus-master, only to then become the possessor of a trinket that embodies further mysteries that follow. In *The Sign of the Twisted Candles*, her cohort George exclaims: "You are always putting yourself out to do a kindness for somebody or other who simply doesn't count in your life at all."[50]

But the young reader knows otherwise. This largesse is the driving force of Drew's energy, the evidential signs of her competence, the marks that matter. The recipients of her benevolence are often women—female prey, hapless victims—much like ourselves. Her ethical sense is quickened by threats to the tokens and tropes of security: material objects that represent a requisite status for survival. Lost heirlooms and relics, the inheritances of poor orphans and spinster sisters, a struggling hostelry, an infamous mantel clock. To the school-age reader, particularly female, Nancy's Drew's heroics provide the construct, the schema of possible change—individually and corporately. They form the backbone of character as well as the essence of adventure as defined by the struggle toward the familiar and recognizable good. Drew's formulaic fiction confirms for the child facing diverse new experiences that a pattern already exists in learning one's way in the adult world. Child readers find solace from the repetition of what Todorov calls the basic structure of childhood narratives: equilibrim/disequilibrim/equilibrim-restored.[51] The reader intuits that this progression occurs in the romance of action (rather than earlier fantasy landscapes) peopled by protagonists, like Nancy Drew, with right traits and right tasks. In her particular strand of moral crusading—her weave of mystery, mayhem, and moral outrage—Nancy is, in the Yiddish words of one editor, "a *mensch*."[52]. We as readers are comforted by such company.

And in the larger company of a series—a succession of books with ritualistic plots and resurgent characters—a young reader knows the enjoyment of books possessed. "My book and heart shall never part," instructs the old *New England Primer*, suggesting the gift nature of literature. Favorite books—selected, savored, preserved—reflect more than commodity choices; they are magical and mysterious in their own right and meaning. Since most young readers, such as myself, found these books apart from libraries, received them from the self-accumulating littleness of allowance, and enjoyed the pleasure of their perpetuity on our shelves, they became relational objects, transitional objects that mark our own passages, that linger in our storied rooms. Series books are property, dearly bought. While my own Nancy Drew collection is dispersed, I remember the spacious act of collecting, where there is always room for one more, and the search is always on. When what is collected is a story, it matters even more in the formation of our own sense of mission, in the story we make of the story of our life. Through this fabulous landscape of stories, readers give themselves what Margaret Meek calls "private lesson."[53] We learn these lessons by texts sweetly devoured. Nancy was my alter ego, a kind of sage older sister, book-smart and street-smart, and very much the missionary (however chair-bound) I yearned to be. I wove Nancy Drew into my Calvinist teachings of original sin and sacrifice, into my middle-class virtues of altruism toward the underprivileged. I learned her lessons well in terms of social work, cultural work, heroics.

What are some of those lessons? In abstract terms, I envision a benign, ever-mysterious universe, governed by a moral code and relational ethic, providing premature certainties for the most optimistic projections of the self in the imagination. In more impish words, this translates to an immense "Yes": I could be Nancy Drew, girl detective, and I could be a writer. Both partake of mystery, of great adventure, of a certain virtue. What is projected is indeed "a sensational design," a vision of that probable flame of hope for order, of the understanding of the self that comes from language. Nancy Drew's serial fiction as essence of heroic possibilities glints around us, then and now, brilliant shards. Nancy Drew's tales offer the adventure and resolution that a lived life often denies a young reader, seeking something in books, rounded and right. The derring-do of Nancy Drew is my looking-glass. Up close, I see another beloved book offering other mysteries. I pretend to be Nancy Drew, Girl Detective, in search of secret gardens.

TEXT AS MYTH

"A book of the new century," so heralds Ann Thwaite in her admirable biography of Frances Hodgson Burnett, *Waiting for the Party*.[54] Indeed, *The Secret Garden* represents, to many converts, a classic full of significance and sentiment, with mythic roots connecting the generations, celebrating creativity and healing, both young and old. England and America each wish to claim the book as its own. An exploration of the critical and commercial reception of the book and its multiple adaptations give evidence to the power of the text as cultural work. Jane Tompkins in her work *Sensational Designs: The Cultural Work of American Fiction, 1790–1860* suggests that certain popular novels resonate with the contemporary cultural discourse: "providing society with a means of thinking about itself, defining certain aspects of a social reality which the authors and their readers shared."[55] A literary text can do this kind of cultural work of reflecting and constructing the world about in a way that matters so deeply that its effects are represented in myriad re-visions.

The Secret Garden's agency in achieving these ends is demonstrated in the ways that people received and revived the text over nearly a century. While the whole story of the history of this one work will encompass a longer exploration, I hope to place the book within its cultural context: the response of reviewers and critics at the book's publication; obituaries of Burnett; new editions of the book; references to the work by other writers remembering childhood reading; literary criticism; and media adaptations. This study is part of a larger project by which I am exploring the classics as a social critique. Writing on *The Secret Garden* is a labor of love, for the book is the fertile ground of my being as writer and gardener of sorts.

A work's reception both reflects and constructs its literary locale. Reception study is a modern approach to literary history that examines the ways in which literary works are received by readers. Related to reader-response criticism, reception theory shares an interest in the relationship between the literary text and its reader. Reception study is distinguished by its greater concern with historical changes affecting the reading public rather than the solitary reader. Literary meaning shifts over time through a series of readings constituting its history of influence. Historicizing the context to a book's reception provides the opportunity to see texts in a different light. *The Secret Garden* reveals its secrets discretely to the audience listening.

The Secret Garden's reception was shaped by its first appearance in serial form in an adult literary magazine. That the book first appeared as a serial was not uncommon at the time; periodicals were often the first format for literary works, and their serial structure influenced how the story emerged, particularly a mystery. *Fauntleroy* first appeared in *St. Nicholas*, that esteemed children's magazine. The difference here is that this text appeared in a mainstream adult journal, the *American Magazine*, the year before book publication. The public perceived the text as adult fiction, likewise its promotion. Advance notice of the book appeared in *Publishers Weekly*, August 12, 1911, announcing in a full page illustrated ad the book's arrival on August 25 and featuring a picture cover by Maria L. Kirk, an illustrator popular with the publisher. The ad read: "Has the tenderness and charm of 'Little Lord Fauntleroy,' the imagination and power of 'The Dawn of Tomorrow,' and the dramatic suspense of 'The Shuttle.' All the qualities which have made Mrs. Burnett the most beloved American storyteller are here, intensified and enriched."[56] Note the emphasis on Burnett as a fiction writer with related titles of recent adult works. This book was marketed as an adult book and was received as such, with some overlap as a juvenile. The first edition must have sold readily as the same magazine featured an ad less than a month later announcing "2nd Large Edition—25,000 Copies" and quoting a blurb from the *Minneapolis Journal* praising Burnett as "a writer of optimistic fiction."[57] An October ad predicted the book to be the most popular of the season and listed the reasons why: "It appeals to both young and old. It combines the qualities of her best works. It is full of optimism, health and joy."[58] While the prediction may have been awry, the rationale was convincing as to its resonant reception: ageless appeal, connection to previous work, and hopeful, healthy theme.

The book was immediately, warmly received by the press. I have read that the book received a lukewarm reception, but my research reveals a hearty initial response, tempered by the text's overshadowing predecessor, *Little Lord Fauntleroy*. The presence of this blockbuster of 1886 dwarfed other works by the author, who was endlessly both blessed and cursed by her *Fauntleroy* fame. *Secret Garden* struggled to assert its own identity as a different kind of story, which spoke to both the romanticism and modernism of a new century. Burnett inscribed in the text some of the popular philosophy of the age, the power of positive thinking, the therapeutic message of health and healing in language and forms that spoke to adults in particular. These ideas found expression in a favorite and familiar subject for Burnett: gardening. While taking up gardening in her new Long Island estate, she recalled the makeover of an abandoned orchard into a rose garden in Kent and an earlier childhood incarnation of an abandoned garden in Manchester, which in her mind's eye was transformed from squalor to splendor. Her first book as a child was *The Little Flower Book*, in which each letter of the alphabet was illustrated with flowers that grew into a garden before her eyes. She also may have been familiar with an earlier garden restoration story published a decade before, *Elizabeth and Her German Garden*, a popular book whose central figure and author was Elizabeth van Arnim, an Australian-born writer who had been raised in England and married a German count. In this book, the character discovers a large neglected garden on her husband's country estate and begins its restoration. Burnett, transplanted to America, recalls her own childhood reverie with green places magically transformed.

While the critics did not connect intertextually with van Arnim, they instinctively did connect to her other writings for adults and children. Her success in both realms and in several genres made her a true crossover author, long before that term circulated. Impressively, the critics did not seem to have Burnett categorized as one type of author with a certain audience in mind. Reviews also suggest that adult readers found pleasure in books on childhood experience, which is not assumed today. The earliest review, in the *Literary Digest* of September 2, 1911, announced its arrival with a sense of eager anticipation. Relating the book to her earlier works, "Glad" and "The Dawn of Tomorrow," the critic lauded its similar "allurement of mystery, the fascination of child-life, and the joyous and sane philosophy of life." Susan Sowerby, Dickon, and Ben Weatherstaff are mentioned glowingly and even the "robin."[59] The *New York Times,* which wrote a lengthy review a day later entitled "What was Hid in a Garden," appreciated the book's dual appeal and the author's rare talent in attracting young people and "their elders who love young things, for whom literary craftsmanship is a source of enjoyment and a quiet, beautiful tale."[60] Next, The *Independent* characterized the author as someone able to speak to children, as in "Fauntleroy" and "Sarah Crewe." While a worthy successor, this book may not appeal as much to more sophisticated readers, who might notice similar themes in her recent play, "The Dawn of a Tomorrow." The book's charm seemed to lie in its "fresh-air gospel" and garden imagery, which might inspire a similar project of one's own, though "the transformation it may work will be less startling."[61] *Outlook* wrote a lengthy summary of the plot and mentioned in particular the "agency of the garden" and the "innocent conspiracy" as factors leading to "an exposition of nature-cure and mental healing." Despite the "unnecessary mysticism" at the end of the story and the "little holding forth by the ex-hysteric," the book was simple, natural, undidactic in its "out-of-door spirit" and poetic tone.[62] The *Nation* mentioned characters' names, the three children, and Mrs. Sowerby and approved of the charming story, with its absence of two objectionable qualities: "the children's faults are not such as to invite imitation; and the young are not reformers of the old."[63] R. A. Whay in the *Bookman* (New York) found it to be a difficult book to review because it was hard to tell who was the leading character and whose story it really was. Relating the various possible heroes or heroines, the other possibility might be the moor itself. After summarizing the story as romance, the critic astutely noted, "*The Secret Garden* is more than a mere story for children; underlying it there is a deep vein of symbolism."[64] The *American Monthly Magazine* found the book to be a worthy if not superior successor to *Little Lord Fauntleroy* in its lack of sentimentality and piety and its appeal to "those grown-up people who love children and out-of-door pleasures, the open moor, and flowers, and sweet scented mystic 'secret gardens.'"[65] The *Dial* mentioned the book in an article appraising the best of the season's juvenile offerings as one among the many "to be accounted permanent."[66]

The book was selected as one of the best of the season in holiday reviews. *The New York Times* published "One Hundred Christmas Books," which included *The Secret Garden* among its regular holiday fare, stating that the book "is so very near to the common lot of humanity that its readers cannot be defined by age, class, or literary taste."[67] One of its picks of the fifty best books of the season, the *Literary Digest* applauded its broad appeal—"I like to believe that every one will get hold of this tale"—and mentions by name the hero, Dickon.[68] The book sold briskly that season, according to monthly reports in *Bookman*, where it was seen in the top six best-selling category for Fiction and occasionally for Juveniles in Boston, Minneapolis, Baltimore, Cleveland, Albany, Washington, D.C., and Providence.

The British press were more sparing in coverage but ardent. The book appeared in October 1911 by Heinemann with illustrations by the distinguished Charles Robinson, aesthetic illustrator of classics. The edition includes a prefatory ad for her earlier adult fiction, *The Shuttle,* with effusive blurbs from six British papers. Recalling the book's earlier serial appearance, the critic Katherine Tynan in the *Bookman* (London) raved: "It is a *hortus inclusus* of a book—a very fragrant book, sweet with the sweets of the Hidden Garden, and with certain other flowers that grow in the soil of the human heart." The author is commended for applying her talents to writing stories for children; the illustrator, Charles Robinson, is cited for his imaging Mary at her various stages of growth. Noting its touch "of the grown-up heart and experience," the book belongs "as much to general literature as to the literature of the schoolroom ... from seven to seventy-seven."[69] The *Athenaeum* reviewed it as a new adult novel with "graceful descriptive writing," a distinctive Yorkshire dialect, and eight illustrations by Charles Robinson.[70] The *Canadian Magazine's* review focused on the crippled boy finding healing "through the most tender and faithful of teachers," presumably either Mary or Mother Nature herself. Appreciating the author's sensitivity for youth, the critic found there to be little plot or narrative but, instead, a lesson of gentle suggestion.[71]

The only negative review I found was by *Booklist*, the reviewing journal of the American Library Association. Covered under the section "Fiction," the reviewer wrote: "The hours spent in rescuing the 'secret garden' from a state of wildness are the means of redeeming the lives of two lonely, selfish English children. A 'new-thought' story, over-sentimental and dealing almost wholly with abnormal people. The moral is obvious but sensible, and both it and the character of the story will appeal to many women and young girls."[72] While the review is idiosyncratic (might I say "abnormal"), it is unique among the reviews I uncovered. The book was a credible success for a season and then languished in obscurity.

Burnett's obituaries in 1924 reveal that *The Secret Garden* was indeed dormant. Commentators aligned Burnett fondly with *Fauntleroy* and added, in the London *Times*: "In her other books and plays Mrs. Burnett was less successfully Dickensian, sentimental, naive."[73] *The New York Times* had three pieces about her. The first was a lengthy review that heralded *Fauntleroy* but omitted any mention of other children's books. The second was a letter to the editor from a friend who extolled her love of gardens, mentioning *The Secret Garden* as a corner of her rose garden at Maytham Hall, Kent. The third, entitled "Fauntleroy," placed this character among "the gallery of immortal children" and made a mistaken reference to "The Secret Orchard" in passing.[74] A long memorial tribute in *St. Nicholas* mentioned several of her juveniles and fiction, without referring at all to *The Secret Garden*.[75] In a tribute titled "A Portrayer of Lovable Children," the *Outlook* mentioned the title as possessing "a singular outdoor charm mingled with much that was mystical."[76] With Burnett's death, the book now considered her masterpiece seemed to have passed as well.

The Secret Garden's revival was a slow fruition. That new generations found the text is evident from references in the literature, despite the lack of interest by some important figures in the library field. The selection bible, the *Children's Catalog*, only began listing *The Secret Garden* as a recommended title in the fourth edition (1930) and only as a secondary title under *Fauntleroy*, which remained the leading title until 1951. The book was absent from the influential *Book Shelf for Boys and Girls*, edited by Clara Hunt from 1918 to 1931; this guide influenced Bertha Mahony who drew upon it to compile the collection for her children's bookstore and for the *Horn Book* magazine, which followed. Mahony did mention the book in her massive tome, *Realms of Gold* (1929), under the category "Home and School Pleasures," with the annotation: "The story of how health and friendships came to a little sick boy in a 'secret' garden."[77] Why such neglect from librarians, who presumably would appreciate such a popular book with children? Where was the strong adult following that the book initially attracted? Louise Seaman Bechtel, the pioneer children's book editor for Macmillan and a mover and shaker in the field, dismissed the book in various speeches published in her work, *Books in Search of Children*, as "sub-literature," and grouped the book with other landmarks "not necessarily a rightful inheritance, however popular."[78] Referring to the results of a 1926 "favorite books" survey in the popular family magazine, *Youth's Companion*, in which *The Secret Garden* ranked twelfth, she bemoaned "the frank indifference to literary quality, the lack of fairy tales, and the conservative staying appeal of the misnamed 'children's classics.'"[79] In an essay on what constitutes a classic, the editor listed the book as one among others unnecessary today as "strange survivals."[80] Another influential figure, *the* Anne Carroll Moore, gave modest mention of the book on one of her recommended lists on "Books for Middle-Aged Children," reprinted in her collection, *My Roads to Childhood:* "One of the first of a new order of mystery stories appealing to girls on the edge of the teens. Its setting is a very lovely garden in Yorkshire. Written many years later than the *Little Princess*, its characters are less distinct. One remembers the garden better than the boy and girl characters. Mrs. Burnett was a lover of gardens."[81] In the first survey of American children's literature, Cornelia Meigs's *A Critical History of Children's Literature*, Elizabeth Nesbitt, notable children's librarian and educator from Pittsburgh, included the book in a discussion of the years of 1890 to 1920, a period she calls "Romance and Actuality," in which she finds in *The Secret Garden* the "combination of the old and the new." Amid the highly romanticized setting is a real problem rarely discussed by writers for children: "It is the conversion into mental and physical health by two children … accomplished by a combination of self-development, the healing qualities of the outdoors and the self-forgetting love of growing things and, of all things, the principles of mental healing." While "over simplified and idealized," the book's thesis remains that "a happy and normal child must care for something and must be cared for."[82] Frances Clarke Sayers, Anne Carroll Moore's successor at New York Public, mentioned the book in her collection of essays and speeches, *Summoned by Books*. Recalling an inveterate young reader of nine or ten years old in a school library Sayers visited, the author was struck by this overheard conversation: "Have you read *The Secret Garden?* she asked, not waiting for a reply, and stroking the back of the book as if she were petting a kitten."[83] This anecdotal evidence illustrates the power of one book being passed to another, without benefit of institutional acclaim or selective tradition.

While the book may have received faint public praise among librarians, it has long garnered acclaim through the tributes of writers recalling their childhood reading. Lois Lowry, Katherine Paterson, Philippa Pearce, Joan Bodger, Jean Little, among others. Another kind of writer has been instrumental in preserving the work's longevity: literary historians and critics. The first to take notice were the British, who tended to claim Burnett as their own, despite her American naturalization in 1905. Before literary criticism existed on children's literature to champion the cause, a lone literary study appeared in 1950: Marghanita Laski's *Mrs. Ewing, Mrs. Molesworth, and Mrs. Hodgson Burnett*. This slender book by a British critic elevated *The Secret Garden* to preeminent status as Burnett's major contribution to children's literature. Laski astutely perceived the metaphorical significance of an introspective, unhappy child figure learning how to cope by cultivating a garden. She, like many other readers then and now, appreciated finding themselves in such an empathetic, comforting work, for which Burnett deserves to be richly remembered: "This is a book for introspective town children. I was such a child myself, and it is therefore the most satisfying children's book I know."[84] The fact that this opinion was somewhat heretical is suggested by a reviewer from *The Saturday Review* who dismissed her literary judgment with this comment: "The test of worth for children's books—Alice and Huck pass such a test—is whether they can be reread by adults. None of the books by the three ladies can. As for Mrs. Hodgson Burnett—how many squirming, sweating boys in velvet pants and lace collars have cursed the creator of Little Fauntleroy!"[85]

Nothing as eloquent as Laski's work on Burnett appeared for over a decade. Following Laski's lead, British readers and critics seemed more receptive. The London *Times* in 1960 organized an exhibition "The One Hundred Best Books for Children," which included the book as its last item due to the overwhelming voice of readers.[86] While Marcus Crouch in *Treasure Seekers and Borrowers* dismissed the book as a period piece in his 1962 history, John Rowe Townsend praised its "powerful effect on children's imaginations" with its feeling for growth and longing for achievement; Roger Lancelyn Green in *Tellers of Tales* and in *Only Connect* affirmed the book's "great individuality and astonishing staying power."[87] And the list goes on of articulate British champions of the book, with the exception of Humphrey Carpenter who borrows the title for his own study of the Golden Age, but begrudges her space in the echelon. Of particular note is the commentary by Fred Inglis in his study of the social values of children's literature, *The Promise of Happiness*, which weaves *The Secret Garden* into his central theme of the radical innocence of the youth and the novelist's vision for the future: "our faith that our children will have a future."[88] To Inglis, the book frames powerful feelings on childhood and England: the secret garden of childhood and of England, a metonymy that shapes cultural ways of thinking and feeling. Ann Thwaite's 1974 biography of Burnett, *Waiting for the Party*, published fifty years after Burnett's death, established Burnett as a major writer and *The Secret Garden* as her most loved book, which enjoyed classic status with young readers as "a living story."[89]

The American critical response to *The Secret Garden* has grown along with the scholarly discipline of children's literature, a phenomenon of the last quarter century. The major scholarly journals in the field—*Children's Literature Association Quarterly, Children's Literature, The Lion and the Unicorn, Children's Literature in Education, Signal*—all hold weighty responses to the work, which resonated with burgeoning feminist consciousness. In 1986, the year the book entered the public domain, Faith McNulty, children's book editor of the *New Yorker,* wrote her own homage and exclaims: "There is hardly a literate female alive who hasn't read and loved it."[90] The list of who has written on the book's generative themes is stellar, including several of our speakers, but the key player in this country is surely Phyllis Bixler, whose literary studies of Burnett and numerous articles, beginning in 1978, have quickened interest in the breadth of Burnett's contributions. Bixler's 1984 critical appraisal of Burnett and her 1996 study of *The Secret Garden* for

Twayne's Masterwork series places the book within the author's body of work and critical and commercial reception. Works like Ann Thwaite's biography, Phyllis Bixler's criticism, and numerous scholarly articles have elevated *The Secret Garden* to academic significance as well as its sentimental stature as beloved text. Literary scholarship has christened *The Secret Garden* as a classic much as have the small hands passing the book along.

The book's bonding to our culture is witnessed as well by its many editions and adaptations, bespeaking its commercial viability and adaptability. *The Secret Garden* I read as a child was the 1949 Lippincott edition illustrated by Nora S. Unwin, which surely charmed me if not Anne Carroll Moore, who expressed displeasure with all that color. In her column "The Three Owls' Notebook" in the *Horn Book*, Moore wrote that the book "remains deservedly popular, for Mrs. Burnett's story is still a good story and might well have been accompanied by fewer pictures reflecting more of its essential atmosphere."[91] The trend toward more illustration was effected through Tasha Tudor's 1962 illustrated edition by Harper & Row. When the book entered public domain in 1986, new editions and adaptations began to emerge, some abridged or transformed into audio books or picture books, illustrated by Graham Rust, Michael Hague, Thomas B. Allen; some adapted to the theater or film, once again. The movie of *The Secret Garden* first appeared in 1949 for Metro-Goldwyn-Mayer, in 1975 for BBC-TV, in 1987 for Viacom TV, and in 1993 for Warner Brothers. The book was adapted to the stage in 1990, with the production winning many top awards of the season. A cataloging search in WorldCat indicates 281 different published editions, 70 sound recordings, and 35 visual materials (VHS and DVD versions). The text's openness to interpretation and invention speaks to its currency and commerce in the culture.

The Secret Garden was indeed a book for the new century, but which century? The book seems poised to play this inaugural role again. Despite the resistance of librarians toward popular reading or the shadow of *Fauntleroy*, the book found its reader, hand upon hand, all ages. The readers led the way that the critics later followed, as academics mapped their own extenuated landscapes of reading. While I like to think how the book early on found so many avid readers, that it appeared at a time when such a book would find a dual audience, I am pleased that adults and children might discover the book today in one of its manifestations. I have no doubt that this is a text rich enough to romance a reader still seeking what is on the other side of the wall, what is the magic beneath the surface. The mythic imagery of a restored garden, of something submerged awaiting discovery, of the secrets we bear, of the mysteries about, all speak to the larger revelations this text offers. The world dwells in Possibility, life-changing, this book promises.

The Secret Garden is a personal as well as a public myth with sensational designs. We walk on fertile ground, those of us who read, write, and revere the literature of childhood. The field of children's literature is a secret garden. To some, it is but a discarded childhood of simple lore, a playground of stories. For those who dare to be the child in the book again, wonders open wide, a garden of Eden. Reading is that secret garden, a sense of place, a social order. Frances Hodgson Burnett left a legacy that we continue to claim as we come close to secret gardens and kneel to kiss the earth.

This felicitous reading—my own paracanon—is the native land of a singular journey as reader, librarian, and scholar. Here, as Wordsworth says, is the world where alone we find our happiness or not at all. The classics for me are the works that somehow persist, that propel me into literary careers, that stir yearnings for outreach, that quicken my conscience for those whose own affair with language has been threadbare. I embrace through these classics not answers—which they are promised to bring—but an infinite set of questions that mark a spacious country. Through their mappings, I relate to a community of readers who know how a text of a book can enter the text of a life. From library history to literary arts, from reception to romance, through all the clouds of witness, I know a secret garden, beside, beneath, and beyond library walls and ivory towers.

Epilogue

"Only connect! Only connect the prose and the passions, *And both will be exalted. . . . Live in fragments no longer!*"
— E. M. Forster, *Howards End*

In *Charlotte's Web*, E. B. White—gentle satirist of the human condition—tells us something about our uses of language in the web Charlotte weaves. To save pig Wilbur's life, Charlotte the spider spins a web over his head with certain words, chosen from the dump by the rat Templeton: "SOME PIG," "TERRIFIC," "RADIANT," "HUMBLE." This absurd laudation succeeds in saving Wilbur's life and suggests the machinations—and miracles—of language. How easily people can be fooled, Charlotte muses, as she notes how gullible people really are: "not as smart as a bug." I read this memorable scene as a wry comment on our credulity with print and conceit with prize: the power of the select words we weave over certain books, such as "GREAT," "BEST," "CLASSIC," "TOUCH-STONE."[1] White suggests such appropriation of language for our own purposes does not transform the object viewed—still a plain old pig—but instead the viewer of the object who envisions a different creation.[1]

That is my "slant of truth" on the canon we have built of children's literature in the twentieth century. Caroline Hewins's guidebook, Anne Carroll Moore's booklists and book columns, Anne Jordan's definitive *Classics*, children's literature anthologies and curriculum, and the Children's Literature Association's *Touchstones* are all efforts to transform children's books into something else—from "book" to "literature"—through valorization of classics. Both groups invested in the faith that evaluating children's books with the same standards as adult books would position them within their institutions and the larger culture. The process of making distinctions inevitably reflects on the institution and its practitioners, who all shine in the reflection of the medal. Choosing greatness must convey greatness, where both awardee and awarder share the prize. What *is* the prize? I believe it is cultural positioning, cultural validation. It's a game where we don't know the rules, or they keep changing. The problem is much more profound

141

than professional pride; the problem is a cultural perception that literature matters more than the child reader in the grand scheme of things. These messages are also unspoken, which adds a dense cover over attempts at communication. Establishing yourself as a critic in a field under-read and unsung is quite a feat. Could it be that writers who write about writing—critics—are somehow diminished by their close brush with creativity, the "*about*" rather than the "*is*"? If critics are themselves writers, what else is needed for cultural authority?

"A fervent relation with the world" is John Updike's rejoinder, his standard for criticism as a high-minded, impassioned pursuit. Children's librarians surely possessed that spirit in their evangelistic fervor in bringing the best books to children. They clearly possessed a vision of a world made better by better books. Anne Carroll Moore's emblem of the three owls, with the critic co-equal with author and artist, is gloriously triumphant. But how equal *is* the critic? How does criticism function as cultural work? Updike characterizes writing literary criticism as "hugging the shore," as contrast to writing fiction and poetry as sailing in the blue yonder. Hugging the shore has its institutional rewards but lacks the intensity of the true sport. As Updike writes: "Hugging the shore, one can always come about and draw even closer to the land with another nine-point quotation."[2] The shore-bound librarian and scholar live a humble existence—like a certain pig we know—as part of the dynamics of a system larger and more imposing. These two professions breathe the same air, part of the veil of ideology too. In acts of valorization, they construct themselves as professionals grounded in tradition with its own rewards. Constructing a canon is a culture-based political act of making literary pasts, of decontextualizing literary works, a process that, validated by the institution, naturalizes its definitions of what literature is—and what they do. As a professional in a validating institution, librarians and scholars claim territory by bestowing honorific authority in an ideology of reading "the best books." I do suspect that as a culture we make a "muchness" of things being minimalized in a disappearing childhood. Perhaps children's literature needs to be canonized when it is slipping away from us.

All in all, I wonder about the anxiety that underlies canon formation. I question the act of canonization, so steeped in privileging class, race, gender, and age, the Other. Inherent is a cultural debate on how to read and what to read: a troubling question for a democratic and free society. I believe that we need to tread lightly on the unstable ground of distinctions, particularly of "value," that heavily laden word with economic resonance. Even "touchstone" refers to a process of testing pure gold or silver: to ready for the marketplace. Jack Zipes's voice is a clarion call to sense our role in the culture industry so much a player in this profession of literature.[3]

The evolution of the word "books" to "literature" reveals the increasing sacralization of discourse on reading for children. For a good long time, "children's books" seemed like a suitable phrase to describe the genre. Even Darton's 1938 landmark history uses the simple title of *Children's Books in England* (with that subtle subtitle: "Five Centuries of Social Life"). I find no mention of "children's literature" in any of the early decades of the *Horn Book* (1924–). Somehow the word changed, grew up from "books" to "literature," somewhere in the 1950s, with the publication in 1953 of two key texts proclaiming literary status: Meigs's *Critical History of American Children's Literature* and Lillian Smith's *The Unreluctant Years: A Critical Approach to Children's Literature*. Both texts highlight the genre as part of literature, although the more common term "books" appears sporadically throughout both. Meigs's text is advertised in a full-page ad in the *Horn Book* proclaiming its rightful heritage as literature; the book itself includes an introduction by Henry Steele Commanger, whose first line proclaims: "Here is something new, a history of children's literature."[4] Smith's *Unreluctant Years: A Critical Approach to Children's Literature* (1953) takes the high ground from the start, not only in the title but also in the foreword where she states: "The aim of this book is to consider children's books as literature, and to discover some of the standards by which they can be so judged."[5] In 1962, the title of the new specialist in the field for the Library of Congress is alternately called "Specialist for Children's Literature" and "Specialist for Children's Books" by the *Horn Book* of that year, with "literature" appearing in the index and "books" appearing in the news report.

I submit that this confusion over titles is critical to the positioning of children's literature—by librarians, by scholars. It was the children's librarians who crusaded for children's books as literature, who established the standard of evaluating the literature with the same standards, a legacy inherited by the academy. Matriarchs were reared on the lofty language of a Horace Scudder. Hear his definition of this "distinct and new form": "as literature in which conceptions of childhood are embodied, and as literature which feeds and stimulates the imagination of children."[6] Literature *about* childhood and yet *in* childhood as imaginative possibility—no wonder the appeal and the ambiguity. Heightened attention to language is integral to cultural validation, ironically even in debating its status as a commodity in the marketplace, where it is indeed a "book." I am wary now with terminology, sensitive to the way I pronounce the "Literature" of "Children's Literature" in hushed tones. Raymond Williams, in defining "literature," speaks of its evolution from meaning polite learning and general literacy to its modern connotations of a rarefied past rather than an active contemporary writing; the Romantics privileged the term as imaginative writing, which the librarians would have surely appreciated.[7] Librarians established the foregrounding of children's books as a rich shared culture of the Golden Age.

This is my understanding of the confluence of librarians and scholars in the construction of the literature. Children's librarians were, first and foremost, pioneer women in the professions. In *A Room of One's Own*, celebrating the value of a women's literary tradition, Virginia Woolf exhorts women writers to "think back through their mothers." The matriarchs of children's literature are the writers, teachers, artists, librarians, publishers who left their mark on us. These women entered a field that was open to them because it was assumed they could take care of children and so, go, *do*. Bring the right book to the right child at the right time. Librarians had more agency than academics in shaping discourse on the "best books"; they were there first, were considered authorities, and were allowed freedom to develop any way they wished. And they had a *place,* a powerful public sphere from which they could create a series of sites: newspapers and periodicals, book publishing, professional associations, and, above all, lists of best books, their professional calling.

Librarians chose "critic" as their role more than teacher of reading or child development expert: literature over literacy. The paradigm chosen was less child-centered than book-centered, although these priorities shifted. They were clearly child-focused in a literary, romanticized shepherding of children to books. This course determined their direction for a half of a century, when they began to lose momentum in the 1960s with challenges to their cultural authority. Investing cultural authority in the position of critic can be risky if your judgments are questioned—in fact, if literature itself is problematic.

The canon was beginning to shake as others questioned the ideology of books for children: the imaginative flights of Anglo-Saxon children in sylvan places. Who was not in the picture? What is children's literature for? Children's librarians began to focus more attention on their annual prizes, however challenged, and the status quo rather than the more expansive synergy of institution building. A spirit of realism in literature challenged their more romanticized ideology, the sanctuary they made now so distant. Librarians had earlier modeled structure: an organization, training, a journal, publishing, publicity, and a network of connections between libraries, publishers, schools, and media. The university seemed remote, apart from these parameters, with children's literature taught more as tool than art in departments of education and library science. The incorporation of children's literature into the academy seemed a fantasy in the 1960s, but times were changing.

Popular culture was a new frontier for academics, and children's literature could sneak in under that low fence. New disciplines were welcomed, and scholarship was intertwining. Men were entering what had been a feminized field. Some disciples of children's books, who saw their appeal with undergraduates, began to coalesce and plan strategy. As the interest in a canon grew, academics began to assume roles held by librarians as cultural critics. Without a past, the academy staked its claims and "discovered" the field. The subject flourished in the reinvigoration of serious study of the literature, the proliferation of journals like *The Lion and the Unicorn,* the interdisciplinarity of research. Children's librarians were limited in carrying the field in this direction, as their connections with the academy were slim, the subject isolated in women-centered fields like education and librarianship. Competing interests favored the academy, which in its humanism and high stature could transform the simple little tale. And so they did, and still do thirty years later. The work is unfinished.

Academic interest in children's literature did propel the field forward. The subject was "coming of age," which seems a bit ahistorical considering its proud heritage over the century. The scholars meant "coming of age in the academy," but higher education is only one world. Children's books can grow up and succeed in other disciplinary professions. They could even learn from each other. When the academics superseded the librarians' authority, like a new edition of an old classic, they built on a tradition already in existence for a half a century. Scholars followed the path of the third owl and became the critic through the means they knew: a professional organization, journals, annual conferences, research scholarships, awards, and, best of all, a canon.

Touching on the Touchstones

Why a canon? I ponder this question as I read the criticism of the *Touchstone* essays as neutrally as I could. I was not as interested in the content of criticism as in the questions raised in me. What does this construct say about us as canon makers? What is the worth of creating a list of touchstones with their own accompanying defense? Is the idea to construct a canon, support it with suitable interpretation, and then censor any challenges that come along? Do we wish to bolster the "popularity" of these books, thereby establishing more firmly their place in future canons and considerations? Is the point to better understand why certain books work to foster the discussion and create better work (and possibly readers)? Will this result in a dialogue between academics and librarians (rather, did it foster that)? What are the statements about meaning implied from these abstracts? Why do some critics discuss illustration more than others? What, then, are the elements of a successful children's book? Would a librarian agree? Would a parent? Would a child? Are these valuations subject to the whims of time and fad? How useful is it to create a list as variable as the text that each reader finds? Can a canon exist if we really believe in reader response?

Not only the big questions, but the small ones matter too. I argue with Perry Nodelman as he rationalizes the canonical process. He speaks of some books being omitted from consideration, at least now, because of their darker nature. Does that imply that certain subject matter is required, perhaps more of a romantic strand? The question of popularity underlies the criticism. The touchstones are said to share the commonality of telling a good story, where popularity of a text is followed by scholarship. In general, I noticed critics referencing a book's popularity when needed, or highlighting its unpopularity when held in contrast to the book's so obvious, although at one point misunderstood, worth. They fail to mention a book's popularity when it does not obviously make a strong statement. So subjectivity is at play. In fact, the story of a writer is always included in the essay. Touchstones are said to have a gap in common: a space unexplained for young readers to discover something about the text. I found this also to be true in reading the essays.

Each essay uses history, time, endurance, and pleasure as measures of a text's worth. Most essays begin with a personal statement about the critic's relationship to the work. Sometimes reception of a work in a classroom is described, the writer's children's response is recounted, and at times a critic will depart from connections with the text. A few of the essays are critical of the work. When a critic is critical of a touchstone's status, it is along standard criteria of race, class, and gender. When a critic romances a work, class might be discussed, race very rarely, but even less so gender.

Perry Nodelman as editor claims the list comes from children and not just literature, but few discuss children in their essays. Nodelman chose to base his judgment on the same criteria used in literature courses. Some of his phrases caught my attention: the touchstone transcends "both pseudo-nostalgia and child psychology;" consists of a "shared context;" and must be "groundbreaking," setting the basis for new conventions while breaking the old. The critic's role is to "separate good from the likeable and the great from the good." Well, the touchstones did provoke some observations and response from this reader, who by now feels very familiar with one canon anyway.

Ways of Being

The classics of children's literature are part of a lost history, or one barely known even to the practitioners. Children's library history tells a story that I believe is sufficiently profound and complex to offer explanations of the origins and development of the cultural history of children's literature. Academics have elevated the subject of children's culture to interdisciplinary influence in the academy, promising new understandings of childhood. The commonality is concern for the child and the culture of childhood, which includes literature and the institutions that select and study texts. We should know each other. Here is a bold suggestion: children's library history deserves a place in foundational courses in related fields of English, women's studies, American studies, education, librarianship. The emergence of childhood studies offers that prospect of configuring the humanities, social sciences, and sciences in a community of research and reflection, stretching the horizons of text and context.

What are alternatives to a selective tradition? Is it possible to operate in innocence apart from corruptions of canonicity? Let's consider many canons, not just one. There does seem to be a human proclivity to make lists, to order existence in some manner of being. If we as professionals engaged in a literature of childhood could resist the language of "best" and instead contextualize and relativize titles in a dynamic relationship with each other, we could uphold standards of a different kind and effect a transformative rewriting and rereading of children's literature. Instead of the Anglocentric pantheon of classics, both fields could create a series of canons reflecting and constructing a variety of cultures and literatures for children. This pluralistic approach would be a dialogue of many voices that contribute to the dynamics of culture—a democratic representation of difference rather than commonality. In a broad cultural forum, parallel professions could expand territorial boundaries in an intertextuality that breaks opens the canon and expands definitions of readers and texts. That could come only with a struggle as the literature is bound up in conventions of subject matter and language conducive to control.

That change could come from viewing children's literature as cultural studies rather than aesthetics. With an anthropological approach, children's books could be read in many directions as cultural work. Robert Scholes in *Textual Power* speaks of the need to teach the cultural text as well as the literary one. Terry Eagleton argues that we have narrowed the concept of literature and need to return literary practices to other cultural practices. Literary categories can so dislocate texts and the pleasures they bear. No text is an island, as Gerald Graff reminds us. Works of literature speak to each other, as Umberto Eco reveals in *The Name of the Rose*. Children's literature is an intersection of two powerful ideological positions: our ideas about childhood and our ideas about literature, ideas often conflicted beyond our knowing. Unfortunately, those ideas are often divided into one or the other: a good reader/nonreader; a reader of classics/a consumer of junk; book people/child people. I want more choices and fewer categories. We need ways to distinguish between books other than those binaries. Think of how reading could flourish if we defined it as pleasure? If instead of the canon, we made a paracanon. I believe fervently that once a child has known an affinity with a book, has captured that away-sense or seen a mirror on the page, once the imagination has captured something in words arranged in unique ways, the child will never be the same. I sense that awakening should come in childhood, for if not, will an adult ever wander into that risky affair again? That gives urgency to reading, a sense that we should offer a wide array of books in the wild gardens of our shelves, where classics converse with comics, Nancy Drew draws sensational designs, and Mary Lennox finds the secret garden once again.

I hear the voice of the child as reader, as critic, as creator of meaning. It may be that children can only claim classics after childhood. And certainly not because they are called such. These books we remember fifty years later struck a chord within us that defined us and left signs of the future. Reading them again as an adult, we look back and feel a connection to our former selves. I don't see that tug as nostalgia but more primal, fierce, protective. This book is part flesh and blood. We work as educators of culture—librarians, academicians—to try to figure out what endures, although the knowledge is incomplete, for we ourselves are part of the configuration. I certainly forgot about *The Secret Garden* until I saw an abandoned garden wall and cried, "Look, the secret garden!" which renewed my romance again. I found the old diary in my basement with little of interest except for the fact that Nancy Drew was the only book mentioned, and I read that I wanted to be Nancy, at age twelve! I have written about how the text of a book can enter the text of a life. It's as if we create canons for ourselves—fellow adults—

who plan to converse through criticism in the public sphere with our theoretical tools of the trade. "Touchstones that touch us" might be a better description of the canon, for its law and logic seem so remote from the lived experience of the young reader receptive to the openness and variety of texts: the potential for a classic to come into our lives, unbeknownst. It's secret like the garden. Each reader knows what makes a classic: a book to return to in your mind if not in another reading, a book with a certain imaginative density. Putting these titles on a list and defending their existence seems so immaterial to what readers do. I truly believe that a child will pass on a beloved text to another child and never see the prescription. That is how texts like *The Secret Garden* survived when the powers-that-be found it unappealing or unsatisfactory. I do see the need to stimulate use, but I sense librarians are closer to their audience than academics may be. If scholars can be scholars sharing children's books without the great judgment from on high, then all is well. All would be even better if the minds met and shared a favorite book or two. It is the recovery of ourselves when new, when books made all the difference, as Graham Greene knew so well: "Perhaps it is only in childhood that books have any deep influence on our lives."[8]

Neither profession has reached the child with such power as the classic that finds the reader, when the books we need are there. Literacies are based on context, on the uses we find for texts. The focus is on literature in the life of the child rather than the child in the life of literature. A classic is a gift. A work of art works within a market economy and a gift economy, says Lewis Hyde in his lovely book, *The Gift: Imagination and the Erotic Life of Property*. An object becomes one kind of property or another depending on how we use it. The spirit in a book can wake our own. The work reaches out to us, as Joseph Conrad says, to a part of our being that is itself a gift and not an acquisition. I like to think that certain books speak to us in this way, in this place. Books converse with books, as do we. When books from another time and place can speak to questions asked years beyond their time, we sense immortality, the closest we may know. What we love in literature speaks to the gift nature of art: "that art that matters to us—which moves the soul, or delights the senses, or offers courage for living, however we choose to describe the experience—that work is received by us as a gift is received."[9] I like the sense of classics as gift not commodity in ways of being.

E. M. Forster in his epigraph to *Howards End* calls us to join the passion and the prose, the disparate parts, into a new being. "Only Connect!" This entreaty to live no longer in fragments "speaks to our condition," as the Quakers say. I dream of a field of literature for children where the professionals in theory and practice center in a discourse of connection, of synergy. This question of linking is part of who we are in this curiously doubled life: both children and literature naming who we are.

Notes

Chapter 1. Best Books: The Librarian

1. Frances Clarke Sayers, *Anne Carroll Moore: A Biography* (New York: Athenaeum, 1972), 47.
2. Frances Jenkins Olcott, *The Children's Reading* (Boston: Houghton Mifflin, 1927), 1.
3. Anne Scott MacLeod, "Literary and Social Aspects of the Twenties and Thirties," in *Stepping Away from Tradition: Children's Books of the Twenties and Thirties*, ed. Sybille A. Jagusch (Washington, D.C.: Library of Congress, 1988), 52.
4. Judith Plotz, "The Perpetual Messiah: Romanticism, Childhood, and the Paradoxes of Human Development," in *Regulated Children/Liberated Children: Education in Psychological Perspective*, ed. Barbara Finkelstein (New York: Psychohistory, 1979), 72.
5. James Holt McGavran, "Introduction," *Romanticism and Children's Literature in Nineteenth-Century England*, ed. James Holt McGavran (Athens: University of Georgia Press, 1991), 7.
6. F. J. Harvey Darton, *Children's Books in England: Five Centuries of Social Life*, 3rd ed., ed. Brian Alderson (Cambridge, U.K.: Cambridge University Press, 1982), 1.
7. Anne K. Mellor, *Romanticism & Gender* (New York: Routledge, 1993), 209.
8. Mitzi Myers, "Reading Children and Homeopathic Romanticism: Paradigm Lost, Revisionary Gleam, or 'Plus Ça Change, Plus C'est La Même Chose,'" in *Literature and the Child: Romantic Continuations and Postmodern Contestations*, ed. James Holt McGavran, Jr. (Athens: University of Georgia Press), 45.
9. Anne Carroll Moore, *Roads to Childhood* (New York: Doran, 1920), 135.
10. Moore, *My Roads to Childhood* (Boston: Horn Book, 1964), 297.
11. Mark Girouard, *Sweetness and Light: The Queen Anne Movement 1860–1900* (New Haven, Conn.: Yale University Press, 1984), 4.
12. Jackson Lears, *No Place of Grace: Antimodernism and the Transformation of American Culture, 1880–1920* (New York: Pantheon, 1981), 145.
13. Barbara Garlitz, "The Immortality Ode: Its Cultural Progeny," *Studies in English Literature* VI (1966): 647.
14. F. J. Harvey Darton, *Children's Books in England: Five Centuries of Social Life*, 3rd ed. Brian Alderson (Cambridge, U.K.: Cambridge University Press, 1982), 179.
15. Darton, 178.
16. Mary Thwaite, *From Primer to Pleasure in Reading* (Boston: Horn Book, 1972), 81.
17. Mildred Batchelder, "The Leadership Network in Children's Librarianship: A Remembrance," *Stepping Away from Tradition: Children's Books of the Twenties* and

149

Thirties, ed. Sybille A. Jagusch (Washington, D.C.: Library of Congress, 1988), 71–72.

18. Betsy Hearne and Christine Jenkins, "Sacred Texts: What Our Foremothers Left Us in the Way of Psalms, Proverbs, Precepts, and Practices," *Horn Book* (September/October 1999): 536.

19. Annis Duff, *Bequest of Wings: A Family Pleasure with Books* (New York: Viking, 1944); Margaret A. Edwards, *The Fair Garden and the Swarm of Beasts: The Library and the Young Adult* (Hawthorn, 1969); Paul Hazard, *Books, Children and Men*, trans. Marguerite Mitchell (Boston: Horn Book, 1944); Bertha E. Mahony and Elinor Whitney, *Realms of Gold* (New York: Doran, 1929); Amelia H. Munson, *An Ample Field* (Chicago: American Library Association, 1950); Frances Clarke Sayers, *Summoned by Books: Essays and Speeches* (New York: Viking, 1965); Ruth Sawyer, *The Way of the Storyteller* (New York: Viking, 1942); Lillian Smith, *The Unreluctant Years: A Critical Approach to Children's Literature* (Chicago: American Library Association, 1953); Ruth Hill Viguers, *Margin for Surprise: About Books, Children, and Librarians* (Boston: Little Brown, 1964).

20. Humphrey Carpenter, *Secret Gardens: A Study of the Golden Age of Children's Literature* (London: Allen & Unwin, 1985).

21. Peter Coveney, *The Image of the Child: The Individual and Society: A Study of the Theme in English Literature* (Baltimore, Md.: Penguin, 1967), xi.

22. "Books for the Young," *Dial* 27 (December 1899): 342.

23. Girouard, *Sweetness and Light*, 139.

24. "Illustrated Juveniles," *Dial* 2 (December 1881): 182.

25. W. E. Henley, "Randolph Caldecott," *Art Journal* 43 (July 1881): 212.

26. R. Gordon Kelly, "Children's Literature," in *Handbook of American Popular Literature* (New York: Greenwood, 1988), 49.

27. Holbrook Jackson, *The Eighteen Nineties: A Review of Art and Ideas at the Close of the Nineteenth Century* (New York: Knopf, 1922), 227.

28. Horace Sutton, "Children and Modern Literature," *National Review* 18 (December 1891): 507.

29. Florence Maccunn, "Children's Story-Books," *Good Words* 44 (1904): 341.

30. "The Point of View," *Scribner's Magazine* 23 (January 1898): 123.

31. "The Point of View: The Child's Garden of Verses and Other Literature," *Scribner's* 9 (April 1896): 519.

32. "Books for and about Children," *Atlantic Monthly* 73 (June 1894): 853.

33. Louise Betts Edward, "The Literary Cult of the Child," *Critic* 39 (August 1901): 167.

34. Horace Scudder, *Childhood in Literature and Art* (Boston: Houghton Mifflin, 1894).

35. Ellen Key, *The Century of the Child* (London: Putnam's, 1909).

36. Carpenter, *Secret Gardens*.

37. James Holt McGavran, *Literature and the Child: Romantic Continuations, Postmodern Contestations* (Iowa City: University of Iowa Press, 1999), 12.

38. Gwendolen Rees, *Libraries for Children* (New York: H. W. Wilson, 1924), 91.

39. Hearne and Jenkins, "Sacred Texts."

40. Mitzi Myers, "Romancing the Moral Tale: Maria Edgeworth and the Problematics of Pedagogy," *Romanticism and Children's Literature in Nineteenth-Century England*, ed. James Holt McGavran, Jr. (Athens: University of Georgia Press, 1991), 113.

41. Anne Scott MacLeod, *American Childhood: Essays on Children's Literature of the Nineteenth and Twentieth Centuries* (Athens: University of Georgia Press, 1994), 117.

42. Jane Tompkins, *Sensational Designs: The Cultural Work of American Fiction, 1790–1860* (New York: Oxford University Press, 1985), xi.
43. Edward E. Hale, "On Writing for Children," *Dial* (December 6, 1884): 267.
44. Paul S. Boyer, *Purity in Print: Book Censorship in America from the Gilded Age to the Computer Age* (Madison: University of Wisconsin Press, 2002).
45. Horace E. Scudder, "American Classics in Schools," *Atlantic Monthly* (July 1887): 88–89.
46. "Literature for the Young," *The Critic* (May 26, 1883): 243–44.
47. *The Critic* (December 1898): 424.
48. Anna Hamel Wiekel, "The Child and His Book," *Education* (May 1900): 547.
49. Sidney H. Ditzion, *Arsenals of a Democratic Culture* (Chicago: American Library Association, 1947), 7.
50. Ditzion, 172.
51. Lawrence Levine, *Highbrow/Lowbrow: The Emergence of Cultural Hierarchy in America* (Cambridge, Mass.: Harvard University Press, 1988).
52. Edward Shils, *Tradition* (Chicago: University of Chicago Press, 1981), 21.
53. Wayne Wiegand, "The Socialization of Library and Information Science Students: Reflections on a Century of Formal Education for Librarianship, *Library Trends* (winter 1986): 389.
54. Andrew Abbott, *The System of Professions: An Essay on the Division of Expert Labor* (Chicago: University of Chicago Press, 1988), 222.
55. Abbott, 219.
56. Wayne Wiegand, "The Politics of Cultural Outsourcing: 'Outsourcing' High Profile Library Positions," *American Libraries* (January 1998): 81.
57. *Library Journal* (June 15, 1989): 5.
58. Wayne Wiegand, "The Politics of Cultural Authority," *American Libraries* (January 1998): 80–82.
59. Sheila Rothman, *Women's Proper Place: A History of Changing Ideals and Practices, 1870 to the Present* (New York: Basic, 1978).
60. Barbara Brand, "Librarianship and Other Female-Intensive Professions, " *Journal of Library History* 18, no. 4 (fall 1983): 391–406.
61. Dee Garrison, *Apostles of Culture: The Public Librarian and American Society, 1876–1920* (New York: Macmillan, 1979), 180.
62. Sara Fenwick, "Library Service to Children and Young People," *Library Trends* 25, no. 1 (July 1976): 329–60.
63. Suzanne Hildebrand, "Ambiguous Authority and Aborted Ambition: Gender, Professionalism, and the Rise and Fall of the Welfare State," *Library Trends* 34, no. 1 (summer 1985): 185.
64. Elizabeth Minnich, *Transforming Knowledge* (Philadelphia: Temple University Press, 1990), 42.
65. Joanne Passet, "The Literature of American Library History, 1991–1992," *Library and Culture* 29, no. 4 (1994): 415.
66. James V. Carmichael, Jr., "Ahistoricity and the Library Profession: Perceptions of Biographical Researchers in LIS Concerning Research Problems, Practices, and Barriers," *Journal of Education for Library and Information Science* 31 (4) (1991), 331.
67. Michael H. Harris and Stanley Hannah, "Why Do We Study the History of Libraries? A Meditation on the Perils of Ahistoricism in the Information Era," *Library & Information Science Research* 14 (1992): 129.
68. Anne Lundin, "The Pedagogical Context of Women in Children's Services and Literature Scholarship," *Library Trends* 44, no. 4 (spring 1996): 840–50.

69. Anne Carroll Moore, "Writing for Children," *Roads to Childhood* (New York: George H. Doran, 1920), 26.
70. Caroline Hewins, "The History of Children's Books," *Atlantic Monthly* (January 1888): 112–26.
71. Alice M. Jordan, "The Ideal Book from the Standpoint of the Children's Librarian," *Children's Library Yearbook,* Number Three (Chicago: American Library Association, 1931), 9–11.
72. Beverly Lyon Clark, *Kiddie Lit: The Cultural Construction of Children's Literature in America* (Baltimore. Md.: Johns Hopkins University Press, 2003), 70.
73. Robert Sink, "Democratic Images," *Biblion: The Bulletin of The New York Public Library* 1, no. 2 (spring 1993), 20.
74. Caroline Hewins, "Old Books and New Books," *Library Journal* (1896): C47–48.
75. Sayers, *Anne Carroll Moore: A Biography,* 61.
76. See Mary Macke, "'No Philosophy Carries So Much Conviction as the Personal Life': Mary Wright Plummer as an Independent Woman," *Library Quarterly* (January 2000): 1–46.
77. Mary Wright Plummer, "Work with Children in Free Libraries, *Library Journal* 22 (1897): 686.
78. Anne Carroll Moore, "Children's Room," *Report of the Free Library for the Year Ending June 30, 1897,* Pratt Institute, Brooklyn, New York, 11.
79. Anne Carroll Moore, "Special Training for Children's Librarians," *Library Journal* 23 (August 1898): 81.
80. *Library Journal* 27, no.12 (December 1902): 989–1004.
81. Sybille Anna Jagusch, "First Among Equals: Caroline M. Hewins and Anne C. Moore. Foundations of Library Work with Children" (diss., University of Maryland College Park, 1990), 286.
82. William E. Foster, "The Appraisal of Literature: Comments and Opinions," *Library Journal* 27 (December 1902): 997–98.
83. Anne Carroll Moore, "Writing for Children," *Roads to Childhood* (New York: Doran, 1920), 27.
84. Moore, 26.
85. See Sayers, *Anne Carroll Moore,* 86.
86. Adele Fasick, "Anne Carroll Moore," *Dictionary of American Literary Biography* (Littleton, Colo.: Libraries Unlimited, 1978), 370.
87. Leonard S. Marcus, *Dear Genius: The Letters of Ursula Nordstrom* (New York: HarperCollins, 1998).
88. Frederic Melcher, "Thirty Years of Children's Books," *Children's Literature Yearbook,* vol. 1. (Chicago: American Library Association, 1929), 5–10.
89. Christine Jenkins, "Does Cream Really Rise to the Top? H. W. Wilson's *Children's Catalog* and the Children's Canon, 1909–1996," Society of the History of Authorship, Reading and Publishing Conference, Madison, Wisc., July 15–18, 1999.
90. Hearne and Jenkins, "Sacred Texts," 539.
91. Dee Garrison, *Apostles of Culture* (New York: Macmillan, 1979), 62.
92. Thomas Kuhn, *The Structure of Scientific Revolutions* (Chicago: University of Chicago Press, 1962).
93. Raymond Williams, *Problems of Materialism and Culture: Selected Essays* (London: Verso, 1980), 39.
94. Wayne Wiegand, *Irrepressible Reformer: A Biography of Melvil Dewey* (Chicago: American Library Association, 1996), 372.
95. Garrison, *Apostles of Culture,* 63.

96. Garrison, 63.

97. Paul Boyer, *Purity in Print: Book Censorship in America from the Gilded Age to the Computer Age* (Madison: University of Wisconsin Press, 2002).

98. Donald L. Wilson, ed. *The Genteel Tradition: Nine Essays by George Santayana* (Cambridge: Harvard University Press, 1967).

99. John Tomsich, *A Genteel Tradition: American Culture and Politics in the Gilded Age* (Stanford: Stanford University Press, 1971), 6.

100. Joan Shelley Rubin, *The Making of Middlebrow Culture* (Chapel Hill: University of North Carolina Press, 1992).

101. Sally Allen McNall, "American Children's Literature, 188–Present," *American Childhood: A Research Guide and Historical Handbook*, eds. Joseph M. Hawes and N. Ray Miner (Westport, Conn.: Greenwood, 1985), 381.

102. MacLeod, *American Childhood,* 122.

103. See Clifford Geertz, "Ideology as a Cultural System" in *Interpretations of Culture: Selected Essays* (New York: Basic Books, 1973), which explores ideology as templates of experience.

104. Hans Gans, *Popular Culture and High Culture: An Analysis and Evaluation of Taste* (New York: Basic Books, 1974).

105. Wiegand, *Irrepressible Reformer,* 95.

106. Barbara Herrnstein Smith, "Contingencies of Value," in *Canons,* ed. R. Von Hallberg (Chicago: University of Chicago Press, 1984), 29.

107. Michael Harris, "State, Class, and Cultural Reproduction: Toward a Theory of Library Service in the U.S.," in *Advances in Librarianship,* vol. 14 (New York: Academic Press, 1986), 241.

108. Wiegand, "Socialization," 389.

109. Wiegand, "Role of the Library," 72.

110. Arthur E. Bostwick, ed., *The Library and Society* (New York: H. W. Wilson, 1920), 5.

111. James Hubbard, "How to Use a Library," *The Library and Society,* 303.

112. Boyer, *Purity in Print,* 31.

113. Boyer, 32.

114. Marjorie Bedinger, "Censorship of Books by the Library," *Libraries* 33 (November 1931): 392–94.

115. Darton, *Children's Books in England,* vii.

116. Lance Salway, *A Peculiar Gift: Nineteenth Century Writings on Books for Children* (Harmondsworth, Middlesex, U.K.: Kestrel Books, 1976).

117. Hearne and Jenkins, "Sacred Texts."

118. Olcott, *The Children's Reading,* 1.

119. Olcott, 16.

120. Hearne and Jenkins, "Sacred Texts, 546.

121. Wiegand, *Irrepressible Reformer,* 372.

122. Cornelia Meigs, et al., *A Critical History of Children's Literature* (New York: Macmillan, 1969), 276.

123. Alice Jordan, *From Rollo to Tom Sawyer and Other Papers* (Boston: Horn Book, 1948), 113.

124. Jordan, 117.

125. Alice Jordan, "Children's Classics," *Horn Book* (January 1947): 9–19.

126. Horace Scudder, "Books for Young People," *The Riverside Magazine for Young People* (January 1867): 44.

127. Scudder, 43–45.

128. Horace Scudder, *Childhood in Literature and Art* (Boston: Houghton Mifflin, 1894), 245.

129. Jordan, *From Rollo to Tom Sawyer,* 118.

130. Caroline Hewins, *Books for Boys and Girls,* 3rd ed. (Chicago: American Library Association, 1915), 64.

131. Horace Scudder, "Nursery Classics in School," *Atlantic Monthly* 59 (June 1887): 800–803; "American Classics in School," 60 (July 1887): 85–91.

132. Scudder, *Childhood in Literature and Art* (Boston: Houghton Mifflin, 1884), 242.

133. Jordan, *From Rollo to Sawyer,* 133.

134. R. Gordon Kelly, *Children's Periodicals of the United States* (Westport, Conn.: Greenwood, 1984), 377.

135. Kelly, *Children's Periodicals,* 379.

136. Kelly, 378.

137. Frederic Melcher, "Characteristics of Today's Children's Books," *Publishers Weekly* (1923): 1363.

138. Moore, *My Roads to Childhood,* 44–45.

139. Moore, 44–45.

140. Sir Arthur Quiller-Couch, *On the Art of Reading* (Cambridge, U.K.: Cambridge University Press, 1920), vi.

141. Quiller-Couch, 65.

142. Quiller-Couch, 210.

143. Quiller-Couch, 211.

144. Quiller-Couch, 212.

145. Quiller-Couch, 217.

146. Quiller-Couch, 226.

147. Moore, *My Roads to Childhood,* 169.

148. Moore, 328.

149. Smith, *Unreluctant Years,* 42–43.

150. Walter de la Mare, *The Cambridge Guide to Children's Books in England* (Cambridge, U.K.: Cambridge University Press, 2001), 201.

151. Sayers, *Anne Carroll Moore,* 187.

152. Sayers, 229.

153. Sayers, 231.

154. Moore, *My Roads to Childhood,* 213.

155. Alice M. Jordan, "Books, Children and Men," *Horn Book* (March/April 1943): 116.

156. Anne Carroll Moore, "The Three Owls," *Horn Book* (January 1945): 29.

157. Alice M. Jordan, *Library Quarterly* (October 1944): 351–52.

158. Paul Hazard, *Books, Children and Men* (Boston: Horn Book, 1944), 42.

159. Hazard, 88.

160. Smith, *Unreluctant Years,* 39.

161. Hearne and Jenkins, "Sacred Texts," 541–42.

162. Melcher, "Characteristics of Today's Children's Books," 1363.

163. John Tebbel, "For Children, with Love and Profit," *Tradition: Children's Books of the Twenties and Thirties,* ed. Sybille A. Jagusch (Washington, D.C.: Library of Congress, 1988), 26.

164. Irene Smith, *History of the Newbery and Caldecott Medals* (New York: Viking, 1957), 64.

165. Michael Patrick Hearn, "Before the Flood: Notes on Early Twentieth Century American Children's Illustration," *The Calendar,* Children's Book Council (November 1979–June 1980), n.p.

166. Leonard S. Marcus, *Margaret Wise Brown: Awakened by the Moon* (Boston: Beacon, 1992), 57.
167. Christine Jenkins, "Youth Services and Professional Jurisdiction," *Library Trends* 44 (Spring 1996): 813–39.
168. Olcott, *The Children's Reading*, 176.
169. Hearne and Jenkins, "Sacred Texts," 546.
170. Smith, *Unreluctant Years*, 8.
171. Smith, 7.
172. MacLeod, *American Childhood*, 121–23.
173. Felicity A. Hughes, "Children's Literature: Theory and Practice," *English Literary History* 45 (1978): 542–61.
174. MacLeod, *American Childhood*, 125.
175. Nancy Larrick, "The All White World of Children's Books," *Saturday Review* (September 11, 1965): 63–65; 84–85.

Chapter 2. Best Books: The Scholar

1. Alison Lurie, *Foreign Affairs* (New York: Random House, 1984), 6.
2. Iona and Peter Opie, *The Classic Fairy Tales* (London: Oxford University Press, 1974), 11.
3. Felicity Hughes, "Children's Literature: Theory and Practice," *English Literary History* 45 (1978): 548.
4. Betsy Hearne, "Problems and Possibilities: U.S. Research in Children's Literature, *School Library Journal* (August 1988): 30.
5. MacLeod, 124.
6. MacLeod, 125.
7. Dee Garrison, *Apostles of Culture: The Public Librarian and American Society, 1876–1929* (Madison: University of Wisconsin Press, 2003).
8. Beverly Lyon Clark, *Kiddie Lit: The Cultural Construction of Children's Literature in America* (Baltimore, Md.: Johns Hopkins University Press, 2003), 74.
9. Ray Lonsdale and Sheila Ray, "Librarianship," *International Companion Encyclopedia of Children's Literature*, ed. Peter Hunt (London: Routledge, 1996).
10. Jack Zipes, *Sticks and Stones: The Troublesome Success of Children's Literature from Slovenly Peter to Harry Potter* (New York: Routledge, 2001).
11. Lawrence Levine, *Highbrow/Lowbrow: The Emergence of Cultural Hierarchy in America* (Cambridge, Mass.: Harvard University Press, 1988).
12. Henry Steele Commager, "When Majors Wrote for Minors," *Saturday Review* (May 1952), 10.
13. Ann Thwaite, *Waiting for the Party: The Life of Frances Hodgson Burnett* (London: Secker and Warburg, 1974), 95.
14. Jerry Griswold, *Audacious Kids: Coming of Age in America's Classic Children's Books* (New York: Oxford University Press, 1992), vii–viii.
15. Clark, *Kiddie Lit: The Cultural Construction of Children's Literature in America*, 48–49.
16. Lance Salway, ed. *A Peculiar Gift: Nineteenth Century Writings on Books for Children* (Harmondsworth, Middlesex, U.K.: Kestrel Books, 1976).
17. Anne Lundin, "Victorian Horizons: The Reception of Children's Books in England and America, 1880–1900," *Library Quarterly* 64 (January 1994): 30–59.

18. Richard Darling, *The Rise of Children's Book Reviewing in America, 1865–1881* (New York: Bowker, 1968).
19. Salway, *A Peculiar Gift,* 11.
20. F. J. Harvey Darton, *Children's Books in England: Five Centuries of Children's Books* (Cambridge, U.K.: Cambridge University Press, 1982), 315.
21. Griswold, *Audacious Kids,* 237.
22. Levine, *Highbrow/Lowbrow,* 223.
23. Mrs. E. M. Field, *The Child and His Book.* (London: Wells, Gardner, Darton, 1892), 8.
24. Kathleen Hines, "Introduction to the Second Edition, " F. J. Harvey Darton, *Children's Books in England: Five Centuries of Social life* (Cambridge, U.K.: Cambridge University Press, 1960), ix.
25. For example, see Mitzi Myers, "Romancing the Moral Tale: Maria Edgeworth and the Problematics of Pedagogy," *Romanticism and Children's Literature in Nineteenth-Century England,* ed. James Holt McGavran, Jr. (Athens: University of Georgia Press, 1991), 96–128.
26. Frances Clarke Sayers, "Introduction to the Revised Edition," *A Critical History of Children's Literature,* ed. Cornelia Meigs et al. (New York: Macmillan, 1969), vii.
27. Anne Lundin, "Text and Context: Special Collections and Scholarship," *College & Research Libraries* (September 1989): 553–56.
28. R. Gordon Kelly, "Children's Literature as a Field of Study," *American Literature and Realism* 6: 2 (1973): 89.
29. Frederick Crews, *The Pooh Perplex: A Freshman Casebook* (New York: Dutton, 1963).
30. Francelia Butler, "The Editor's High Chair," *Children's Literature: The Great Excluded: Critical Essays on Children's Literature,* vol. 1, ed. Francelia Butler (Storrs, Conn.: [s.n.] 1972): 8.
31. R. Gordon Kelly, *Mother Was a Lady: Self and Society in Selected Children's Periodicals, 1865–1890* (Westport, Conn: Greenwood, 1974); Roger Sale, *Fairy Tales and After: From Snow White to E.B. White* (Cambridge: Harvard University Press, 1978).
32. "Panel Discussion: Developing a Canon of Children's Literature," *Proceedings of the Annual Conference of the Children's Literature Association,* Villanova University, Villanova, Pa., 1980.
33. Perry Nodelman, "Grand Canon Suite," *Children's Literature Association Quarterly* 5: (Summer 1980): 1–6.
34. Matthew Arnold, "The Study of Poetry," *Essays in Criticism: First and Second Series.* Everyman's Library (New York: Dutton, 1964), 241–42.
35. Perry Nodelman, "Introduction: Matthew Arnold, a Teddy Bear, and a List of Touchstones," *Touchstones: Reflections on the Best in Children's Literature,* vol. 1, ed. Perry Nodelman (West Lafayette, Ind.: Children's Literature Association, 1985), 2, 5, 7, 8.
36. Nodelman, 1.
37. Lawrence R. Sipe, "The Idea of a Classic," *Journal of Children's Literature* 22, 1 (Spring 1996): 31.
38. Deborah Stevenson, "Sentiment and Significance: The Impossibility of Recovery in the Children's Literature Canon or, The Drowning of the Water Babies," *The Lion and the Unicorn* 21 (1997): 112–30.
39. Michael Steig, "Canon Report," *ChLA Quarterly* (Winter 1983): 38.
40. Peter F. Neumeyer, "Canon Report: Spanish Kids Got No Books?" *ChLA Quarterly* (Summer 1983): 35.
41. Peter Hunt, *Understanding Children's Literature* (London: Routledge, 1999), 11.

42. Margaret Meek, "Symbolic Outlining: The Academic Study of Children's Literature," *Signal* 35 (May 1987): 99.
43. Clark, *Kiddie Lit*, 14.

Chapter 3. Best Books: The Reader

1. Graham Greene, *The Lost Childhood, and Other Essays* (London: Eyre and Spottiswoode, 1951), 13.
2. Eudora Welty, *One Writer's Beginnings* (Cambridge, Mass.: Harvard University
Press), 9.
3. Fay Weldon, *Letters to Alice on First Reading Jane Austen* (New York: Carroll and
Graf, 1984), 77–78.
4. Catharine R. Stimpson, "Reading for Love: Canons, Paracanons, and Whistling Jo
Marsh," *New Literary History* (1990): 958.
5. Stimpson, 961.
6. Stimpson, 964.
7. Louise Rosenblatt, *Literature as Exploration* (New York: Modern Language Association, 1984), 133.
8. Terry Eagleton, *Literary Theory* (Minneapolis: University of Minnesota Press, 1983),
74.
9. Stanley Fish, *Is There a Text in This Class? The Authority of Interpretive Communities* (Cambridge, Mass.: Harvard University Press, 1980).
10. Hans Robert Jauss, *Toward an Aesthetic of Reception,* trans. Timothy Bahti
(Minneapolis: University of Minnesota Press, 1981).
11. Jane Tompkins, *Sensational Designs: The Cultural Work of American Fiction,
1790–1860* (Oxford: Oxford University Press, 1985), xviii.
12. Janice Radway, "Reading Is Not Eating: Mass-Produced Literature and the Research
Quarterly: Theoretical, Methodological, and Political Consequences of a Metaphor,"
Book 2 (1986): 26.
13. John Fiske, *Understanding Popular Culture* (New York: Unwin Hyman, 1989).
14. Gerald Graff, *Professing Literature: An Institutional History* (Chicago: University of
Chicago Press, 1987), 10.
15. Eudora Welty, *The Eye of the Story: Selected Essays and Reviews* (New York: Vintage,
1979), 118.
16. Margaret Drabble, *A Writer's Britain: Landscapes in Literature* (London: Thames
and Hudson, 1979), 8.
17. Annie Dillard, *Pilgrim at Tinker's Creek* (New York: Harper's Press, 1974), 12.
18. Dillard, 142.
19. J. B. Jackson, *Discovering the Vernacular in Landscape* (New Haven, Conn.: Yale
University Press, 1984), 5.
20. D. W. Meinig, *The Interpretation of Ordinary Landscapes: Geographical Essays* (New
York: Oxford University Press), 228.
21. Umberto Eco, *The Name of the Rose* (New York, Warner, 1980), 342.
22. J. R. R. Tolkien, *Tree and Leaf* (Boston: Houghton Mifflin, 1965), 80.
23. Joyce Thomas, "Woods and Castles, Towers and Huts: Aspects of Setting in the
Fairy Tale," *Only Connect: Readings on Children's Literature*, 3rd ed., ed. Sheila Egoff,
et al. (New York: Oxford University Press, 1996), 128.
24. L. Frank Baum, *The Wizard of Oz* (Chicago: Rand McNally, 1900), 10.

25. B. Attenburg, "Oz," *The Wizard of Oz*, ed. M. P. Hearn (New York: Schocken, 1983), 281.
26. Michael Bracewell, "The Never Ending Story," *The Times Magazine* (January 29, 1994): 18–19.
27. Fred Inglis, *The Promise of Happiness: Value and Meaning in Children's Fiction* (London: Cambridge University Press, 1981), 109.
28. Frances Hodgson Burnett, *In the Garden* (Boston: Medici Society of America, 1925), 30.
29. E. B. White, *Letters of E. B. White*, ed. Dorothy Lobrano Guth (New York: Harper and Row, 1976), 367.
30. Annie Dillard, *An American Childhood* (New York: Harper and Row, 1987), 3.
31. Carolyn Heilbrun, *Writing a Woman's Life* (New York: Ballantine, 1988), 18.
32. Mauren Reddy, *Sisters in Crime* (New York: Continuum, 1988), 8.
33. Elaine Showalter, *A Literature of Their Own: British Women Novelists from Brontë to Lessing* (Princeton, N.J.: Princeton University Press, 1997), 158.
34. Nancy Miller, *Subject to Change: Reading Feminist Writing* (New York: Columbia University Press, 1989), 7.
35. Heilbrun, *Writing a Woman's Life*, 18.
36. Carol Gilligan, *In a Different Voice* (Cambridge, Mass.: Harvard University Press, 1982), 22, 173.
37. Heilbrun, *Writing a Woman's Life*, 46.
38. Deborah Felder, "Nancy Drew: Then and Now," *Publishers Weekly* (May 30): 31.
39. Nicholas Tucker, *The Child and the Book: A Psychological and Literary Exploration* (Cambridge, U.K.: Cambridge University Press, 1981), 121–22.
40. Tucker, 127.
41. J. A. Appleyard, *Becoming a Reader: The Experience of Fiction from Childhood to Adulthood* (Cambridge, U.K.: Cambridge University Press, 1991), 82, 259.
42. Margaret Meek, *How Texts Teach What Readers Learn* (South Woodchester, U.K.: Thimble Press, 1988), 158.
43. Appleyard, *Becoming a Reader*, 59.
44. Northrop Frye, *Anatomy of Criticism: Four Essays* (Princeton, N.J.: Princeton University Press, 1957), 186, 193.
45. Brian Sutton-Smith, *The Folkstories of Children* (Philadelphia: University of Pennsylvania Press, 1981); Kristin Wardetsky, "The Structure and Interpretation of Fairy Tales Comprised by Children," *Journal of American Folklore* 103 (1990): 169.
46. Alison Lurie, *Don't Tell the Grownups: Subversive Children's Literature* (Boston: Little Brown, 1990), x.
47. Carolyn Keene, *The Secret of the Old Clock* (New York: Grosset and Dunlap, 1930), 17, 36–37.
48. Carolyn Keene, *The Clue in the Diary* (New York: Grosset and Dunlap, 1932), 11.
49. Carolyn Keene, *The Bungalow Mystery* (New York: Grosset and Dunlap, 1930), 114.
50. Carolyn Keene, *The Sign of the Twisted Candles* (New York: Dunlap and Grosset, 1933), 11.
51. Tzvetan Todorov, *The Poetics of Prose* (Ithaca, N.Y.: Cornell University Press, 1977).
52. Felder, "Nancy Drew," 32.
53. Meek, *How Texts Teach*, 7.
54. Ann Thwaite, *Waiting for the Party: The Life of Frances Hodgson Burnett* (Boston: David R. Godine, 1991), 221.

55. Jane Tompkins, *Sensational Designs: The Cultural Work of American Fiction, 1790–1860* (New York: Oxford University Press): xi.
56. *Publishers' Weekly* (August 12, 1911): 768.
57. *Publishers' Weekly* (September 16, 1911): 1040.
58. *Publishers' Weekly* (October 14, 1911): 1446.
59. *Literary Digest* (September 2, 1911): 361.
60. *The New York Times,* September 3, 1911, 526.
61. *The Independent* (September 7, 1911): 547–48.
62. *Outlook* (September 16, 1911): 136.
63. *Nation* (September 28, 1911): 547–48.
64. *Bookman* (New York) (October 1911): 183–84.
65. *American Monthly Magazine* (December 1911): 342.
66. *Dial* (December 1, 1911): 457.
67. *The New York Times,* December 3, 1911, 793.
68. *Literary Digest* (December 2, 1911): 1041.
69. *Bookman* (London) (December 1911): 102—3.
70. *Athenaeum* (November 18, 1911): 621.
71. *Canadian Magazine* (February 1912): 398–99.
72. *Booklist* (October 1911): 76.
73. *The Times* (London), October 30, 1924, 16.
74. *The New York Times,* October 30, 1924, 19; October 31, 1924, 18; November 4, 1924, 11.
75. *St. Nicholas* (January 25, 1925): 306–10.
76. *Outlook* (November 12, 1924): 397.
77. Bertha E. Mahony and Elinor Whitney, *Realms of Gold in Children's Books* (Garden City, N.Y.: Doubleday, Doran, 1929):605.
78. Louise Bechtel, *Books in Search of Children* (London: Macmillan, 1969), 28.
79. Bechtel, *Books in Search,* 145–47.
80. Bechtel, 174.
81. Anne Carroll Moore, *My Roads to Childhood: Views and Reviews of Children's Books* (Boston: Horn Book, 1961): 238.
82. Elizabeth Nesbitt, "A Rightful Heritage," *A Critical History of Children's Literature,* ed. Cornelia Meigs, et al. (New York: Macmillan, 1953), 264, 377.
83. Frances Clarke Sayers, *Summoned by Books* (New York: Viking, 1965), 152–53.
84. Marghanita Laski, *Mrs. Ewing, Mrs. Molesworth, and Mrs. Hodgson Burnett* (New York: Oxford University Press, 1951), 88.
85. *The Saturday Review* (March 29, 1952): 33.
86. Qt. In *Children's Books in England: Five Centuries of Children's Books.* 3rd ed., ed Brian Alderson (Cambridge, U.K.: Cambridge University Press, 1982), 329.
87. Marcus Crouch, *Treasure Seekers and Borrowers* (London: The Library Association, 1962), 14; John Rowe Townsend, *Written for Children,* 3rd ed. (New York: Lippincott, 1987), 71; Roger Lancelyn Green, "The Golden Age of Children's Books," *Only Connect: Reading on Children's Literature,* ed. Sheila Egoff, et al. (Toronto: Oxford University Press, 1969), 11.
88. Fred Inglis, *The Promise of Happiness,* 111.
89. Thwaite, *Waiting for the Party,* 220.
90. Faith McNulty, "Children's Books for Christmas," *The New Yorker* (December 1, 1986): 115.
91. Anne Carroll Moore, "The Three Owls' Notebook," *Horn Book* (November/December 1949): 521–22.

Epilogue

1. I am indebted to Marjorie Garber's *Symptoms of Culture* (Routledge, 1998) for her illustrative use of *Charlotte's Web*.
2. Peter Neumeyer notes in a sidebar comment in his *Annotated Charlotte's Web* that White was uncomfortable with awards and resisted such honors (p. 159).
3. John Updike, *Hugging the Shore: Essays and Criticism* (New York, Vintage, 1984), xv.
4. Jack Zipes, *Sticks and Stones: The Troubling Success of Children's Literature from Slovenly Peter to Harry Potter* (New York: Routledge, 2001).
5. Cornelia Meigs, et al., *A Critical History of Children's Literature* (New York: Macmillan, 1952), vii.
6. Lillian Smith, *The Unreluctant Years: A Critical Approach to Children's Literature* (Chicago: American Library Association, 1953), 7.
7. Horace E. Scudder, *The Child in Literature and Art* (Boston: Houghton Mifflin, 1894), 216.
8. Raymond Williams, *Keywords: A Vocabulary of Culture and Society* (New York: Oxford University Press, 1976), 183–88.
9. Graham Greene, *The Lost Childhood and Other Essays* (London: Eyre and Spottiswoode, 1951), 13.
10. Lewis Hyde, *The Gift: Imagination and the Erotic Life of Property* (New York: Vintage, 1983), xii.

Selected Bibliography

Books

Abbott, Andrew. *The System of Professions: An Essay on the Division of Expert Labor.* Chicago: University of Chicago Press, 1988.

Adorno, Theodor. *The Culture Industry: Selected Essays on Mass Culture,* ed. J. M. Bernstein. London: Routledge, 1991.

Appleyard, J. A. *Becoming a Reader: The Experience of Fiction from Childhood to Adulthood.* Cambridge, U.K.: Cambridge University Press, 1991.

Bechtel, Louise Seaman. *Books in Search of Children.* London: Macmillan, 1955.

Beckett, Sandra L., ed. *Reflections of Change: Children's Literature Since 1945.* Westport, Conn.: Greenwood Press, 1997.

Bostwick, Arthur E., ed. *The Library and Society.* New York: H. W. Wilson, 1920.

Boyer, Paul S. *Purity in Print: Book Censorship in America from the Gilded Age to the Computer Age,* 2nd ed. Madison: University of Wisconsin Press, 2002.

Calvino, Italo. *Why Read the Classics?* trans. Martin McLaughlin. New York: Vintage, 2000.

Chambers, Aidan. *Booktalk: Occasional Writing on Literature and Children.* New York: Harper & Row, 1985.

Clark, Beverly Lyon. *Kiddie Lit: The Cultural Construction of Children's Literature in America.* Baltimore, Md.: Johns Hopkins University Press, 2003.

Committee on Library Work with Children of the American Library Association, *Children's Literature Yearbook,* 1–4. Chicago: American Library Association, 1929; 1930; 1931; 1932.

Darling, Richard L. *The Rise of Children's Book Reviewing in America, 1865–1881.* New York: R. R. Bowker, 1968.

Darton, F. J. Harvey. *Children's Books in England: Five Centuries of Social Life,* ed. Brian Alderson. 3rd ed. Cambridge, U.K.: Cambridge University Press, 1982.

Davidson, Cathy N. *Reading in America: Literature & Social History.* Baltimore, Md.: Johns Hopkins University Press, 1989.

Ditzion, Sidney H. *Arsenals of a Democratic Culture.* Chicago: American Library Association, 1947.

Donoghue, Denis. *Speaking of Beauty.* New Haven, Conn.: Yale University Press, 2003.

Egoff, Sheila. *Only Connect: Readings on Children's Literature,* 2nd ed. Toronto: Oxford University Press, 1980.

Fasick, Adele M., Margaret Johnston, and Ruth Osler. *Lands of Pleasure: Essays on Lillian H. Smith and the Development of Children's Libraries.* Metuchen, N.J.: Scarecrow, 1990.

Fenwick, Sara Innis. *A Critical Approach to Children's Literature.* Chicago: University of Chicago Press, 1967.

Field, Mrs. E. M. *The Child and His Book.* London: Wells Gardner, Darton, 1891.

Fraser, James H., ed. *Society & Children's Literature.* Boston: Godine, 1978.

Frey, Charles and John Griffith. *The Literary Heritage of Childhood: An Appraisal of Children's Classics in the Western Tradition.* Westport, Conn.: Greenwood, 1987.

Garber, Marjorie. *Symptoms of Culture.* New York: Routledge, 1998.

Griswold, Jerry. *Audacious Kids: Coming of Age in American Classic Children's Books.* New York: Oxford University Press, 1992.

Gross, Elizabeth H. *Public Library Service to Children.* Dobbs Ferry, N.Y.: Oceana, 1967.

Hawes, Joseph M. and N. Ray Hiner. *American Childhood: A Research Guide* and *Historical Handbook.* Westport, Conn.: Greenwood, 1985.

Hazard, Paul. *Books, Children, and Men.* Boston: Horn Book, 1944.

Hazeltine, Alice, ed. *Library Work with Children.* New York: H. W. Wilson, 1917.

Heins, Paul, ed. *Crosscurrents of Criticism: Horn Book Essays, 1968–1977.* Boston: Horn Book, 1977.

Hewins, Caroline. *Caroline M. Hewins: Her Book.* Boston: Horn Book, 1954.

Hildebrand, Suzanne, ed. *Reclaiming the American Library Past: Writing the Women In.* Norwood, N.J.: Ablex, 1996.

Hunt, Peter, ed. *Children's Literature: The Development of Criticism.* London: Routledge, 1990.

———. *Criticism, Theory, and Children's Literature.* London: Blackwell, 1991.

———., ed. *Literature for Children: Contemporary Criticism.* London: Routledge, 1992.

———., ed. *International Companion Encyclopedia of Children's Literature.* London: Routledge, 1996.

———. *An Introduction to Children's Literature.* Oxford: Oxford University Press, 1994.

———. *Understanding Children's Literature.* London: Routledge, 1999.

Hürlimann, Bettina. *Three Centuries of Children's Books in England.* Cleveland, Ohio: World, 1968.

Hyde, Lewis. *The Gift: Imagination and the Erotic Life of Property.* New York: Vintage, 1983.

Inglis, Fred. *The Promise of Happiness: Value and Meaning in Children's Fiction.* Cambridge, U.K.: Cambridge University Press, 1981.

Jordan, Alice M. *From Rollo to Tom Sawyer and Other Papers.* Boston: Horn Book, 1948.

Jagusch, Sybille A. "First among Equals: H. Hewins and Anne C. Moore: Foundations of Library Work for Children." Ph.D. diss., University of Maryland, 1990.

———., ed. *Stepping Away from Tradition: Children's Books of the Twenties and Thirties.* Washington, D.C.: Library of Congress, 1988.

Katz, Bill, ed. *Readers, Reading and Librarians.* New York: Haworth, 2001.

Kelly, R. Gordon. *Children's Periodicals of the United States.* Westport, Conn.: Greenwood Press, 1984.

———. "Children's Literature." *Handbook of American Popular Literature,* ed. M. Thomas Inge. Westport, Conn.: Greenwood, 1988. 45–74.

———. *Mother Was a Lady: Self and Society in Selected American Children's Periodicals, 1865–1890.* Westport, Conn.: Greenwood Press, 1974.

Kermode, Larry. *The Classic.* London: Faber and Faber, 1975.

Levine, Lawrence. *Highbrow/Lowbrow: The Emergence of Cultural Hierarchy in America.* Cambridge, Mass.: Harvard University Press, 1988.

Long, Harriet G. *Public Library Service to Children: Foundations and Development.* Metuchen, N.J.: Scarecrow, 1969.

Lundin, Anne. *Teaching Children's Literature.* Jefferson, N.C.: McFarland, 1995.

———. *Victorian Horizons: The Reception of the Picture Books of Walter Crane, Randolph Caldecott, and Kate Greenaway.* Lanham, Md.: Children's Literature Association/ Scarecrow Press, 2001.

Lundin, Anne and Wayne Wiegand, eds. *Defining Print Culture for Youth: The Cultural Work of Children's Literature.* Westport, Conn.: Libraries Unlimited, 2003.

Lurie, Alison. *Boys and Girls Forever: Children's Classics from Cinderella to Harry Potter.* New York: Penguin, 2003.

———. *Don't Tell the Grown-Ups: Why Kids Love the Books They Do.* Boston: Little Brown, 1990.

MacLeod, Anne Scott. *American Childhood: Essays on Children's Literature of the Nineteenth and Twentieth Centuries.* Athens: University of Georgia Press, 1994.

McGavran, James Holt, Jr., ed. *Literature and The Child: Romantic Continuations and Postmodern Contestations.* Iowa City: University of Iowa Press, 1999.

———. *Romanticism and Children's Literature in Nineteenth-Century England.* Athens: University of Georgia Press, 1991.

Marcus, Leonard. *Margaret Wise Brown: Awakened by the Moon.* Boston: Beacon, 1992.

May, Jill, ed. *Children's Literature and Critical Theory.* New York: Oxford University Press, 1995.

———. *Children and Their Literature: A Readings Book.* West Lafayette, Ind.: Children's Literature Association, 1983.

Meek, Margaret, Aidan Warlow, and Griselda Barton. *The Cool Web: The Pattern of Children's Reading.* Toronto: Bodley Head, 1977.

Meigs, Cornelia, et al. eds. *A Critical History of Children's Literature.* New York: Macmillan, 1969.

Moore, Anne Carroll. *My Roads to Childhood: Views and Reviews of Children's Books.* Boston: Horn Book, 1964.

———. *Roads to Childhood.* New York: George Doran, 1920.

———. *The Three Owls, Third Book: Contemporary Criticism of Children's Books, 1927–1930.* New York: Coward-McCann, 1931.

Munson, Amelia H. *An Ample Field: Books and Young People.* Chicago: American Library Association, 1950.

Murray, Gail Schmunk. *American Children's Literature and the Construction of Childhood.* New York: Twayne, 1998.

Nell, Victor. *Lost in a Book: The Psychology of Reading for Pleasure.* New Haven, Conn.: Yale University Press, 1988.

Nikolajeva. *Children's Literature Comes of Age: Toward a New Aesthetic.* New York: Garland, 1996.

Nodelman, Perry and Mavis Reimer. *The Pleasures of Children's Literature,* 3rd ed. Boston: Allyn & Bacon, 2003.

———. *Touchstones: Reflections on the Best in Children's Literature.* Vols. 1–3. West Lafayette, Ind.: Children's Literature Association, 1985—1989.

Olcott, Frances Jenkins. *The Children's Reading.* Boston: Houghton Mifflin, 1927.

Olson, Joan Blodgett Peterson. "An Interpretive History of the *Horn Book,* 1924–1973." Ph.D. diss., Stanford University, 1976.

Power, Effie. *Work with Children in Public Libraries.* Chicago: American Library Association, 1943.

Quiller-Couch, Sir Arthur. *On the Art of Reading.* Cambridge, U.K.: Cambridge University Press, 1920.

Radway, Janice. *A Feeling for Books: The Book-of-the-Month Club, Literary Taste, and Middle-Class Desire.* Chapel Hill: University of North Carolina Press, 1997.

————. *Reading the Romance: Women, Patriarchy, and Popular Literature.* Chapel Hill: University of North Carolina Press, 1991.

Rahn, Suzanne. *Rediscoveries in Children's Literature.* New York: Garland, 1995.

Rees, Gwendolen. *Libraries for Children: A History and a Bibliography.* New York: H. W. Wilson, 1924.

Reynolds, Kimberley. *Children's Literature in the 1890s and the 1990s.* Plymouth, U.K.: Northcote/British Council, 1994.

Roggenbuck, Mary Jane. "St. Nicholas Magazine: A Study of the Impact and Historical Influence of the Editorship of Mary Mapes Dodge." Ph.D. diss., University of Michigan, 1976.

Rosenblatt, Louise. *Literature as Exploration,* 4th ed. New York: Modern Language Association, 1976.

Ross, Eulalie Steinmetz. *The Spirited Life: Bertha Mahony Miller and Children's Books.* Boston: Horn Book, 1973.

Rubin, Joan Shelley. *The Making of Middlebrow Culture.* Chapel Hill: University of North Carolina Press, 1992.

Ruoff, Gene W., ed. *The Romantics and Us: Essays on Literature and Culture.* New Brunswick, N.J.: Rutgers University Press, 1990.

Sadler, Glenn Edward, ed. *Teaching Children's Literature: Issues, Pedagogy, Resources.* New York: Modern Language Association, 1992.

Said, Edward. *Tradition.* Chicago: University of Chicago Press, 1981.

Salway, Lance, ed. *A Peculiar Gift: Nineteenth Century Writings for Children.* Hammondsworth, Middlesex, U.K.: Kestrel, 1976.

Sayers, Frances Clarke. *Anne Carroll Moore: A Biography.* New York, Athenaeum, 1972.

————. *Summoned by Books.* New York: Viking, 1968.

Scholes, Robert. *Textual Power: Literary Theory and the Teaching of English.* New Haven, Conn.: Yale University Press, 1985.

Scudder, Horace. *Childhood in Literature and Art.* Boston: Houghton Mifflin, 1894.

Smith, Irene. *A History of the Newbery and Caldecott Medals.* New York: Viking Press, 1957.

Smith, Lillian. *The Unreluctant Years: A Critical Approach to Children's Literature.* Chicago: American Library Association, 1953.

Spufford, Francis. *The Child That Books Built.* New York: Henry Holt, 2002.

Thomas, Fannette H. "The Genesis of Children's Services in the American Public Library: 1875–1906." Ph.D. diss., University of Wisconsin, 1982.

Tompkins, Jane. *Reader-Response Criticism: From Formalism to Post-Structuralism.* Baltimore, Md.: Johns Hopkins University Press, 1980.

————. *Sensational Designs: The Cultural Work of American Fiction, 1790–1860.* New York: Oxford University Press, 1985.

Thwaite, Mary F. *From Primer to Pleasure in Reading.* Boston: Horn Book, 1963.

Townsend, John Rowe. *Written for Children,* 3rd ed. New York: Lippincott, 1987.

Vandergrift, Kay E. *Children's Literature: Theory, Research, and Teaching.* Englewood, Colo.: Libraries Unlimited, 1990.

Walter, Virginia. *Children & Libraries: Getting It Right.* Chicago: American Library Association, 2001.

Watson, Victor, ed. *The Cambridge Guide to Children's Literature in English.* Cambridge, U.K.: Cambridge University Press, 2001.

Weldon, Fay. *Letters to Alice on First Reading Jane Austen.* New York: Carroll and Graf, 1984.

Wiegand, Wayne. *Irrepressible Reformer: A Biography of Melvil Dewey*. Chicago: American Library Association, 1996.

Williams, Raymond. *Keywords: A Vocabulary of Culture and Society*. New York: Oxford University Press, 1983.

Yolen, Jane. *Touch Magic: Fantasy, Faerie and Folklore in the Literature of Childhood*. New York: Philomel, 1981.

Zipes, Jack. *Sticks and Stones: The Troublesome Success of Children's Literature from Slovenly Peter to Harry Potter*. New York: Routledge, 2001.

Periodicals

Aiken, Susan Hardy. "Women and the Question of Canonicity." *College English* 48, 3 (March 1986): 288–301.

Bush, Margaret. "New England Book Women: Their Increasing Influence." *Library Trends* 44, 4 (Spring 1996): 719–35.

Butler, Francelia. "The Great Excluded." *Children's Literature* 1 (1972): 7–8.

Clark, Beverly Lyon. "Kiddie Lit in Academe." *Profession* (1996): 149–57.

Guillory, John. "Canon." *Critical Terms for Literary Study*, ed. Frank Lentricchia and Thomas McLaughlin. Chicago: University of Chicago Press, 1990.

Harris, Michael. "State, Class, and Cultural Reproduction: Toward a Theory of Library Service in the United States." *Advances in Librarianship* 14 (1986): 211–52.

Haugland, Ann. "The Crack in the Old Canon: Culture and Commerce in Children's Books." *The Lion and the Unicorn* 18 (1994): 48–59.

Hearne, Betsy and Christine Jenkins. "Sacred Texts: What Our Foremothers Left Us in the Way of Psalms, Proverbs, Precepts, and Practices." *Horn Book* (September/October 1999): 536–61.

Jenkins, Christine. "Professional Jurisdiction and ALA Youth Services Women: Of Nightingales, Newberies, Realism, and the Right." *Library Trends* 44, 4 (Spring 1996): 813–39.

———. "The History of Youth Services Librarianship: A Review of the Research Literature." *Libraries & Culture* 35, 1 (Winter 2000): 103–40.

Jordan, Alice M. "Children's Classics." *Horn Book* 23, 1 (January/February 1947): 9–20.

Lundin, Anne. "Anne Carroll Moore: 'I Have Spun Out a Long Thread.'" *Reclaiming the American Library Past: Writing the Women,* ed. Suzanne Hildebrand. Garden City, N.J.: Ablex, 1996, 187–204.

———. "A Delicate Balance: Collection Development and Women's History." *Collection Building* 14, 2 (1995): 42–46.

———. "The Pedagogical Context of Women in Children's Services and Literature Scholarship." *Library Trends* 44, 4 (Spring 1996): 840–50.

Nodelman, Perry. "Grand Canon Suite." *Children's Literature Association Quarterly* 5, 1 (Summer 1980): 2–7.

Radway, Janice. "Beyond Mary Bailey and Old Maid Librarians: Reimagining Readers and Rethinking Reading." *Journal of Educational for Library and Information Studies* 35, 4 (Fall 1994): 275–98.

Sipe, Lawrence R. "The Idea of a Classic." *Journal of Children's Literature* 22, 1 (Spring 1996): 31–33.

Smith, Barbara Herrnstein. "Value/Evaluation." *Critical Terms for Literary Study*, ed. Frank Lentricchia and Thomas McLaughlin. Chicago: University of Chicago Press, 1990.

Stevenson, Deborah. "Sentiment and Significance: The Impossibility of Recovery in the
    Children's Literature Canon or, The Drowning of the *Water Babies.*" *The Lion and
    the Unicorn* 21 (1997): 112–30.
Stimpson, Catharine R. "Reading for Love: Canons, Paracanons, and Whistling Jo March."
    New Literary History 21, 4 (1990): 957–76.
Tucker, Nicholas. "Keeping Children's Classics Alive and the Case of Beatrix Potter." *Signal*
    99 (September 2002): 183–88.
Wiegand, Wayne. "Tunnel Vision and Blind Spots: What the Past Tells Us about the
    Present; Reflections on the Twentieth-Century History of American Librarianship."
    Library Quarterly 69, 1 (January 1999): 1–32.
Zipes, Jack. "Down with Heidi, Down with Struwwelpeter, Three Cheers for the Revolu-
    tion." *Children's Literature* 5 (1976): 162–80.

Index